P9-DGS-274

Knut Hamsun

Twayne's World Authors Series

Scandinavian Literature

Leif Sjöberg, Editor

State University of New York at Stony Brook

TWAS 715

KNUT HAMSUN
(1859–1952)
Etching by Edvard Munch, 1896
Courtesy of the Munch Museum, Oslo

Knut Hamsun

By Harald Næss

University of Wisconsin–Madison

Twayne Publishers • Boston

Knut Hamsun

Harald Næss

Published by Twayne Publishers
A Division of G. K. Hall & Company
70 Lincoln Street
Boston, Massachusetts 02111

Book Production by Marne B. Sultz

Book Design by Barbara Anderson

Printed on permanent/durable acid-free
paper and bound in the United States of
America.

Library of Congress Cataloging in Publication Data

Naess, Harald.
Knut Hamsun.

(Twayne's world authors series; TWAS 715)
Bibliography: p. 175
Includes index.
1. Hamsun, Knut, 1859–1952—Criticism and
interpretation. I. Title. II. Series.
PT8950.H3Z745 1984 839.8′236 83–18343
ISBN 0–8057–6562–X

Contents

About the Author

Harald Næss is Torger Thompson Professor of Scandinavian Studies at the University of Wisconsin where he has taught since 1959. Born in Kristiansand S., Norway, he was educated at Oslo University and taught for six years at King's College, University of Durham, England, before coming to the United States.

Professor Næss is a former president of the Society for the Advancement of Scandinavian Study and served as editor of its journal *Scandinavian Studies* 1974–78. He is the author and editor of several books and articles on Norwegian literature (including especially Knut Hamsun) and Norwegian-American immigrant culture.

Preface

Thomas Mann, trying to place Hamsun in a European context, spoke of him as a disciple of Dostoevski and Nietzsche.[1] He could also have mentioned Rousseau, whose attitude to the ill effects of civilization Hamsun shared, and Strindberg, who looked down upon emancipated women in much the same way as Hamsun. Among Norwegian writers Hamsun admired above all Bjørnstjerne Bjørnson—"for his tremendous vitality in all things."[2]—yet his own development really resembles more that of another countryman, Edvard Munch, who did for Norway's pictorial arts what Hamsun did for its literature. In a manifesto from 1889 Munch repudiated the school of Norwegian naturalist painters: "No longer were interiors to be painted, pictures of people reading and women knitting—there would be living people breathing and feeling, suffering and loving. I felt I should do this—it would be so easy. The flesh would take shape and the colors would live."[3] Less than a year later and in much the same manner Hamsun turned against the literary establishment in Norway, which included Ibsen:

> Now what if literature on the whole began to deal a little more with mental states than with engagements and balls and hikes and accidents as such? Then one would, to be sure, have to relinquish creating types, as all have been created before, "characters" whom one meets every day at the fishmarket. . . .But in return . . . we would experience a little more of the secret movements which are unnoticed in the remote places of the soul, the capricious disorder of perception, the delicate life of fantasy held under the magnifying glass, the wandering of these thoughts and feelings out of the blue; motionless, trackless journeys with the brain and the heart, strange activities of the nerves, the whispering of the blood, the pleading of the bone, the entire unconscious life.[4]

In his great works from the 1890s—*Hunger, Mysteries, Pan, Victoria*—Hamsun was able to put these theories into practice, so that seventy-five years later Isaac Bashevis Singer could write of him: "He is the father of the modern school of literature in his every respect—his subjectiveness, his fragmentarism, his use of flashbacks, his lyricism. The whole modern school of fiction in the twentieth century stems from Hamsun."[5]

By the time of World War I those two revolutionaries, Munch and Hamsun, had adopted more "classical" forms, Munch completing his Oslo University Aula murals, and Hamsun his *Growth of the Soil.* However, while Munch's work from this period and later has always been considered important, Hamsun's entire twentieth-century production—including his Nobel Prize–winning *Growth of the Soil*—has generally been said by critics to mark a decline in the author's creative powers.

I hope to show that this view is narrow and unjust. My aim in the present volume has been to present, however briefly, *all* of Hamsun's work, including what I feel has often been neglected in other surveys—the early production before and after the formative years in America, the plays and poetry of the middle period, the novels of his later years, and his last moving memoir, published when the author was ninety. Even with the Promethean spirit gone, Hamsun—like Munch—was able to renew his style and produce exciting work throughout a long career.

For help in preparing this introduction to Hamsun, I am indebted to my friend and colleague, Dr. Faith Ingwersen.

Harald Næss

University of Wisconsin–Madison

Chronology

1859 Knut Pedersen born 4 August at Lom in Gudbrandsdal.

1863 Moves with family 600 miles north to farm Hamsund at Hamarøy in Nordland.

1873 Moves back to Lom to work in store of distant relative.

1874 Confirmed in Lom church. Returns to Hamarøy to work in store of Mr. Walsøe.

1875 Peddler in North Norway.

1877 *The Enigmatic Man.*

1878 *Bjørger.*

1880 Works on highway construction north of Oslo.

1882 February, arrives in Madison, Wisconsin. Begins using name Hamsund.

1884 Works as assistant to the Reverend Kristofer Janson in Minneapolis. Fall, returns to Norway.

1885 Works as postal clerk in Aurdal, Valdres. Begins using name Hamsun.

1886 August, arrives in Chicago.

1887 In Minneapolis. Begins series of lectures on modern literature.

1888 Arrives in Copenhagen. November, part of *Hunger* appears in journal *Ny Jord.*

1889 *The Cultural Life of Modern America.*

1890 *Hunger.* "From the Unconscious Life of the Mind."

1892 *Mysteries.*

1893 *Editor Lynge* and *Shallow Soil.* Moves to Paris.

1894 *Pan.* Meets Strindberg in Paris.

1895 *At the Gate of the Kingdom,* first part of a play trilogy.

1896 *The Game of Life,* part two of play trilogy. Returns to Norway.

1897 *Siesta,* a collection of short stories.

1898 *Victoria.* Marries Bergljot Bech.

1899 Travels to Russia and the Middle East.

1902 *Friar Vendt,* a verse play.

1903 *In a Wondrous Land,* a travel book; *Brushwood,* a collection of short stories; *Queen Tamara,* a play.

1904 *Dreamers; The Wild Chorus,* a book of verse.

1905 *Struggling Life,* a collection of short stories.

1906 Divorced from Bergljot Hamsun.

1907 *Under the Autumn Star* (*The Wanderer,* vol. 1).

1908 *Benoni* and *Rosa,* novels.

1909 *On Muted Strings* (*The Wanderer,* vol. 2). Marries Marie Andersen.

1910 *In the Grip of Life,* a play.

1911 Settles at Hamarøy as a farmer and a writer.

1912 *Look Back on Happiness.*

1913 *Children of the Age.*

1915 *Segelfoss Town.* "The Child" appears in *Morgenbladet.*

1917 *Growth of the Soil.*

1918 Settles at estate Nørholm, near Grimstad, south Norway.

1920 *The Women at the Pump.* Receives Nobel Prize for literature.

1923 *Chapter the Last.*

1926 Receives psychoanalytic treatment in Oslo.

1927 *Vagabonds.*

1928 12 December, "Festina lente," in *St. Louis Post Dispatch.*

1930 *August.*

1933 *The Road Leads On.*

1935 Visits Germany and France. Publishes article on Ossietzky.

1936 *The Ring Is Closed.*

1940 Norway occupied by German troops. Hamsun writes pro-German articles.

1943 Attends Journalist Convention in Vienna. Meets Hitler at Berchtesgaden.

1945 Interned at Landvik Old Age Home and later examined by Professor Langfeldt at the Oslo Psychiatric Clinic.

1946 Leaves the Psychiatric Clinic; diagnosed as having "permanently impaired mental faculties." Begins writing his memoirs.

1947 Hamsun tried before the Grimstad Municipal Court and sentenced to pay $80,000 in fines.

1948 Supreme Court of Norway upholds Grimstad sentence, though with a $20,000 reduction in fines.

1949 *On Overgrown Paths.*

1952 Hamsun dies on 19 February.

Chapter One

Hamsun's Life: Youth and Old Age

Knut Pedersen, who later took the name of Hamsun(d), was born on 4 August 1859 at Lom in Gudbrandsdal.[1] This is the heart of Norway. The highest peaks in the mountain range Jotunheimen are nearby, and the old trail across the mountains to west Norway runs right through Lom. It is also a center of old Gudbrandsdal culture, with medieval churches, fine examples of rustic art, and several outstanding writers, notably Olav Aukrust, one of Norway's greatest twentieth-century poets. Hamsun's birthplace, Garmotreet, was only a small holding, but it had earlier belonged to Garmo, one of the largest estates in the district, where people had lived as prosperous farmers since the Middle Ages. Through his mother, Tora, Hamsun was related to the Garmos, and though as a young man he failed to show much interest in his home parish, in later life, when he had himself become a farmer after "wasting" years in the cities, he often liked to emphasize his old ties with rural Norway. Hamsun's father, Peder Pedersen, came from a family of small holders and artisans in the neighboring parish of Vågå. He was a quiet and friendly person who had done some traveling and learned the trade of a tailor; during one of his visits to Lom he met Hamsun's mother and had a child by her. Later they married and settled at Garmotreet, where in a two-room cottage they raised a family of six—besides Knut, three older sons and two younger daughters.

Two contrasting features in Hamsun's social makeup—the conservatism of the farm culture at Garmo and the roving spirit of artisans—were exemplified in his two maternal uncles. Ole Olsen, the older, was a farmer and a shoemaker, utterly charming, handsome, athletic, popular with women, and full of strange stories and ideas, but also totally irresponsible, a vagabond given to drink. Hamsun admired him and later used him as a model for many of his characters. The other uncle, Hans Olsen, was a pious and hard-working tailor and merchant, ill liked by his relatives, who were soon to become his dependents, and a hard taskmaster to his nephew Knut when he began working at his house. Hamsun's beautiful handwriting, his incredible pedantry in minor matters, and some of his artistic discipline may well have been acquired in the service of his tyrannical uncle Hans.

In the summer of 1863 the family of ten left Garmotreet and emigrated to Hamarøy in Nordland, a good hundred miles north of the arctic circle and six hundred miles north of their original home. At that time Hans had been in Hamarøy for some years. He rented part of the vicarage there, where he set up a tailor's shop as well as a post office and a library, and invested his money in the farm Hamsund, a few miles to the west, which he let to Peder and his household. Like other immigrants, the Hamsund people preserved the old patriarchal ways. The older members of the family retained their dialect, Gudbrandsdal lived more vividly than ever in their memories, and the cloudy days there soon became silver lined. For Knut the case was different. Since he was only four when his family arrived at Hamsund, he learned the dialect of Nordland, and even though he never became a genuine *nordlending,*[2] he knew the ways of these people as well as any native and used them in his works. In some respects life at Hamsund was an enlarged copy of life at Lom. Hamarøy is one of the most beautiful regions in northern Norway, idyllic, with a rich vegetation and many little fjords and inlets. The surrounding areas are all mountainous. Across the West Fjord one can see the breathtaking Lofoten Range, rising out of the ocean with rugged snow-capped peaks, as beautiful as any in Jotunheimen. Not only is Hamarøy more open and friendly than Lom, but during the summer, when the sun never sets, it presents a unique experience to all strangers. But there is also a gloom and oppressiveness when winter begins, with weeks of fog and snowstorms and daily reports of disaster at sea. The people of this harsh winterland are different from their countrymen further south. In Norwegian literature, when some fantastic scenery or personality is called for, north Norway is normally made to provide it, as in the setting of Bjørnstjerne Bjørnson's finest play, *Beyond Our Power,* or Ibsen's character Rebecca West, and there are important writers, like Jonas Lie, who owe their literary careers to the inspiration of a stay in Nordland. Even more than Jonas Lie, though, Knut Hamsun is the novelist of Nordland. Of his thirty-three books, twelve have a Nordland setting. In another seven part of the action takes place there. Not only are the curious mannerisms of Hamsun's humorous characters typical of the *nordlending,* but also the romantic mixture of arrogance and humility in his early protagonists. And the intense experience of Nordland's natural beauty—as in *Pan*—is only conceivable in a person who spent his impressionable years there.

As a boy Hamsun loved nothing so much as being a shepherd. He would lie on his back among the birch trees for hours, dozing in the sun, while distant cowbells lulled him to sleep. He marveled at the clouds and saw in their curious shapes the promise of a great future, like being chief of the world's bravest robber band.[3] The novel *Victoria,* which contains one of Hamsun's few childhood descriptions, owes its charm to such memories. Very different is the kind of angst evoked in "An Apparition," in which Hamsun tells of a dead person who came to him one night in his dreams and demanded back a tooth Hamsun had found the day before in the graveyard.[4] The story has been analyzed by a German psychologist who found it to be a typical expression of castration angst. However that may be, the account of that apparition, which haunted Hamsun for years and nearly drove him to suicide, also illustrates the unbelievably cruel treatment Hamsun suffered at the hands of his mother's youngest brother, Hans. Uncle Hans, because of his failing health, needed someone to help him on his farm and in his shop, and being a parsimonious man, looked for a servant who could be had free of charge. Because his sister and brother-in-law owed him money, he was able to force them to give up their son Knut, who had for his nine years both considerable strength and an excellent handwriting. Knut was given little to eat, though he worked hard both in the field and at the desk, and he was regularly beaten and scared with hellfire sermons by that overzealous educator. According to a recent theory Uncle Hans is responsible for Hamsun's repulsive pictures of old men, and, by association, for Hamsun's hatred of the English (the old colonial oppressors).[5] At least he must have been important in the same way as the ghost with the missing tooth, of whom Hamsun wrote: "He was one of the first reasons why I learned to clench my teeth and make myself hard. Later in life it has sometimes stood me in good stead."[6]

For the next forty years Hamsun followed the example of his vagabond uncle Ole, by traveling in many lands, from Turkey to North Dakota. His first trip was to Lom, where he went through confirmation ceremonies, which meant admission to adult life and the completion of whatever little schooling country people then received. Back in Hamarøy after a year, he came into the service of a Mr. Walsøe, one of those powerful merchants of north Norway who ruled their districts like the kings in the Norwegian fairy tales. Hamsun has described their "courts" and their daughters, the "princesses," in several of his novels. In retrospect those merchants impressed him more and more as he grew older and found himself increasingly surrounded by the petty bourgeois and by organized labor. A photograph from the year 1874 shows Hamsun with his hat set rakishly over one ear and sporting a new silver watch chain (there was no watch). He even had hopes of winning the affection of his master's youngest daughter, Laura, when everything suddenly ended in catastrophe: Mr. Walsøe went bankrupt, and Laura found another sweetheart. During the following year (1875) Hamsun and a friend traveled in the counties of Nordland and Troms as peddlers. They had much the same ups and downs as Edevart and August experienced in the novel *Wayfarers* (1927), and in the end Hamsun had to give up peddling because of pressure from his family: he was sixteen and had not yet learned a trade. A year (1876) in Bodø, where he was supposed to work as a shoemaker's apprentice, also seemed wasted. He soon gave up mending shoes and began working in the docks, but in between jobs he spent his time on what became his first book, a naive story called *The Enigmatic Man* (1877). The publisher was a "business connection" from Hamsun's peddling period, and in his ninetieth year Hamsun still remembered him: "In a letter he told me that he had corrected some of the worst things in this 'scribbled nonsense.' It hurt me. After that I had nothing printed at Kjeldseth's."[7]

Hamsun writes ironically about his hurt feelings, but they must have been real. Whatever *The Enigmatic Man* is—ludicrous, pathetic, naive in the extreme—it is not slapdash, but the result of a hard struggle with what was to Hamsun literally a foreign language: at seventeen he had no other formal training than elementary reading and spelling. The thirty-one pages are constructed like a primitive pageant in eight acts. The first two chapters, "Åbakken" and "The Acquaintance," set the scene and give the necessary exposition. In a completely stylized country landscape we meet the mysterious character Rolf, the son of a tenant farmer. In the chapters "Guesswork about Rolf Andersen" and "The Receipt" the suspense is increased—Rolf's polite manners and neat handwriting now confuse the local people, and in "The Townspeople" and "Adventures at Night" the conflict reaches its climax: the rich landowner Ole Aae invites a student to his house so that he can meet his daughter, but she prefers the tenant farmer's son who, in the chapter "The Secret is Disclosed," also reveals himself to be a wealthy and well-educated businessman named Knud Sonnenfield. The last chapter, "Great Changes: The Homecoming," tells how Rolf/Knud and his young wife move to the city, where they live "in love and prosperity, generous and kind to the poor and needy." It is the usual story of the prince who seeks his princess and, in order to find a person who loves him for his own sake, disguises himself as a pauper. The book shows an early stage in Hamsun's social striving, his dream of one day revealing himself as something more than even a student—as a true prince of literature. It also demonstrates how the stilted official jargon of Hamsun's employers became his first guide to what he considered good literary style. But even if *The Enigmatic Man* is scribbled nonsense, it contains the beginnings of the romantic irony that characterizes all Hamsun's art and that is already fully developed in his great novels of the 1890s. It also shares with these novels Hamsun's expressed ambition to arrive in a small town completely unannounced, live there incognito for some time, and then disappear as mysteriously as he came.[8]

Early Years in Norway and America

From Bodø Hamsun moved north again, this time to Vesterålen, where he worked for two years (1877–79), one year as a grade school teacher and another as an assistant to the local bailiff. In the bailiff's house Hamsun had access to a greater variety of books than his pious uncle had provided in Hamarøy public library. The influence of writers such as Hans Christian Andersen, Henrik Ibsen, and Bjørnstjerne Bjørnson is not difficult to detect in Hamsun's literary work from that period—a poem, "The Reunion," and a second novel, *Bjørger,* both published in Bodø in 1878 under the full name of Knud Pedersen Hamsund.[9] "The Reunion" is a melodramatic tale of a German murderer, once shipwrecked in North Norway and now living there as an old man in a cabin by the sea. One day he saves a young woman from drowning and takes this as a sign of God's forgiveness, whereupon he dies in peace, clutching in his hand "die hellihge schrift." The poem is written in the meter of Heine's "Lorelei" and probably has as its inspiration the sentimental rhetoric of Ibsen's "Terje Vigen," which Hamsun loved to recite as a very young man. In contrast to "The Reunion," *Bjørger* is an important early work, with at least two interesting characters and a prose style which marks a great step forward from that of *The Enigmatic Man. Bjørger* is the story of a young boy who grows up in quite unusual circumstances. His mother dies in childbirth, his father commits suicide, and his adult brother becomes insane and lives like a recluse in the neighborhood. Bjørger is an extraordinary boy, brilliant at school and poetically gifted, and he impresses his school mates, among them Laura, the daughter of the merchant in whose service Bjørger is employed (cf. Hamsun at Walsøe's). The young couple become sweethearts, but after a while Laura gives up Børger for a newcomer to the district, an older, manlier, more prosperous, and better educated man. Bjørger falls critically ill, and when, after his long reconvalescence, Laura returns to him to ask his forgiveness, he first refuses to see her; only gradually is the old relationship established. Unfortunately Laura has in the meantime contracted tuberculosis and dies soon afterward. Bjørger leaves his home valley, where he has experienced so much pain, but he feels confident that it will inspire him to new poetry in years to come.

The most interesting aspect of *Bjørger* has to do with its language. Somewhere in the text Kristofer Janson's story *Torgrim* is mentioned, and it is clear that Hamsun's model for good prose is no longer the style of contemporary business letters, but rather the pithy language of Bjørnson's and Janson's rustic novels, with short sentences imitating dialect and the syntax of the old Icelandic sagas. The influence of Hans Christian Andersen's light conversational tone as well as the heavy rhythm of the Bible is also evident in the style of *Bjørger,* which is much more flexible than that of *The Enigmatic Man* and has appropriate changes whenever dialogue is interwoven with descriptive and lyric passages. Certain stylistic figures, such as repetition, are used excessively and probably derive from his rhetorical models, but they also anticipate Hamsun's lifelong preoccupation with euphony in language. Hamsun developed this talent into mastery during his stay in America. There he also learned to apply his sense of humor. In the last resort, what best characterizes *Bjørger,* as also *The Enigmatic Man,* is the total absence of a smile. These heroes are to be taken seriously and so seem to have little in common with either the comical-pathetic protagonist of *Hunger* (1890) or the many ironic self-portraits to be found between Rolandsen (*Dreamers,* 1904) and August (*Wayfarers,* 1927).

Toward the end of his two years at Vesterålen Hamsun was busy writing a third novel, *Frida,* but his duties as schoolteacher and bailiff's assistant did not leave him sufficient time and quiet to complete his work. Probably his own classroom presentation of Wergeland's ecstatic poem "Hardanger" made him think of that southwest fjord landscape as particularly inspiring for young writers, and with a donation from a wealthy Nordland merchant, he set out for the town of Øystese, where he was indeed looked upon as a poet—peculiarly dressed as he was, with a gold-rimmed pince-nez recently acquired for the occasion. He changed his name to Pederson (with *o,* instead of the usual Norwegian *e*) and appeared in the local press with an article criticizing the hymn singing in Vikør church. The editor of the paper left out all Latin quotations in Hamsun's text, but the readers still understood that here was a person of youthful arrogance and self-taught wisdom intoning the old song about farmers being stupid, coarse, and lacking in taste.

By that time *Frida* was completed (1879), and Hamsun traveled to Copenhagen, where Norwegian writers of importance still published their books. *Frida* was not accepted by the director of the Gyldendal publishing house, nor was it commended by Bjørnstjerne Bjørnson, whom Hamsun went to see after his return to Norway. "In Distress," a poem about a wounded songbird which Hamsun published at this time in a family journal,[10] describes his disillusionment: one year after he had left Nordland with a substantial donation and great hopes for the future, he found himself not only in Kristiania, "this city that no one leaves without being marked by it," but indeed in much the same miserable plight as the protagonist of *Hunger.* Like him, Hamsun therefore gave up his literary plans for the time being and began working on highway construction north of Oslo (Kristiania), where he soon regained his health and good humor. He wrote in the local paper (this time his target was a fundamentalist preacher), borrowed books from the local library, and was himself something out of literature with his unusual background, peculiar dress, and manners. He impressed his fellow workers as well as the local minister's daughter, who referred to him as Poet Pederson, and made some useful contacts, in particular with Nils Frøsland, a young clerk who often invited Hamsun to his home and during Christmas vacation even to the family farm in the village of Torpa.

By this time Hamsun had resumed his old plans for a literary career. Now he wanted to write for his countrymen in America, where he had friends and relatives who had settled and seemed to be doing well. In those days the Norwegian newspapers, particularly the liberal ones, commented in great detail on the political and economic progress of the United States. There were also enthusiastic reports from immigration agents and successful farmers, and sober accounts of experienced travelers who praised the material welfare and free institutions of the great republic across the ocean. Of intellectuals from Norway there were several who seemed to prosper. The Norwegian poet Kristofer Janson had a large following as minister to the Unitarians in Minnesota; a Mr. Boyesen from Stavanger was a prominent journalist, author, and university lecturer at Cornell and Columbia, and in Wisconsin a young man Rasmus Anderson, who had not even finished his college training, was appointed professor of Scandinavian studies at the university in Madison. In the winter of 1880–81 Bjørnstjerne Bjørnson traveled in the Midwest, and his articles in *Verdens Gang* and *Dagbladet* further confirmed Hamsun's new belief that America was now the only place for him.[11] In the course of the Christmas celebrations at Torpa, Hamsun recited Ibsen's "Terje Vigen" for the guests. They were a grateful audience, and Frøsland's mother wanted to help Mr. Pederson become a minister. When Hamsun asked that she rather pay his way to America, she agreed to lend him a hundred dollars. Frøsland, writing to Bjørnstjerne Bjørnson, secured a letter of recommendation for Knut Hamsun, and the German shipping firm Nord-Deutscher Lloyd provided him with a free ticket, not only to New York, but to Elroy, Wisconsin, where Hamsun had his oldest brother, Peter. He arrived there in February 1882.[12]

On his way to Elroy Hamsun stopped in Madison, where he delivered Bjørnson's letter of recommendation to Rasmus B. Anderson. Anderson was a Norwegian immigrant's son who, in spite of having a poor education and little support, other than what his own tenacity and ambition gave him, had managed before his thirtieth year to establish and personally hold a chair in Scandinavian studies at the University of Wisconsin. At the time Anderson had too many problems of his own (a threatened libel suit from Chicago) to fully understand a naive Norwegian country boy who wished to write poetry for his compatriots in America. If, as he later claimed, he supplied Hamsun with a recommendation to a general dealer in Elroy, that was the extent of his help. In a letter to a friend Hamsun commented, "Professor Anderson is not the man to come to if you are stuck. He cut me short and said that in America every man must help himself."[13] In his hopes for a great future in America Hamsun suffered a second setback when he discovered that his brother was not as prosperous as his letters home had indicated. Peter Hamsun, rather than following the example of his farming father-in-law, set himself up as a tailor. Although considered a first-rate craftsman, he was better known among the Norwegian settlers as a merry fiddler and heavy drinker at Scandinavian wedding parties. Gradually he became a restless vagabond like his Norwegian uncle Ole. He could not keep jobs for any length of time and was unable to help his brother Knut when he turned up in Elroy.

During the spring of 1882 Knut Hamsun worked as a farm hand on the prairie a little east of the town. He was lonely, did not understand the language, and apparently found the local girls unattractive, though he still remembered one of them, Bridget, when he published his memoirs at the age of ninety. Elroy held greater attractions for him than farm life on the prairie, and during the summer of 1882 he moved into town, where he began working for its most powerful businessman, Edmund Hart, banker, postmaster, and general dealer. Mr. Hart's sons Harry and John, who were boys of fourteen and twelve at the time, have both written about their impressions of the colorful new clerk in their father's store.[14] He apparently was also thought highly of by the young ladies of the town and by the teachers at the local schools. Henry M. Johnston, the high-school principal, taught him English, and William T. Ager, a grade-school teacher, became his roommate, friend, and admirer. Hamsun told him about his books and articles, his interview with Bjørnson, and his literary ambitions, and there can be no doubt that Ager encouraged him to resume his writing. By December 1882 it seems Hamsun had not only regained his old confidence in himself but even managed to stake out a new course for his literary activities. After studying Tom Paine's *Age of Reason* he penned his own "Elroy Manifesto" in Harry Hart's poetry book:[15]

"My *life* is a peaceless flight through all the land my religion is the moral of the wildest naturalism but my *world* is the aesthetical literature."

A first careful step toward this demand for a break with old romantic ideas can be seen in Hamsun's lectures in the spring of 1883, first in Elroy, later in Stoughton. He spoke about Bjørnson, and it is apparent that he wanted to restore some of the dignity to what was, for the Norwegian immigrant, a fallen idol. Bjørnson's rustic tales had been widely read by Norwegians in the Midwest, who looked up to the author as a modern—a liberal and a democrat—but at the same time an upholder of the best qualities in Norway's century-old farm culture. However, after his religious crisis in the 1870s followed by public attacks on church and Christianity, the Norwegian ministers in America warned their parishioners against his godless writings and sabotaged his tour of the states during the winter of 1880–81. Though Hamsun had advertised his lecture in the Stoughton press, there were less than a dozen people present, many of them drunk and none of them interested in Bjørnson.[16] Hamsun later tried to reach a wider audience by printing a summary of his main points in the Chicago paper *Skandinaven.*[17] He explains Bjørnson's fall from Christianity as a refusal to accept such ideas as the divinity of Christ and eternal punishment and emphasizes instead his humanism, his attempt to build a better society by fighting hypocrisy and old prejudice. His general tone is mildly ironic, but in no way revolutionary. Hamsun was certainly not rushing headlong into his "wildest naturalism."

He had left Norway in the 1880s, which was not only a golden age in Scandinavian literature, but indeed the only age in which Danes, Norwegians, and Swedes have contributed in a massive way to world literature, with names like Bjørnson, Brandes, Ibsen, and Strindberg. By the time *Bjørger* had appeared, the leading critic in Scandinavia, Georg Brandes, had already turned against Bjørnson's rustic tales as giving an over-idealized view of the Norwegian farmer. From his home town of Copenhagen Brandes preached the gospel of European positivism and demanded of Scandinavian writers that they discuss modern problems, such as the relationship between the sexes, church and religion, property and social conditions.[18] Both Bjørnson and Ibsen had accepted the challenge. Bjørnson had written Scandinavia's first realistic play, *A Bankruptcy,* back in 1875 and Ibsen was already busy writing *A Doll's House,* which was to be followed two years later by *Ghosts* (1881), a play so radical in its subject matter (religious hypocrisy and venereal disease) that it provoked a storm of protest which scared even Ibsen. To people who thought of *Ghosts* as an appropriate standard for modern literature, American realism under Howell's leadership would naturally appear somewhat passé, not to speak of the literary tastes of the Midwest. As an educator for his countrymen there, Hamsun had little success when he tried to advance beyond Ibsen's early romantic poetry, and this realization goes a long way to explain his fits of depression. In his hotel room, which he shared with Ager, he covered one third of the plastered ceiling with a pencil drawing representing the Angel of Night spreading veils of darkness over the world, and under a portrait of himself on one of the walls he repeated his old credo about his life being a peaceless flight. Ager recalls that Hamsun would place a light on a chair near his pillow before retiring and then read until sleep overcame him. When Ager returned late at night, he would often find a cigar lying by the light. "On several occasions he left an open clasp knife on the chair with a note addressed to me and reading 'Smoke the cigar and stick the knife into my heart. Do it quickly, surely and kindly if you value my friendship.' Signed Knut H. P.S. 'This note shall be your defense in court.' "[19]

During the summer of 1883 Henry Johnston left Elroy High School to try his luck at something more remunerative than teaching. He bought a lumber yard in Madelia, Minnesota, and asked Hamsun to come west and look after the business while he and his wife traveled in the East. In the little sketch "Fright," Hamsun has described his short stay in Madelia, where, he claimed, Jesse James had just been caught and killed.[20] Hamsun was not only treated in an unfriendly manner there, but was even attacked in the dead of night by a group of unknown men whom he managed to scare away with Johnston's gun. One day in Madelia Hamsun met a Norwegian minister named Kristofer Janson. He knew him well: in Norway Janson was a famous poet and novelist, and Hamsun had read his work with great admiration. Janson had been favorably impressed with what he saw of the United States during a visit in 1879 and published his views in a book entitled *American Conditions* (1880). While he was appalled at the petty power struggle and widespread intolerance among the Norwegian ministry of the Midwest, the ideas of the Unitarians Channing, Parker, and Clarke appealed to him and when, after a year in Norway, he was asked to head a unitarian congregation in the Midwest, he accepted and moved with his family to Minneapolis. From there he made regular excursions to other churches in the vicinity, and on one such occasion he met Hamsun at the Madelia Railway Station, heard about his plans to become a writer, and asked him to come and work with him in Minneapolis.

Hamsun stayed in the Janson home for half a year (April to September 1884), a period which was to be of immense importance for the development of his literary career.[21] Not only did he now have at his disposal a library containing most of the controversial works of his times, but Janson was himself an author and a critic who knew Bjørnson, Ibsen, and other writers personally and could speak with authority about their works. Moreover, Janson loved to share his enthusiasm with others and arranged literary evenings in his home, assisted by his gifted wife. Hamsun's admiration for Mrs. Janson, who was musically accomplished and full of vitality, is said to have been mutual. According to Rasmus Anderson she claimed it was "bracing and invigorating, both mentally and physically, to be in the same room with Knut Hamsun."[22] Drude Krog Janson did not find satisfaction in her work as a housewife. She wanted to be creative and looked with boundless admiration on some of the colorful artists who visited their home. Bjørnson and Hamsun were struck by something genuine and refreshing in her personality, but while Bjørnson also appreciated the naive, almost saintlike temperament of her husband, Hamsun more and more looked upon Janson's Christianity and democratic ideas as an obstacle to the creation of free men and a free literature. The development of Hamsun's disenchantment with Janson was gradual, and ideological rather than personal. He never forgot what he owed that fine man, and he showed it in his letters to him.

Hamsun worked as a kind of secretary to Kristofer Janson; in particular, he was hired to translate English articles into Norwegian for a church periodical Janson planned to publish. However, since Hamsun's knowledge of English was still rudimentary, Janson used him more and more for his church activities. On two occasions he had him give public lectures, and on several others he asked him to contribute to entertainment evenings or bazaars with humorous talks. In the summer of 1884 Hamsun fell ill. What was a severe case of bronchitis was mistakenly diagnosed as "galloping consumption." He was given up by the doctors and wished to return to Norway to die at home. In his autobiography Rasmus Anderson has described how, during a visit to the Janson home, he went upstairs, pulled Hamsun out of his bed, and ran with him around the block. That cured him, Anderson claimed; he also said he collected sufficient funds from friends to pay Hamsun's way back to Norway.[23] These, and other of Anderson's accounts of Hamsun in America, for example, that Anderson was the one who gave Hamsun (earlier Pedersen/Pederson) his name, have been emphatically denied by Hamsun himself.[24] Nevertheless, Anderson seems to have been the first person to understand Hamsun's disease properly. By the time Hamsun reached Oslo, he was told by the doctor that all he now needed was rest and fresh air.

That he found in Aurdal, Valdres, where he became a friend of the local post clerk, Erik Frydenlund, whose job he even took over for a period of several months while Frydenlund did his military service.[25] In Valdres Hamsun also lectured with great enthusiasm on Ibsen and Bjørnson. Clearly he was not only completely recovered from his disease but more productive than he had been since he brought out *Bjørger.* He had been in Norway for a couple of months only when his story "Fragment of a Life, by a Young, Unknown Author" appeared in *Dagbladet.*[26] In his description of a young rake (Harald Storm) who, on a peaceless flight through all the land, is finally smitten by an incurable disease, Hamsun clearly tries to imitate Ibsen's "wildest naturalism" in *Ghosts*—and Zola's in *Nana* (Storm admires a lady by the name of Nana)—but the story is humorless and pathetic. More interesting are three articles on America which Hamsun published in *Aftenposten* a few weeks later.[27] Compared to what he later wrote about America, these articles show a friendly disposition—and they contain the first traces of Hamsun's humor. In order to obtain the greatest effect, Hamsun emphasizes colorful aspects of the United States, its things of great size as well as the intricate mechanisms of its newest and most startling inventions. He does deplore the average American's conservative taste in literature and the arts, but he is decidedly pro-democracy and, like Bjørnson and Janson, praises America's famous free institutions. Of special interest in his third *Aftenposten* article on America is a belletristic account of how Hamsun, on New York's Cherry Street, is taken in by an elderly gentleman, seemingly poverty stricken, yet of dignified appearance. The story also contains the first mention of the electric hymnbook which Hamsun later used in *Hunger.*

During the spring of 1885 Hamsun published a series of three articles on Mark Twain.[28] Evidently he had not read much of that author, except *The Innocents Abroad,* which he criticized for its provincial attitudes, but he was nevertheless able to give striking characterizations of Mark Twain ("that pale pessimist"), probably because he felt temperamentally related to him. Reading Mark Twain (and listening to him?) also taught Hamsun something about the importance of humor in a lively literary style. This is evident in two stories from 1886, "Sin" and "On a Lecturing Tour," both published in *Dagbladet.*[29] "Sin" contains a story within a story and deals with a little girl who is told by her dying sister that, when she is buried, the girl must take the flowers from her grave, sell them, and buy herself a pair of shoes. But the little girl is caught by the police and later in life becomes a prostitute. Although the inner story is in itself a typical piece of mirthless naturalism, the person who relates it to the narrator of the frame story is not unlike that gentleman from Cherry Street, New York, who made a fool of Hamsun. This can be seen more clearly in Hamsun's revised version of "Sin." Here the teller of the inner story first confuses the narrator with his philosophic discourse, thereafter moves him to tears with his story of the stolen flowers, then perplexes him further by relating how he went to bed with the girl, and finally manages to steal the narrator's watch from him. He is, as the new title of the story indicates, "An Arch Scoundrel."[30]

This new ability to laugh at himself, which Hamsun had first demonstrated in his Cherry Street incident, is more central in the story "On a Lecturing Tour," about Hamsun's experiences as a lecturer in the city of Drammen. The author here describes himself in a number of absurd situations whose comic effects depend on the contrast between the protagonist's naiveté and his attempts to preserve a degree of dignity. The method is very much that of Mark Twain's "Trying Situation," which Hamsun may have heard the author read. The Norwegian writer Arne Garborg (1851–1924), to whom Hamsun showed the manuscript of "On a Lecturing Tour," complained that Hamsun imitated the Russians too much. He must have had in mind the depressing naturalism which colors the whole of "Sin" and at least the opening paragraph of "On a Lecturing Tour." As later in *Hunger,* the humorous whims of the protagonist/

author stand in strange contrast to his otherwise utterly depressing life: Hamsun himself was actually traveling around giving lectures at the time, and it exhausted both his funds and his good spirits. People did not turn out for his talks, and even though a few enthusiasts came, there were not enough of them to pay for his expenses. In September 1886 he wrote his Valdres friend Erik Frydenlund about his last miserable months in Norway—from Chicago, where he had been working for some weeks at one of the new cable car lines.[31]

Hamsun had returned to America, not to stay this time but to earn enough money so that he could finally settle in Norway, pay his creditors, and live as a writer. After a period of hard labor in the streets of Chicago he became a conductor on the Hallsted and Cottage Lines and worked as such until the spring of 1887. The short story "Feminine Victory" gives an interesting picture of his conductor days. However, with seven dollars a week, of which he paid four for board and lodging he was not able to put aside any money. As a matter of fact, in order to get away from the big city, he applied to no less a person than Philip Armour for help, received twenty-five dollars and left for Minnesota. On 17 May (Norway's Constitutional Day) he addressed the Norwegians in Minneapolis and in the following days renewed his old contacts with the Janson family, besides making new friends who not only supported him in various trivial ways during his last year in America but, since this was also the final and most decisive stage in his apprenticeship, actually helped prepare his breakthrough as a writer. There was the druggist Yngwar Laws, with whom he often shared his literary discoveries, and the two editors, Hallvard Askeland and John O. Hansen, in whose abolitionist paper *Felt-Raabet (The Battle Cry)* Hamsun wrote two editorials. More perceptive than they were Krøger Johansen, a young editor with anarchist leanings who later wrote the first article on Hamsun in America,[32] and Victor Nilsson, writer of literary articles for a Swedish Minneapolis paper, *Svenska Folkets Tidning,* and of all Hamsun's friends probably the one who was most familiar with the new literary trends.

The following year Hamsun wished to devote to literary studies and in order to do so spent the summer of 1887 working on one of the bonanza farms in North Dakota. To judge from what Hamsun later wrote about his time there, North Dakota must have impressed him more than any other part of America. Not only was he fascinated by the vastness of the prairie and its glorious sunsets, but his working comrades were a bunch of strange vagabonds who have since lived on in his fiction, in short stories such as "Zachæus," "On the Prairie," and "Vagabond Days," in parts of *On Overgrown Paths,* and, more distantly, in the characters of August (August trilogy, 1927–33) and Abel (*The Ring is Closed,* 1936). After Hamsun had returned to Minneapolis, he began preparing a series of lectures on modern literature, which were delivered on eleven consecutive Sunday evenings, from 11 December to 12 February 1888. He began by speaking about Balzac, Flaubert, and Zola, continued with the Scandinavian writers Bjørnson, Ibsen, Lie, Kristofer Janson, Kielland, and Strindberg, and ended with two lectures on impressionism and criticism. The lectures were reviewed in *Felt-Raabet* and *Svenska Folkets Tidning,* and it is clear that they contained little of that rebellious spirit with which Hamsun later debunked the whole of Norway's established literature (in his lecture tour of 1891–92, and in the novel *Mysteries*). According to Krøger Johansen, they were inspired by deep admiration for the great authors of earlier generations. In little intermezzi, however, the rebel in him did come out, against Bjørnson's moralizing, or Ibsen's fake profundity. On 28 March 1888 Hamsun gave a last lecture, entitled "Aesthetic Reflexions—Life in Minneapolis," which is the first version of two lectures Hamsun held one year later for students at Copenhagen University and which was afterward published as a book.

With the help of his faithful friends Hamsun managed to get away from America in the summer of 1888. Hallvard Askeland got him a free ride on the railway, and John O. Hansen went with him to Chicago and helped him place an article on Strindberg (the first English tribute to the great dramatist) in the weekly paper *America.*[33] In the middle of the Atlantic Hamsun also met his old enemy Rasmus B. Anderson, when this person, who was now the U.S. minister to Denmark, ventured into the steering class quarters of the S.S. *Thingvalla.* On hearing that a black ribbon Hamsun wore was not there to show his sorrow over some dear departed relative, but to protest the execution of the Chicago anarchists, Anderson knew that all his old suspicions and antipathies were justified: "From that moment Knut Hamsun was in my mind an anarchist and I had no use for people of that ilk," he wrote in his memoirs many years later.[34] When the *Thingvalla* docked at Oslo (Kristiania), Hamsun, remembering only too well the miserable time he had spent in that city, did not go ashore but continued to Copenhagen. From here he wrote to Victor Nilsson: "How I find this country agreeable! I assure you, the whole existence—way of life—here is in deep harmony with my temperament, my nature. Here is Europe, and I am a European, thank God!"[35] These must have been strong convictions, for Copenhagen in the fall of 1888 treated him little better than Kristiania had during the winter of 1881 or summer of 1886. He was finally saved from starvation by a newspaper editor, Edvard Brandes (brother of Georg Brandes), who read the second part of *Hunger* and lent him a small sum of money, and by Carl Behrens, who printed a section of *Hunger* in his periodical *Ny Jord* and also arranged for Hamsun to address the Danish Students' Association with two lectures about his experiences in the New World (15 December 1888; 12 January 1889). On the basis of those lectures Hamsun wrote *The Cultural Life of Modern America* (April 1889), which, with the published section of *Hunger,* finally established his reputation as a writer of considerable promise.

In America Hamsun had done some traveling and tried a variety of occupations; yet for all that his experiences were rather limited. His friends—small holders, artisans, clerks, and schoolteachers—were mostly Scandinavians, and so belonged to an ethnic group of little prestige among America's elite; even within the Norwegian ranks they were far below the ruling class of ministers, politicians, and prominent businessmen. Thus Hamsun never met America's leaders in industry, politics, or the arts. In 1880–81 Bjørnstjerne Bjørnson had been appalled to see the ignorance and bigotry among the Scandinavians in America, but he had also visited the East and met people like Longfellow, Emerson, and Holmes. "Whoever has lived among the men and women of New England," he wrote, "has enjoyed the world's best company. An American Gentleman . . . is the noblest thing there is."[36] Hamsun, on the other hand, spent his years in America in a pioneer district, where men and women after the struggle of the day devoted their time to nationalistic and religious trivialities. His experience among those people could hardly give him adequate material for a book on American civilization, which he also treated unfairly. The sins of America, as Hamsun saw them, had all been enumerated by earlier European travelers and fell into the categories of restlessness, which destroys people's peace of mind; democracy, which reduces all standards of excellence; and national pride, which leads to isolationism and cultural stagnation.

The only field Hamsun could speak about with some degree of authority was American literature, but the fact that in his treatment he left out Mark Twain, an American writer he always admired, indicates that Hamsun's goal this time was to debunk. Nevertheless, *The Cultural Life of America* is both a very amusing book and, as we shall see in the following chapter, a document of considerable importance for understanding Hamsun's later development.

In a brief autobiography, written in 1894, Hamsun laments all his troubles in Norway and America and ends with the line "wrote the first published chapter of *Hunger* (1888). Then things got better."[37] And they did. Hamsun's later life is mostly the story of his books, which appeared over the next forty-eight years at average intervals of sixteen months, but since to write them he needed new impressions and therefore had to travel, his life continued to be the old "peaceless flight through all the land." There were the obligatory journeys to the cultural centers—Scandinavia's Copenhagen, which he visited many times between 1892 and 1904, and Europe's Paris, where he stayed during 1893–96, though apparently without learning anything interesting about the French. Then there were the journeys of his personal choice, a major trip to Finland, Russia, and the Orient in 1898–1900, which resulted in two travel books, and his sentimental journey to what was by then an equally exotic place, his childhood home at Hamarøy, which he had not seen in twenty-five years. Immediately before World War I he mentioned the possibility of a lecture tour of America,[38] and in the late 1930s he thought again of visiting the United States to gather material for a second volume of his recent book, *The Ring is Closed* (1936), but it came to nothing, and he gave up the idea of completing the novel. Tore Hamsun tells us that his father even thought of traveling to Palestine to see the Jewish colonizing projects there; instead, during the spring of 1938, he visited Italy and Yugoslavia, with the idea of writing a travel book. He visited Germany several times during World War II, and though he had always feared heights, even to the extent of being unable to climb trees during his childhood, he began to enjoy the excitement of air travel. On his trips he also met unusual people, including famous men—Strindberg in Paris, Edvard Munch in Munich, Sibelius in Helsingfors, and Johannes V. Jensen in Copenhagen.

Hamsun never cared for panoramic views, and traveling did not so much mean going to exciting places, as simply getting away. As a writer he remained a vagabond, even after he built a home and established a family—any neighboring town, however small and insignificant, could inspire him or at least provide the peace he needed to concentrate on the one thing necessary, which was his art. Because of his nomadic nature, a stationary life at first did not appeal to him. Hamsun was forty when he first married, forty-three when his first child was born, forty-six when he built his first home, fifty when he remarried, and fifty-two when he finally returned home to Hamarøy—as he believed, for good—to cultivate the soil on his new farm Skogheim (1911). But even at Skogheim, where he began to refer to himself as a farmer, he had his actress wife take charge of the chores, while he stayed in a neighboring town writing a book and there received news that his wife had given birth to his first son. In 1918 he moved with wife and four children to the estate of Nørholm, near Grimstad in south Norway, where he spent the remainder of his life, though he continued to stay for longer or shorter periods away from home, in Oslo or one of the small towns on the South Coast.

He was also a farmer, and possessed a considerable theoretical knowledge of farming.[39] Still, it was gentleman farming. He increased his cultivated land area, planted thousands of trees, bought modern farm machinery, all of which cost large sums of money and added to his worries. Running Skogheim had made him so nervous that he had to sell it, though soon after he acquired the much larger farm of Nørholm. Occasionally he would honestly admit that his real work was writing, but more often in his letters during and after World War I he would emphasize the fact that he was a farmer. There is no doubt but that his own family suffered from having to live with an artist. His wife found him nervous and unreasonable, and to his children he was irritable and pedantic. On the other hand, he could be extremely generous, inviting friends to come and stay for days on end or inviting guests for evening parties, at which Tore and the other children would be surprised to see their father in an extraordinarily happy mood over a poker game.[40]

Hamsun had written and lectured disdainfully about the general overestimation of great poets, and now he was himself one. He did not seek fame, shunning both newspaper reporters and biographers, to one of whom he wrote (1926): "I shall not read it—but then it is not intended for me. This is already the sixth book about me, and I have not read any of them. I can't bear to read them: praise makes me embarrassed and helpless. . . ."[41] On the other hand, he knew who he was and the Scandinavian custom of always using titles sometimes infuriated him, as did misspellings of his name: " 'Author, Mr. Hamsun': A Man is not 'Author, Mr.' when he is close to seventy and in addition Me. . . ." "I am not the farm Hamsund . . . no more than Anatole France is the same as the country of that name."[42] On two occasions he brought a suit against people who, he felt, had tried to usurp the name of either Hamsun or Nørholm. Hamsun without the *d,* he insisted, was his own invention, and with the purchase of his estate in 1918 went the sole right to use its name of Nørholm.[43]

Even if Hamsun was never a public person in the same sense as, say, Bjørnstjerne Bjørnson, he felt the need to publicize his opinions and on several occasions got involved in polemics that harmed his reputation among his countrymen. An article from 1910,[44] deploring the difficulty of getting ministers to the churches of north Norway (since most civil servants, then as now, hoped to find a position in the south), was relatively harmless, likewise his S.O.S. (1913, 1918) to the public about defending Norway's official language, *Riksmål,* against the attack of eager language reformers. The article "Barnet" (The child, 1915),[45] with following polemics, directed against the government's lenient treatment of unwed mothers who had killed their babies, showed more clearly Hamsun's conservative attitude, as did his pro-German articles during World War I. Nevertheless, Hamsun remained a popular writer in his social-democratic homeland as well as abroad, even in communist countries. He won the Nobel Prize in 1920 and on his seventieth birthday nine years later received a festschrift in which many prominent writers of his generation paid their respects to a great novelist: John Galsworthy, André Gide, Maxim Gorkij, Gerhard Hauptmann, Thomas Mann, Jacob Wassermann, H. G. Wells, Stefan Zweig, and others. Czechoslovakia's president, Thomas Masaryk, wrote: "Among the many names of Scandinavian literature, whose works I have studied, I give Knut Hamsun the place of honor. Of late I enjoyed his analysis of the primitive colony of pioneers, a splendid modern Robinsonade of the near north. To me it is a reassuring lesson, how the small Scandinavian nations so largely contribute to world literature."[46] On his seventy-fifth birthday in 1934, he was offered the Goethe Prize; however, considering the economic difficulties of Germany, a country he had come to love and admire, he refused the 10,000 marks award, but accepted the Goethe Medal. His eightieth birthday, celebrated less than a month before Germany attacked Poland, received somewhat less attention, but the Gyldendal publishing company, since it could not hope to announce a new novel by Hamsun, brought out a collection of his articles. These show how, during three decades, Hamsun the critic had something important to tell his countrymen: from introducing the unknown Strindberg in 1889 to praising the new vitality of American literature in 1928.[47] All would have been well if Hamsun had died at that ripe old age as the most respected and most beloved of all Norwegian novelists, and no one would have remembered his sometime intemperate journalism or paid attention to those critics, like Leo Lowenthal, who tried to prove that there was a fascist streak in all of Knut Hamsun's writings.[48]

Last Years

On 9 April 1940 Hitler's soldiers attacked Norway, and during the following five years of occupation Hamsun wrote more than a dozen articles, which ruined the remaining years of his life and threatened to destroy his reputation for all time.[49] Hamsun's political persuasion differed from that of his countrymen not so much in its general conservatism—not all Norwegians were social democrats—as in his peculiar Anglophobia. Even before World War I he had begun to look upon Germany as a new vigorous country kept down by old England's colonial power, and that sympathy for the young nation he later transferred to Hitler's Germany. A forecast of what was coming was seen by some in 1935, when the Norwegian government contemplated giving the Nobel Prize for Peace to Carl von Ossietzky, then a prisoner in one of Hitler's concentration camps. Hamsun attacked the proposition as an insult to a whole nation. The Norwegian Authors' Union, however, strongly supported the Norwegian government, with the result (so many believe) that Ossietzky received the prize.[50] Four and a half years later, the first of Hamsun's infamous wartime articles appeared. "Et Ord til os" (A word for us) was published on 19 April, only ten days after the German attack. Basically the article attempted to convince Norwegians that, whereas England was their enemy and had always been their enemy, Germany was not at war with Norway but with the western powers: Norway was still neutral, and Germany had occupied the country in order to guard its neutrality. More particularly Hamsun criticized Norway's king and social-democratic government for having fled the country, though at this point he still seemed to hope the king would return.[51]

A second article, entitled "The Cabinet," criticized the cabinet for having mobilized (and there was virtually nothing to mobilize), since the result was that young Norwegians had to die in vain.[52] Finally on 4 May, while Norwegians were still fighting in north Norway, Hamsun published the notorious "Nordmenn!" (Roll Call), addressed to his Norwegian countrymen. "When the English penetrated into the Jøssing Fiord and broke our neutrality," it said, "you did nothing, likewise when the English placed mines along our coast. But when the Germans occupied Norway in order to prevent the war from coming here, then you sided with our runaway king and his private cabinet and mobilized." He went on to tell them their warfare was useless. "Throw away your guns and go home. Germany is fighting for all of us and will soon break England's tyranny against us and all neutrals."[53] During the summer of 1940 Hamsun also brought in the name of Quisling, a man he had not met, but long known from his writings, "a man all Norwegians now ought to support." Hamsun apparently was fully aware that not all Norwegians shared his opinions, for he mentions a number of anonymous letters in which he was accused of being a traitor—people even told him they had burned his books. That news seemed not to affect him though: the article is inspired by the contempt for the common man, which had long ago begun to lead him astray.[54] More than a year later, when Hamsun was asked why he was a member of the Norwegian Nazi party (which he actually was not), he mentioned again his thoughts on Quisling. The article was directed above all against England. The Norwegians, he said, would have to learn to reorient themselves toward Germany and stop being exploited by the long-toothed Britons. But even the English, he added, might one day be part of Hitler's national socialism. Of all people, he concluded, Hitler had spoken most directly to his heart.[55] Later in the same year, 1941, Hamsun appeared to have new ideas about young Norwegians losing their lives in battle. He was then writing for the Norwegian Legion fighting with the Germans on the Eastern Front. The Legion, he said would form the nucleus of a future Norwegian defense.[56]

One side of Hamsun's wartime activity was concerned with propaganda for Hitler's Germany and the Norwegian Nazi party; quite different was his work for Norwegians who had been imprisoned by the occupation forces for their political convictions. On 15 January 1941 Hamsun met with Joseph Terboven, the Reichskommissar for Norway, and the subject of their conversation was the arrest of a Norwegian writer, Ronald Fangen. Apparently Hamsun's publisher, Harald Grieg, had asked that Hamsun do something for his colleague. Fangen was transferred to a hospital, and later that year was released, probably because of Hamsun's intervention.[57] On 13 February 1943, in an article entitled "Nu igjen—" (Now once more) and dealing with letters Hamsun had received from parents whose sons had been sentenced to death for collaboration with the enemy, Hamsun deplores the situation, not only that these men have sided with England, but that they are young and must die. He tries to convince them that their sacrifice has been worthless and illogical, since they claim to know England will win even without their help. Nevertheless, the article seems inspired by genuine pity, and it is reasonable to think that Hamsun saw Terboven as a man Norway did not need, a person who should be removed.[58] On 19 May of the same year Hamsun visited Joseph Goebbels in Berlin. Goebbels in his diary describes the visit as successful and moving. Hamsun believed completely in German victory, he said; right from his childhood he had hated the English, he had also lived in America for many years and described people there as completely lacking in culture. Hamsun apparently returned the warm feelings of the Goebbels family. He spoke afterward about Mrs. Goebbels and their six children, and one month later he sent his host his Nobel medal, which he had received in 1920.[59] In June 1943 Hamsun was out traveling again, this time to Vienna, where he attended the Press Congress and in a speech repeated his old phobias about the English: "I am deeply and intensely anti-British, and I cannot remember that I have ever been anything else. . . ."[60]

Two days later Hamsun met Adolf Hitler at Berghof in Obersalzberg. After polite introductory remarks, the conversation turned to politics, in particular to Terboven, whom Hamsun tried to criticize. His manner apparently did not please Hitler, although he too had reason to be dissatisfied with Terboven's methods. Noting Hitler's displeasure, the Norwegian interpreter interrupted the conversation with a long description of the Norwegian Nazi party, which further tired Hitler. Hamsun noticed it, and not having understood anything of what was being said, he suddenly remarked in a very loud voice: "The Reichskommissar does not suit us. His Prussian manner is not acceptable to us, and then all these executions—it's enough!" Hamsun repeated his accusations against Terboven, and Hitler promised that after the war Terboven would continue as Gauleiter of Essen. Hamsun added other complaints, many of which were not translated, but finally asked the interpreter to tell Hitler "We believe in you." By that time Hitler had interrupted the conversation and gone out on the terrace. Hamsun wept, and Hitler asked the interpreter to calm down the old poet and left the meeting.[61]

Over the radio Hamsun in 1944 sent out an appeal to Norwegian sailors in English service: "I know that it is dangerous for you to try and break your chains and come home, but I know that Norwegian sailors have done dangerous things before and will do them again when they have the opportunity."[62] On 12 June 1944, after the Allies had landed in France, Hamsun wrote for *Aftenposten* a brief note with the headline "Tyskerne holder Europas redning i sin hånd" (Germany holds the salvation of Europe in its hands) and was then silent for a whole year, until 7 May 1945, when the war was over and he published the following obituary: "I am not worthy of speaking in a loud voice about Adolf Hitler, and his life and works do not invite sentimental emotions. He was a warrior, a warrior for mankind and a preacher of the gospel of right for all nations. He was a reformer of the highest order and his historical fate was to be active in times of extraordinary aggression, which finally felled him. This is the way the ordinary west European looks at Hitler, and we, his close followers, bend our heads at his death."[63]

"What will you do with Hamsun when the war is over?" Molotov asked the Norwegian minister of justice. "He will be treated like other Nazi-sympathizers." "Oh, but he has written such beautiful books!"[64] Three weeks after Hamsun had published his eulogy of Hitler (and explained it to his son Tore as an example of his will to be consistent), he and his wife Marie were interned at their estate Nørholm. Another three weeks thereafter, on 14 June, Hamsun was transferred first to Grimstad Hospital, and three months later to Landvik Old Age Home, a short distance from the town. On two occasions he was interrogated by the magistrate at Grimstad. Hamsun did not deny his sympathy for Germany. He had worked for Germany because he believed that was best for Norway. He did not consider himself guilty of treason, because his conscience told him he had worked for his country. When he was accused of being a member of the *Nasjonal Samling* party and of having supported Germany through his articles, he again denied the accusations. The result of the hearing was, however, that Hamsun was indicted in accordance with a new law concerning treason, whereby membership in the *Nasjonal Samling* was punishable with prison or fines of up to one million Norwegian crowns. Nørholm was confiscated and Hamsun placed under arrest until 22 September, when his release was further postponed until 6 November. However, before the charges were brought against him by the magistrate, Hamsun on 15 October was moved to the Psychiatric Clinic in Oslo, where he was examined by Professor Gabriel Langfeldt and Dr. Ørnulv Ødegård. Whether the attorney general actually had doubts about Hamsun's ability to stand trial, or whether, like Molotov, he just wished to see the Hamsun case shelved, is not known. After general questioning, at which Hamsun seemed to answer perfectly well for himself, Professor Langfeldt on 1 November stated that a proper mental observation was called for, with the result that Hamsun's case was further postponed until 12 January 1946. Professor Langfeldt apparently felt something was the matter with Hamsun's marriage, which he wished to look into further.[65]

Mrs. Hamsun—then in prison and awaiting her trial—was brought to the Psychiatric Clinic and there interrogated by Professor Langfeldt, who urged her to report the most intimate scenes from her marriage. Feeling this was the best way to save her husband from prosecution, she told details that showed him to be tyrannical and emotionally unstable, and Knut Hamsun, when he discovered his wife at the Clinic, felt instinctively what she had been up to. The quarrel that followed was heard throughout the corridors and ended with "Good bye, Marie, we shall not see each other again," a promise he kept for more than four years. On 11 February 1946, after what Hamsun later described as four terrible months at the Psychiatric Clinic, he was returned to the Old Age Home at Landvik. Doctors Langfeldt and Ødegård sent out a declaration saying they did not consider Hamsun to be insane or to have been insane at the time of his offensive actions, but that they considered him to be—and the phrase has since become famous in Norway—"a person with permanently impaired mental faculties." Two weeks later the attorney general announced that though Hamsun, since he was not insane, must be considered to be responsible for his actions, the government did not wish to bring a criminal case against him—because of his permanent mental impairment and the fact that the old man was practically deaf. However, the directorate for reparations would be responsible for the reparations question. What the statement meant was that Hamsun would not be sent to prison, but might lose his money.

He had to wait for almost two years before his case came up. On 16 December 1947 Hamsun in a moving speech explained why he had written the articles: it had been to save Norwegian lives. He had also sent innumerable telegrams to Terboven and to Hitler, asking for clemency. Somewhat less diplomatic was his statement that he had the best conscience and that he held Norwegian justice in high regard—but that his own perception of what was right and wrong was even higher. The prosecutor was able to show that Hamsun had been duly warned by well-meaning Norwegians. The counsel for the defense concentrated her efforts on proving that Hamsun had not strictly been a member of the party; neither party, however, brought in Hamsun's important visit to Hitler. The jury, consisting of the judge and two jurors, found Hamsun to be guilty. Even though he had perhaps not technically been a member of the *Nasjonal Samling* he had supported the enemy throughout the war, a transgression all the more serious since Hamsun had a high social position in Norway. It is interesting to note that the verdict was not unanimous: Judge Sverre Eide himself voted not guilty. Hamsun was sentenced to pay a fine of 425,000 Norwegian crowns, which was eighty-five percent of what the court considered him to be worth. Two years later Hamsun published a moving and brilliant account of his trial, *On Overgrown Paths,* which was well received by the critics and made readers wonder what Dr. Langfeldt had meant by "permanently impaired mental faculties."

Hamsun, who was now ninety-one and sat most of the time in an old wicker chair in his room upstairs at Nørholm, was completely isolated from his family and had no other company than two portraits of Goethe and Dostoevski looking down at him from the walls. In April 1950 he suddenly began thinking about his wife, whom he had not seen in more than four years. A telegram was sent to Oslo, to his son Tore, with whom Marie had stayed after serving her prison sentence, and she arrived less than a week later. She found it ironic that he should keep repeating "I cannot live without you"—something he had assured her of many times in love letters more than forty years earlier—since the words now had real meaning: he was rather helpless and she nursed him like a difficult child for the next two years. He clearly appreciated what she and others did for him—attention that now seems no more than his due. Very encouraging for the old artist were the news of his election to the exclusive Mark Twain Society and, particularly, a message from his old publisher Harald Grieg that Gyldendal would now begin republishing and advertising his books. "Daddy wept for joy," Marie wrote to her younger daughter Cecilia, and told her at the same time that she was now writing her memoirs, trying to make her husband as attractive as possible: "I mustn't expose him to the point where people can no longer sympathize with him—after all there was much to respect and love in him as long as he remained his old self."[66] In her letters she otherwise kept referring to another aspect of the irony in Hamsun's situation: "a man who despised old age and really was heartless against all those that allowed themselves to become old and helpless. It's perhaps 'his nemis' as an old woman in our prison said. The ugly always repulsed him. He could see nothing at all beautiful in an old face, but claimed there was always something beautiful in every young one. Not to speak of what he found unappetizing about senile people. And exactly this now strikes him."[67] As late as December 1951 she still thought her husband could live for a few more years, but when she finally realized that the end was near, her main concern was whether the family would be able to take care of the funeral expenses. She wrote to Cecilia on 18 February: "I look upon poverty as the worst of all curses, almost all sorrows and difficulties can be resolved for those who have money. At this point Hamsun is being played and read in the world. They call him the greatest of living writers, and we do not have the money to get him buried. And he is lying in rags on his death bed now."[68] Only a few hours after those lines were written, on 19 February 1952, Knut Hamsun died at the age of ninety-two.

Chapter Two

The Whispering of the Blood

The most important decade in Hamsun's writing career are the ten years between 1888 and 1898, beginning with his return from America and ending with his journey to Russia. This eastward movement also seems to characterize his literary production, which is marked by its diminishing "American" quality and its increasing use of what Hamsun referred to as "the dreamlike, lingering poetry of the Orient."[1] If, in *Hunger* (1888–90), some of the humor and "manly seriousness"[2] of Mark Twain is clearly present, this is no longer the case in *Victoria* (1898). But, as we shall see, there are certain features of Hamsun's style which he developed during the 1880s, which are typical enough to be referred to as "American," and which stayed with him throughout his life. It is true that Hamsun on his return from America used every opportunity to ridicule the Yankees. On the other hand, it is equally true that his colleagues in Scandinavia looked upon him as "American." His need to be in the news and to attack the old and clear the ground for the young, for instance, was seen as an American characteristic—indeed, a word often applied to him during the early 1890s was "Yankee."[3] In this sense Hamsun is not unlike Ibsen's Peer Gynt, who denounced the trolls but actually wrote their motto behind his ear, and lived accordingly.[4]

When Hamsun returned to Copenhagen in the summer of 1888, Georg Brandes had altered his signals. Rather than calling for a literary treatment of social problems, he now honored the elitism of Friedrich Nietzsche, about whom he had recently given a series of lectures which led to a lively public discussion among his old utilitarian followers.[5] What Nietzsche did to Georg Brandes, America in the meantime had done to Knut Hamsun. He had arrived in the New World in 1882 full of confidence in its egalitarian principles, but he soon felt that democracy could never favor his most immediate concern—the field of literature and the arts—and returned to Scandinavia in 1888 as an elitist, an unwitting disciple of Nietzsche and a soon-to-be leader of a literary movement against the positivism of the 1880s. What he still shared with the old positivists, however, was a firm stand against the idealization of life which filled American literature but which was happily absent in American newspapers. In the *Cultural Life of Modern America* he writes, "American journalism is still the most distinctive and vigorous intellectual manifestation of the American people. In its boldness, its realistic intensity, it is also from a literary standpoint the most modern."[6]

Even if Hamsun's concern in *The Cultural Life* was how best to amuse an audience of Copenhagen students, he was also fighting for a realistic art: "I am not asking for madness and the great sin—that is a question of morals, an issue by itself. I am asking for life, for bodies alive in their clothes—that is a question of art."[7] Provoked by the romantic in American literature (Longfellow and others) and guided by the realistic tone of the American press, Hamsun during the 1880s launched his attack upon puritanism in literature. Already his "Elroy Manifesto" ("My religion is the religion of the wildest naturalism"), several short stories—such as "Feminine Victory" and "Livets Røst" ("The Call of Life")—and finally the novel *Hunger* show that a completely unhampered realism was Hamsun's first condition for a viable modern literature.

According to Hamsun, it followed from the edifying principle of American literature that its fictional heroes would have to be psychologically simple. In his own writing he wanted instead to reintroduce a complex Byronic hero of the kind whose "life is a peaceless flight through all the land" ("Elroy Manifesto"), but his early attempts to shape that new hero were unfulfilled because they lacked humor. As mentioned earlier, Mark Twain's type of self-directed irony Hamsun used successfully for the first time in the short story "On a Lecturing Tour," which has a peculiar mixture of reckless farce and, on the other hand, drab, almost depressing realism. In the story are three subordinate characters—a cripple, an old shipwrecked captain by the name of Happolati, and an impoverished girl—all of whom later appear in some form in *Hunger,* but the repulsion or compassion aroused by such characters places Hamsun closer to Strindberg and Dostoevski than to Mark Twain. In his pioneering article on Strindberg from 1888, Hamsun shows how the Swede rejected Hippolyte Taine's concept of the *faculté maî-*

tresse—the idea that a literary personality will normally have one leading characteristic. Like Strindberg, Hamsun during the 1880s wished to create characters with a more complex psychology, and he remembered his missionary spirit even sixty years later, when he was examined by the psychiatrist Gabriel Langefeldt and described his fictional personae as being all "without so-called character. They are split and complex, not good, not bad, but both, subtly differentiated in their natures, changing in their actions."[18]

This concept of a new fictional hero, a special type of character unheard of in contemporary Scandinavian novels, Hamsun expounded in a series of lectures and in the important program article "Fra det ubevidste Sjæleliv" ("From the Unconscious Life of the Mind"), which he published in the journal *Samtiden* in 1890. In it he spoke about "the delicate life of fantasy held under the magnifying glass, the wanderings of these thoughts and feelings out of the blue; motionless, trackless journeys with the brain and the heart, strange activities of the nerves, the whispering of the blood, the pleading of the bone, the entire unconscious intellectual life."[9] None of Hamsun's heroes exemplifies his new literary program better than Johan Nilsen Nagel of *Mysteries*—a favorite book with many Hamsun specialists (including the American Henry Miller), though at its appearance in 1892 it was seen first and foremost as an example of Hamsun's childish need for publicity, what Arne Garborg called "this breathless, hellish Yankee-manner, which knows of no higher literary value than that of the hocus-pocus."[10]

Expressions like "the whispering of the blood, the pleading of the bone" tell us that Hamsun was interested not only in the unusual fictional character, but also in a special kind of language that would suit an unusual temperament. His Elroy claim, "but my world is the aesthetical literature," is fully endorsed by Kristofer Janson in his review of *The Cultural Life:* "I have never met anyone who has had as morbid a passion for aesthetic beauty as he and whose whole way of thinking has been to that extent dominated by that passion."[11]

In his article about August Strindberg Hamsun had deplored that a writer whom he so admired was not really a fine stylist. On the other hand, it seems that, if Hamsun had nothing to learn from the ideas of American authors, they had at least something to teach him in the way of literary style. Longfellow's rhythms did not leave him entirely cold, and though he ridiculed Walt Whitman's "I Hear America Singing" in *The Cultural Life,* he is not above using the same kind of enumeration of euphonic names in some of his own work. Furthermore, his cavalier treatment of Emerson in the same book shows that, though he thought nothing of the man as a thinker, he admired at least his lecturing style: "During a deadly calm he surprises us with a sentence that whips like a silken banner in the wind."[12]

Hamsun had experimented with prose rhythm in his early novels, but particularly during his stay in America, where he listened to lecturers and lectured himself, he developed a sense for the effectiveness of repetition, of questions and answers and antithetical constructions. *The Cultural Life of Modern America* shows that rhetorical style better than any other work by Hamsun, and while it is true that this particular book was originally composed as a lecture, some of its oratorical style always colored Hamsun's journalism and also carried over into his creative writing, characterizing his style till the end of his days.[13] The following two quotations, more than fifty years apart, show Hamsun's lifelong ambition to write sentences that whip "like a silken banner in the wind":

> This other loved him as a slave, as a mad man and as a begger. Why? Ask the dust of the road and the leaves that fall, ask the mysterious God of Life; for none other knows these things. She gave him nothing, no nothing did she give him and yet he thanked her. She said: "Give me your peace and your reason." And he grieved only that she did not ask his life.[14]

> Even now I have reminders of what my stay there at Psychiatric Clinic in Oslo destroyed for me. It cannot be measured; it has nothing to do with weight and measure. It was a slow, slow pulling up by the roots. Where does the blame lie? No one person, no one thing; a system. Domination over a living being, regulations lacking mercy and tact, a psychology of blank spaces and labels, a whole science bristling defiance.[15]

Hunger

Hunger (1890),[16] next to *Growth of the Soil,* is Hamsun's most widely known novel, and many would argue that it is also his best. Like many first novels it contains all the central elements of its author's later fiction—a tragic love story, poetic rendering of natural scenery, a sense of shockingly realistic detail—related in a manner that reveals the special lability of a youthful temperament: the book has humor, exuberance, hope, and despair in a combination never fully repeated by the more mature Hamsun. For students of Hamsun's biography there is also a documentary value to the story: the customary hangouts of the protagonist and the destinations of his many exploratory missions are all identifiable localities in Kristiania (Oslo), reminding us that the hunger described in these pages was indeed Hamsun's own during several sojourns in that city. Hamsun wrote his friend Frydenlund about his stay in Oslo 1885–86: "Things went so far with me Erik (and don't repeat this) that I had to sleep in the City Jail, and I spent several nights up in Møller Street in an abandoned tinsmith's shop. And do you think I had something to eat every single night? Oh, no, I was spared that all right."[17] And three years later he wrote Frydenlund from Copenhagen: "Good Lord, what a life I have led. You can't imagine how my intestines have been whining, both in America and here. Have lived day in and day out on a meal which I might have had sometime at the beginning of the week. Have been sitting chewing match ends. . . ."[18] Edvard Brandes, who finally "discovered" Hamsun in Copenhagen in the fall of 1888, told a friend: "I have rarely seen a more wretched human being. Not only that his clothes were tattered. But that face! I'm not sentimental, as you know, but that face moved me."[19]

This book, then, is more directly autobiographical than is usually the case with fiction of the naturalistic school and explains partly why Hamsun had chosen to use the first-person narrative as the most appropriate form. And he identified with his protagonist in a way which was not then common among the established writers. Arne Garborg's *Bondestudentar* (Peasant students, 1883) shared with *Hunger* its Kristiania milieu and autobiographical background, but Garborg in his novel did not "sing himself" the way Hamsun does in his. Not only was this a form more natural for Hamsun than for Garborg, but he had seen it practiced during his stay in America, in Whitman's poetry and in August Strindberg's autobiography, *Son of a Servant,* the second volume of which fell into his hands in Minneapolis.[20] There he also discovered that Strindberg had recommended the autobiographical documentary as the only acceptable novel of the future.[21] The subtitle of Strindberg's *Son of a Servant* (1886)—"The Growth of a Soul"—nevertheless points out a major difference between *Hunger* and the Swedish autobiography. Hamsun's intention was not to show *Entwicklung* but rather a soul's dialogue with its alter or superior ego. Indeed, he was so much interested in his protagonist's inner monologues that the novel suffers from lack of development. The author claimed he had aimed at that effect by playing, as he put it, his whole plot on one single string:

> What interests me is the endless sensitivity of my little soul; I felt I had described moods in *Hunger* whose total strangeness would not be likely to tire the reader by its monotony. Also, there is from the first to the last page not one single feeling which is repeated, none that resembles either the previous or the following. My book is not to be looked upon as a novel. There are lots of people who write novels when they describe hunger, from Zola to Kielland. All of them do it. And if it is the absence of the conventional structure of a novel which makes my book monotonous, then that is only a recommendation.[22]

Even though Hamsun was gradually to give up the first-person narrative in his fiction, his use of this form in *Hunger* was innovative. Thus,the protagonist's seeming alienation from himself ("I heard myself speak this gibberish but took in each word I spoke as if it were coming from another person"[23]) points toward the preoccupation with problems of identity in twentieth-century literature.

A first reading of *Hunger* will confirm Hamsun's claim that, with regard to plot, he is indeed playing on one string. The four parts that make up the novel seem much alike, both in mood and content. They tell of a young man's search for food, lodging, and part-time work in a big unfriendly city, where he wishes to try his luck as a writer but where, gradually, he finds himself with no place to stay and nothing to eat. His attempts to get a job are all unsuccessful, but in each of the four parts, when catastrophe is close, he is saved by a newspaper editor who buys an article or by an old friend who has a dollar to spare or, at the end, by taking a job on a ship and sailing away from the city.

The novel, like others by Hamsun *(Mysteries, Pan, The Wanderer),* describes an "experiment in living," here on the most elemental level: how to support the body—with food, rest, sex—in order that it can support an exceptional mind. The experiment is, as in most of Hamsun's early work, unsuccessful for the protagonist, whose body and soul are finally at the point of breaking down. The reader, however, will follow its course with special fascination, watching the interplay of crass realism in the description of his physical decline and, on the other hand, the astounding turns of his sparkling imagination. This mixture of naturalism and romanticism singles *Hunger* out among Hamsun's works. Its continuous flow of scenes, showing the protagonist's pain or repulsion, and his euphoria as he acts out his caprices, illuminates the central character and enlivens the tale, but it is also possible to discern in it a certain structuring of the events. Thus the first expository part of the novel offers the general pattern: the search for food, money, and work. Part 2, describing a night spent in a cell at the city jail, marks the first low point in the protagonist's misery and shows how easily his hunger pains are overshadowed by his fear of death. Part 3 contains the climax, with the expectation and excitement of the two meetings with "Princess" Ylajali, and part 4 the catastrophe in which, after losing Ylajali and tearing up his drama, the protagonist gives up the whole experiment. Such a horizontal development, despite Hamsun's wish to obtain the synchronic effect of an orchestral score, is evident also in other ways. The change of time from fall to winter, the change of the protagonist's residence from Oslo's west to its east end, the drop in his social status from having belonged in the company of the city's intellectual elite (when Ylajali first saw him in the theater) to a position where even servants laugh at him, and, finally, his own moral fall where he accepts unearned money—all this reinforces the impression of a planned steady decline. It is true that in part 4 the protagonist does not suffer from a lack of food the way he did in the earlier sections, but we have already learned that there are worse pains than hunger. The ugliness of his human surroundings and, particularly, his own inability to produce beauty in any form finally leave this hero completely without hope.

He is, of course, a special hero—handsome, nearsighted, with strong hands, as Hamsun could have described himself—but more particularly he is an artist-hero of the kind certain psychologists might refer to as schizoid, manic depressive, sadomasochistic, etc. Ibsen's statement that "to be a poet is to see" applies to this hero in an extraordinary degree, for under the influence of hunger, in mental states which today might well be called "psychedelic," he registers objects and events with the fidelity of the most sensitive camera: "Nothing escaped my eyes, I was sharp and my brain was very much alive, everything poured in toward me with a staggering distinctness as if a strong light had fallen on everything around me."[24] Despite the many illustrations of states of mind where the hero is described as being in the power of forces beyond his control, he is not always a mere medium. He can analyze the workings of the camera that he is, so that by creating special conditions he can make it yield extraordinary impressions, sometimes dreamlike, sometimes grotesque.

This hero is definitely an aesthete: the sight of an invalid, a toothless woman, or an old man, strikes him with a revulsion that he tries unsuccessfully to counteract with his daydreams of beauty—of Princess Ylajali reclining on a bed of yellow roses.[25] In his desperate fight to preserve his life he cannot avoid the constant reminders of death—fearful in the prison scene, grotesque in the newspaper advertisement for shrouds, peaceful in the book's many graveyard scenes. He sees life as irony—on the first page we find him reading advertisements for newly baked bread and for shrouds—and he practices such irony by his endless play acting. He simulates in order to confuse his enemy, who are the various representatives of the Kristiania bourgeoisie, but it is at the same time a compulsive make-believe: the hero pretends to be experiencing real life, whereas in fact he is a voyeur, deriving his vicarious pleasures and pains (except for his hunger pains) from observing others. On two occasions, by referring to the citizens in the capital as animals, he shows that underneath his peaceful appearance he considers himself a Nietzschean superman. Generally he is kind and compassionate and goes out of his way to render his fellowmen a service. However, it is all done as part of his ambition to remain unaffected by circumstances. His obsession with the notion of personal sovereignty gives him a pride that often assumes ridiculous forms, yet it marks the basic stance of all Hamsun's fictional heroes: the more ludicrous their life, the more they hope to leave it honorably—to die standing is their ultimate ambition.

In his fight for personal freedom the protagonist finds himself surrounded by allies and adversaries. God, who provides his artistic inspiration, is *for* him; the citizens, to the extent that they exist at all, are *against* him since they do not appreciate his art. *Hunger* is the one novel by Hamsun in which the concept of a personal God is still central. Actually it is also the novel in which Hamsun rejects the Christian God, and he was not a little proud of it: "The scene where the I of the novel throws his fury at Heaven has mainly left in your mind [Brandes's] the memory of the word Scum; but the whole scene is still the wildest protest against Heaven that I have ever seen in print."[26] The plot has overtones of the story of Job (and of Ibsen's *Master Builder* of two years later): God's servant being tried beyond his capacity. Like Job, Hamsun's protagonist has worked for some time in accord with God, but for reasons unknown to him—unless it is the usual: that God is jealous of his creative powers—he falls from grace and suffers bodily ills that finally break his spirit. Religious imagery abounds in the book—in its many references to God, to graveyards, church towers, and to the character of Christie (where the association to Christ is strong in Norwegian), who could have saved the protagonist but rejected him because of a trifling writing error. One critic has regarded the protagonist himself as a kind of Christ symbol, a naive and innocent soul, suffering injustice in the hands of people who do not wish to accept his message.[27]

The policemen, who play a central part in the novel, may be thought of symbolically as representatives of the Godhead—they tell the protagonist how much still remains of his alloted time span—but they also represent the city of Kristiania, the other pole in the protagonist's universe. This universe is peopled with a variety of types, cobblers, cake women, merchants, and at least two real humans, both of them touched by the protagonist's message: the newspaper editor, who sees his talent, and Ylajali, who is in love with him. These two personalities recur in much of Hamsun's work, one as a God/father/benefactor, the other as a potential, but invariably unsuccessful, savior. A common weakness of the first-person narrative is its one-sided character analysis, and if, as here, the narrator happens to be the protagonist, the views and behavior of secondary characters are often only sketched. Hamsun, however, can be both economical and fair. His sympathetic portrait of the "Commander" (modeled on the *Verdens Gang* editor Olav Thommesen) is a little masterpiece, and Ylajali is the first of Hamsun's many interesting women. Like Ibsen's Hedda Gabler, she is the daughter of a military man, presumably strictly brought up, but with a great appetite for the excitement of "adult" life. She had first seen the protagonist laughing with friends at the City Theater—in his happy West End days—and picked him out as a colorful philanderer. When she discovers that his eccentricities are real, that he *does* starve and *is* a poet, she, who is deep down just "an average Kristiania girl" with correct views, decides that she cannot throw her lot in with a person on his way out of society. At the end of the novel the protagonist sees her arm in arm with one of the city's prominent gynecologists. Idols—God and women—fall here as in *Pan* and other Hamsun novels, though there is no clear indication, as claimed by one critic,[28] that Ylajali has become a prostitute.

The real antagonist is still Kristiania, the city no one leaves until it has left a mark on him, and in *Hunger* it assumes personality, as in few other Norwegian novels. Actually, there is little description of the city as such, only glimpses from endless walks in the streets, one or two drab interiors, an occasional view from a window, or else a lyric snapshot from the harbor quarters, where the sea shines like mother of pearl. This highly accomplished impressionism gives way, when hunger affects the protagonist, to expressionism, whereby inanimate objects assume personality, people become animals and incidents symbolic—he experiences his shoes as an old friend, as a soft whispering sound coming toward him; the fall roses seem to have taken on a fever, their leaves a strange and unnatural flush; silent couples and noisy groups on Karl Johan remind him of mating times, of a warm swamp, of cats making love with high-pitched shrieks, and he sees his own predicament in the following scene:

> A small boy had been sitting, playing by himself on the far sidewalk; he was playing peacefully, expecting no harm—fastening together some long strips of paper. Suddenly he jumped up swearing; he walked backwards out on the street, keeping his eyes on a grown man with a red beard who was leaning out of a second-story window, spitting down on his head. The child sobbed with anger, and, unable to do more, swore up at the window, while the man laughed in his face—five minutes perhaps went by this way. I turned away so as not to see the boy sobbing.[29]

As the plot progresses, it becomes increasingly difficult to decide whether it is God or the city that brings about the protagonist's final defeat. The hero's drama—about a prostitute sinning at the high altar of a church—looks like an attempt to get even with God, but the incident with the red-bearded man and the little boy quoted above also seems like an allegory of how the unfriendly city of Kristiania treats its well-meaning visitors. Typically—and all Hamsun heroes have this touch—the final act of the protagonist before his departure is to "set his house in order": he leaves his last cake, even though he is still hungry, for the unknown little boy.

Hunger could be read as an example of Scandinavian naturalism from the late 1880s. Hamsun wanted to be direct in his new novel, and for stark realism some of its scenes are still unsurpassed in Norwegian literature. But the book also marks the end of the naturalistic period in the north. The hero is finally felled by inner and outer circumstances, but in his attempt to overcome the weakness of his body, there is a victory for the free human spirit. The hero studies the "crimes of the future" and is himself a potential lawbreaker insofar as he brings with him a revaluation of all values. He is concerned with the unconscious (that is, the intuitive: "my blood understood this greeting"), and he is suspicious of Christian humility (seeing an old cripple: "I never saw a more sinful back"). But even more than its hero (whose Nietzschean qualities are still only latent), the style of Hamsun's *Hunger* brought something new. The message was transmitted in a medium in which the old romantic rhetoric with its emphasis on color and rhythm came to life in a new way: the sentence "I tried to liven up the dead points with a colorful word" applies not only to the artist-hero of *Hunger,* but also to Hamsun's writing of the novel, as do the kind words of the newspaper editor: "there is too much fever in all you write." However, what makes the style of *Hunger* different from that of other "rhetorical" books by Hamsun, such as *Pan,* is its humor, which gives a special irony to scenes that would otherwise have been merely pathetic or theatrical. The "Russian" quality of *Hunger* has often been pointed out—that gray resigned despair that appears in Dostoevski's work and in Edvard Munch's "Sick Girl" (1885)—but equally important is a sense of frivolous absurdity in the style of Mark Twain. This above all singles out *Hunger* as the "classical" Hamsun novel, not only in the sense of being his first great novel or indeed a novel of some historical significance, but in its wonderful balance—of naturalism and romanticism, of humor and despair—which Hamsun never quite achieved again.

Mysteries

When it appeared in 1892, *Mysteries,* the most ambitious of Hamsun's early novels, was much less of a success than *Hunger.* It is a difficult book, but highly readable and increasingly recognized as central in Hamsun's production.[30] Its many connections with *Hunger* are useful guides for the interpreter. It has the same outsider hero carrying out his experiment in living among the philistines. However, it is an experiment that ends this time not in flight, but in suicide. Also, this time the setting is not the big city, but the unfriendly small town.

Hamsun once referred to Sarpsborg as the setting for *Mysteries*.[31] However, it seems more likely, judging from contemporary letters and articles by Hamsun, that the action takes place in Lillesand in south Norway, where Hamsun spent the summer of 1890. The identification of this locality is further supported by the personal names in the novel, many of them authentic Lillesand names, and by such topographical details as the location of the parsonage.[32] Indeed, it would not be wrong to view much of the novel's action as actual descriptions of Hamsun's own experiences in that little coastal town. He arrived there in June, probably with the intention of preparing for publication a volume of short stories, but soon the place provided him with material for a whole novel, and many details in this material are referred to in his correspondence.[33] He speaks there of a barber (in the novel a theologian) who is said to have committed suicide. He also talks of his endless walks to the parsonage, of visits to the cemetery, and of frightening a young lady by speaking to her without first introducing himself (as in the novel). Then there is the mysterious little man whom he sees walking in the lonely streets late at night. This person is further developed as Tønnes Olai in the short story "Småbyliv" (Small town life, 1890) and later as Oliver in *Women at the Pump* (1920), but first and foremost he is the model for the important character The Midget in *Mysteries*. Even the story of Kamma in chapter 12 may be an autobiographical incident thrown in as a caprice: Hamsun was visited in Arendal that summer by a mysterious lady, who turned out to be the Australian writer George Egerton (pseudonym of Mary Chavelita Dunne). She has celebrated this visit herself in a short story, "Now Spring Has Come" (from *Keynotes*, 1893), which corresponds in many ways with Hamsun's description in *Mysteries*.[34] Finally there are Hamsun's attacks on Gladstone, Tolstoi, Ibsen, and other famous people: similar attacks can now be seen in a recently discovered series of lectures which Hamsun prepared during his stay in Lillesand.[35]

Mysteries, then, like *Hunger*, is to a considerable extent disguised autobiography, and since the point of view is nearly always that of the protagonist (Nagel), the first-person narrative could as easily have been used. Actually, the special advantage of the third-person format—the opportunity it affords the author to render the thoughts of all his characters—has been largely overlooked. Nagel's thinking is shown intermittently throughout the novel, as well as in two long soliloquies, while the views of the other characters are presented only in conversation. Hamsun, therefore, seems to have had other, or additional, reasons for choosing the greater distance of the third-person narrative. Already in *Hunger* the protagonist was occasionally shown as a split personality, with one (narrating) ego watching the other. In *Mysteries* Hamsun has developed this phenomenon further. Here, in the interaction of two distinct characters, the narrator records one part of a personality (Nagel) as watching another part (the Midget) of that same personality. *Mysteries* differs from *Hunger* also in being an apologia for the author's iconoclasm, his "Yankee style," as it was referred to by his detractors: in this novel Hamsun, so to speak, steps back to the third-person narrative in order to take a second, more objective, look at himself.

The monotony which bothered certain readers of *Hunger* is nowhere to be felt in *Mysteries*. The author plays on many strings by developing his plot on several levels: Nagel, a disillusioned young man (29) traveling along the south coast of Norway on a steamer, is struck by the idyllic appearance of a small town and persuades himself to try life there one final time. He has already sized up the place and its inhabitants, whom he keeps confused with his curious dress and odd behavior, when he falls in love with a young woman (19), Dagny, of extraordinary charm and beauty. She finds him interesting, but since she is already engaged to a naval officer now on cruise and decides to remain faithful to him, Nagel's wooing is unsuccessful, and in despair or in spite he proposes to an older woman (41), the spinster Martha, with whom he hopes to live a simple cotter's life. However, because Dagny prevents this union, Nagel is cut off on all sides and ends his life by drowning himself. The denouement sees the two survivors, Dagny and Martha, walking arm in arm and commenting on the unusual qualities of the departed protagonist. Even though this love story has its drama and development, it is remarkable more for the manner in which it supports another aspect of the novel, which might be called "the detective story."

The mystery, practiced by such different writers as Dostoevski and Conan Doyle, was not cultivated by Norwegians until the twentieth century, and then by other writers than Hamsun. As an author of psychological novels Hamsun naturally shared the detective's concern with motives, but it is only in one book, *Mysteries,* that he brings in anything resembling a private investigator. On the other hand, he was always fascinated by crime as a sovereign act, inspired by courage or a sense of refinement, and in his book on America devotes considerable time to discussing it. The humiliation of the exposed criminal also moved him, as in an early short story where he describes the facial expression of an escaped swindler at the moment when the police officer puts his hand on his shoulder and places him under arrest (the motif is also referred to in *Mysteries*).[36] Furthermore Hamsun was interested in the concept of a "battle of the brains," then a popular literary idea, illustrated particularly in works by Strindberg, such as "Tschandala." A similar intellectual hide and seek lies behind much of the action in *Mysteries.*

Nagel, on his arrival in the small town, acts like a police inspector, studying the thickness of the walls and the height of the rooms and investigating the streets and the surrounding countryside by day and by night. He also interrogates his landlord about the details of a recent suicide by a man named Karlsen and questions the Midget's alibi: "where were you on June 6?" His method, however, differs from that of the ordinary detective in that he crosses territories where the readers cannot follow him and arrives at conclusions which would be unusual in conventional mystery stories. Thus, from the dilapidated appearance of Dr. Stenersen's house Nagel concludes that there is also something the matter with the doctor's marriage. And in the case of the Midget—the main object of his investigations—Nagel's chief reasons for suspecting him seem to be the cripple's bodily defect and his humble ways. As a detective story *Mysteries* is unsatisfactory, not only because symbolism and depth psychology take the place of simple induction, but more particularly because the reader is provided with no solutions. At the end of the book he still does not know whether Karlsen was murdered, nor does he know what happened to the Midget and what kind of crime he is supposed to have committed. Perhaps this is so because the detective story is only a part of the larger psychological novel: to solve the little mysteries would divert our attention from the major mystery, which is the character Johan Nilsen Nagel.

In 1890 Hamsun wrote to a friend: "It has always been my ambition to suddenly turn up somewhere and after a while leave as mysteriously as I came."[37] That ambition stayed with Hamsun throughout his life. It inspired his first book, *The Engimatic Man,* and his last complete novel, the trilogy about August. The point was never to be found out, but rather to keep stirring people's imagination—like August in Hamsun's novel of that name, who after his death lived on as a character in a folk ballad. In *Mysteries* Hamsun's ambition to become a myth is particularly well exemplified, for the protagonist certainly leaves as mysteriously as he came. Nagel, who is broad-shouldered but small of stature and described as having a soft, rather feminine mouth, exemplifies that mixture of male and female qualities which Hamsun found particularly fascinating in Strindberg's personality and which we later see generally in the sadomasochistic heroes of other Hamsun novels. On the one hand, Nagel is arrogant and aggressive and, on the other hand, humble and generous. He is drawn to the solitude of the woods, yet he yearns for the company of festive people whom he can entertain, sometimes with bawdy stories, sometimes with charming poetic tales. He wears a rough iron ring, while on his luggage belt the initials J. N. N. are embroidered with pearls. Nagel calls himself a living contradiction, and the author has taken care to show him to be consistently ambivalent in his relationship to other characters.

Dagny is young and beautiful, with a voice like music. She is said to be a happy person, kind to everyone and a good listener. Furthermore she is intelligent, proud, correct; and these qualities appeal to Nagel, though they also provoke him to confuse and embarrass her. He realizes he might not respect her if she were to break her pledge to the naval officer. Yet he still woos her, using a very special method: he deprecates himself, belying his generosity and his heroism, and hopes thereby to rise in her estimation—whereupon he discloses his "method" to her and in this way, by being honest about his dishonesty, betters his case even more. Dagny, like Ylajali, is at first fascinated by the man and his poetic ways, but, being bourgeois at heart, she misunderstands him, finds him too eccentric, and finally withdraws her favor. What follows is a prolonged period of recriminations, so typical of the Hamsun love story. When Nagel later proposes to Martha, Dagny shows the same kind of jealousy as the woman in one of Nagel's tales—of a man who, being unsuccessful with a beautiful damsel, turned to her crippled sister. But the proud lady had prevented that union: if he could not have her, neither should he have her sister.

The crippled sister in *Mysteries* is Martha Gude. Actually, she is not crippled, only older (41), with perfectly white hair. Nagel refers to her once as his guardian angel. On the one hand, she is a mother image—he wishes to bestow upon her the favors of a son by supporting her in her old age—on the other hand, she has fiery black eyes that indicate she may not be too old to be his partner in life. In his relationship to Martha Nagel again employs one of his "methods." He wishes to be generous, but since generosity creates indebtedness in the favored person, he must cover it up by pretending to be the receiver rather than the giver. Hence he buys from Martha a worthless chair at a high price, claiming he has now acquired a valuable piece of furniture. But what of his honesty when he suggests they should marry and live happily somewhere in the country? Since it is clear he cannot love Martha the way he loves Dagny, Nagel does not promise more than he can keep—they will live as companions, comrades, leaving behind them their dreams of passion. Still, the feeling that Martha is being used to help Nagel bury his sorrows is not far away. One of Nagel's many stories concerned a blind girl living in a tower with her demented father. Nagel had spent a night in the tower and in his dreams heard beautiful music from a chorus of blind angels. Some days later he found the blind girl lying crushed to death on the ground: she had fallen or jumped from the tower. The blind girl did not know Nagel, yet she loved him, became his guardian angel and died for him. This is a variation of a story told to Nagel by a woman he had met in a San Francisco opium den. Nagel lent her money so that she did not have to sell her necklace with a cross of precious stones to buy the opium she badly needed. In his opium dream he saw her lying dead at the bottom of the sea and later found out that during the night she had indeed jumped into the harbor. Some years later, when Nagel was in mortal danger, she had appeared before him again and saved his life. The idea of the woman who gives her lover all, including her life, is not developed realistically by Hamsun until Eva in the novel *Pan*. However, to the extent that Martha is the person alluded to in Nagel's tale of the blind girl in the tower, she is a precursor of Hamsun's humble woman, whose features are perhaps best portrayed in the short story "Slaves of Love" ("Kjærlighetens slaver," from *Kratskog,* 1903).

The blind girl lived in fear of her terrible father, and their relationship resembles that of Martha and the Midget. The latter are both of good family background, though life has lately been hard on them—Martha, Captain Gude's daughter, has no fortune or income, and the Midget, son of the Reverend Grøgaard, has suffered an accident at sea which has crippled him and made him sterile. Martha and the Midget have known each other since childhood, and although he has become attached to her, she tries to free herself from him. The book mentions, but does not explain, some crime that the Midget is supposed to have committed against Martha—it could be a crime concerned with either sex or money—the Midget, at least, tries to keep Martha in his power. Nagel's relationship to this character is the most interesting and most intriguing aspect of *Mysteries*. Soon after Nagel's arrival in town his acquaintance with the crippled man begins, and ends when Nagel calls him a swindler, but even then Nagel bestows gifts upon him and weeps when the Midget refuses to accept them. The Midget does small menial jobs or else he entertains his fellow citizens by grinding his teeth or dancing barefoot for money. He is servile and speaks well of all people. Nagel helps him in various ways, though he suspects him of having murdered Karlsen and, presumably, of having sexually molested Martha Gude. The Midget, on the other hand, guards Nagel's local reputation by wiping out a frivolous verse Nagel has scrawled on Miss Meek's gravestone and later saves Nagel's life by emptying a bottle of cyanide with which he intended to end his days. The Midget is said by some to be a harmless fellow, by others to be an exceptionally good person, and exactly such verdicts are what makes Nagel suspect him. Altruism as egoism was a paradox that intrigued Hamsun at the time he wrote *Mysteries*. In the Scandinavian scene of the 1890s it was also part of an intellectual discussion dominated by Georg Brandes's recent (1888) discovery of Nietzsche.

George Egerton's reference to Nietzsche in *Keynotes* (1893) is said to be the first mention of him in English literature.[38] Hamsun, with whom she discussed the German philosopher, was introduced to his ideas five years earlier. He was then working on *Hunger* and an important article on Kristofer Janson, whose middle name, incidentally, was Nagel. Of Janson Hamsun wrote: "As a leader he lacks completely the cold vehemence that can clutch an antagonist and the glowing breath in words that can ignite. . . . He is a hospital doctor whom they have given the position of a field marshall."[39] In the article Hamsun did not lack sympathy for Janson but called him a nobleman, in reference not only to his upper-class background, but to a certain nobility of mind. Henrik Ibsen, on a visit to Norway in 1885, had addressed the assembled workers of Trondheim and mentioned a new kind of nobility, which he found to be necessary for human progress. He believed that its formation would depend on the influence from two groups that had so far not been heard, namely, women and workers, and in the following year he brought out some of those ideas in his play *Rosmersholm*. However, by the time Hamsun read that play (1890) he had changed his mind about nobility. He now ridiculed Rosmer, that weak humanist, whose forefathers had been great warriors—a man, like Kristofer Nagel Janson, who could not strike—and he called Ibsen's portrait a caricature of the concept of nobility.[40]

At a party Nagel describes a dream he once had of an old man who was stuck in a marsh. He looked like a tormented and dangerous animal, and Nagel taunted him more and more recklessly until he was caught by him and expected to be torn to pieces. But the old man—whom the listeners at the party have finally recognized as the Midget—kissed the ground and thanked Nagel for not having tortured him more.[41] In their essays about Nietzsche both Georg Brandes and the Swedish writer Ola Hansson describe his *Toward a Genealogy of Morals*—in which Nietzsche shows how man's natural instincts were perverted to a new sense of sin—but of the two Hansson does it more graphically, translating almost verbatim from Nietzsche's book: "This animal man, which one wishes to domesticate, and which bloodies itself against the bars of its cage, this languishing, despairing captive, which has been cut off from its original animal state, now views its old instincts as something which must be overcome, suppressed, destroyed. Thus, what was once the essence of nature, becomes our bad conscience."[42]

In the novel there is mention of a young woman, Mina, with the unusual surname of Meek (the English word for humble?), a local saint, who—Nagel maintains—has never used her body but denied her natural instincts by communicating at all times with God. Christian humility, which other people in the village praise as a virtue, Nagel—like Nietzsche—sees as a form of emasculation. The Midget's fall from the mast in this respect is symbolic: his real name of Grøgaard was once the most respected in the small town. Now he is everybody's fool. But Nagel goes beyond deploring this kind of fall: he associates it with criminality. Brandes's essay on Nietzsche contains several references to the philosopher's warnings against so-called good people, and Hamsun, in one of the public lectures he gave at the time, discussed the example of a serene-looking old man whom a writer friend wished to use in a novel; but, as Hamsun was able to prove, the old man looked that way not because he was good, but because he had been stealing cheese from his married daughter's pantry.[43] Similarly, as we have seen, Nagel suspects the Midget of a secret sin, and his suspicion is proved correct, even if the reader never learns what the sin is. In his new hero, then, Hamsun has, as it were, taken Kristofer Janson's middle name of Nagel and endowed its possessor with the elitist qualities of a field marshall, while the hospital doctor—that is, the Christian kindliness which Janson exemplified—has been turned into Nagel's caricature in the form of the humble character known as the Midget.

The combination of Christianity and buffoonery probably refers generally to Nietzsche's "slave morality," and more particularly perhaps to the kind of artist/politician who wishes, like Kristofer Janson and Johannes Rosmer, above all to serve the common man. In the novel Nagel tries to save the Midget from his dumb show by appealing to his aristocratic background, and for a while he succeeds, but seeing one day the Midget resume his old clownery in the marketplace finally convinces him that life is ugly and not worth living. But then death can be equally ugly. Like Ibsen's Hedda Gabler, Nagel has dreams of freedom and beauty, at least dreams of a beautiful death, which in his case means a harmonious reunion with peaceful Nature. His planned suicide in the woods, however, turns into a caricature, and when he finally dies it is in the sea, where his friend from San Francisco found her fearful death. Nagel's dream of liberating others (that is, liberating the Midget) did not come true; whether he was able to liberate himself—that is, by eliminating the Midget in him—we do not know. His suicide, again like that of his San Francisco friend, seems to have been the result of fever and confusion. Again, in this respect the novel offers no resolution.

In *Hunger* Hamsun wanted to demonstrate in fictional form his theory of a new hero. In *Mysteries* theories are discussed throughout, both in and between the lines, and Hamsun in later life criticized this *chef d'oeuvre* of his youth for having "too much talk."[44] What is being debated is mostly the importance of great men. Nagel, like Nietzsche, turns against the kind of greatness—exemplified by people like Gladstone, Ibsen, and Tolstoi—that, by the commonplace mind, is ranked according to its measure of fellow feeling. Instead Nagel looks up to the unknown artist or to the political genius whose emergence in history changes its course. However, he does not accept most modern poets, who are described as a scurf on society, arrogant and irritable longbeards demanding to be treated gently. Strangely, Bjørnson, despite his many theories *à la* Tolstoi, fares well in these debates, probably because Nagel considers him closer to that aspect of life which is pulsating and unpredictably mysterious and which cannot be mapped with the help of natural or social science. William Blake's view of Newton as a destroyer of life's poetry is restated by Nagel in his attack on the liberal Dr. Stenersen, whose patients are cured, not by the doctor's science, but by their own superstition. Through the character of Nagel, who wears fetishes and believes in signs and symbols and who appears to be right in most of his suppositions, Hamsun turned against the positivist thinking that characterized Scandinavian literature in the 1880s and instead focused his attention on the importance of dreams and instincts. Nagel arrives in the town with a violin case, which turns out to contain nothing but dirty linen—yet, as he later proves, he can play. He can also pay: the landlord, who cannot sight a single banknote in Nagel's many-pocketed billfold, immediately thinks of him as a swindler, but the landlord is mistaken: when he opens the right compartment he finds it full of money. Nagel walks around in a yellow suit, and since in some traditions, including Scandinavian, yellow is the color of falsehood, many critics have taken it to mean that Hamsun considered Nagel to be a liar and a charlatan. But yellow is more generally the color of sunshine (Apollo) and signifies magnanimity, intuition and intellect.[45] It is also the color of romanticism and the regency style, which Hamsun loved: Ylajali *(Hunger)* reclines on a bed of yellow roses, and Victoria *(Victoria)* is at her most fascinating in her yellow dress. More than mere falsehood, Nagel's yellow therefore also represents a poet's dream of freedom and beauty.

Many modern poets—writers have been particularly attracted to *Mysteries,* not only because of its central character with his dreams, crazy stories, and buffoonery, or because of its inexhaustible wealth of developed and undeveloped Hamsun ideas, but because of the magic of its language, which turns even the most distressing events into song.[46] Henry Miller recalls how a page of Hamsun "frequently would yield the same mysterious harmonies of enchantment as a walk by the canal. . . . Perpetual sunshine. And remembered music, toned down to blend with the hum of insects and the rustle of leaves. Joy, joy, joy. The intimate presence of flowers, of birds, of stones which have preserved the record of similar magical days."[47] The elitism of *Mysteries* does not go well with the political radicalism of today's Norwegian writers,[48] but few of those who once read and admired the book will deny its beauty and its basic message of joy, so evident in the following passage, where Nagel's euphoria has been temporarily upset by the sight of a farmer on his way from the market:

> But when he came back to the docks and saw the bustling activity all around him, his spirits gradually brightened and he again began singing to himself. The weather was glorious, a beautiful June day, no reason to feel depressed. The little town, shimmering in the sunshine, looked like an enchanted city.
>
> When he entered the hotel, his caustic and bitter mood was gone. His heart was free of rancor, and in his mind's eye he again saw the boat of scented wood, with a light blue silk sail in the shape of a half moon.[49]

Pan

In December 1893 Hamsun wrote from Paris to a friend in Bergen: "My new book will be so beautiful. It takes place in North Norway, a quiet and red love story. There will be no polemics, only people living in a strange landscape."[50] *Pan* is indeed Hamsun's most beautiful book, and it is remarkable how it grew naturally from a bitter controversy Hamsun had been engaged in with his detractors and former friends during the previous two years. Olav Thommesen—the admired "Commander" of *Hunger*—had called him a charlatan after his literary lectures, and Hamsun responded, first by drawing a picture of himself as a "charlatan" in *Mysteries,* then by using Thommesen as a model for another kind of charlatan, Editor Lynge in the novel of that name. *Editor Lynge* (April 1893) in turn received a vicious review by Arne Garborg, an older colleague and adviser.[51] Both he and Hamsun were friends of Bolette Pavels Larsen, and in their correspondence with her it is not difficult to detect a tone of mutual jealousy and suspicion. In 1892 Hamsun had been accused of plagiarizing Dostoevski, and he believed that the accusation had originally come from Garborg. Only three weeks before

Garborg's infamous review of *Editor Lynge*—upon his receiving reports of Hamsun's appearance as a lecturer in Copenhagen—he had attacked Hamsun in an article entitled "Svært til Kar" (Braggadocio).[52] By then Hamsun had written the short story "Glahns Død" ("Glahn's Death"),[53] which reports the murder of a certain Lieutenant Thomas Glahn by his companion on a hunting expedition in India. Glahn, who had recently received a letter from a woman he once loved, apparently wished to die and provoked the shooting, which was all the easier since his hunting companion already hated him for stealing his girl friend. The story is written in a strangely pedantic manner, totally (and, of course, intentionally) unlike Hamsun's style, and Glahn, whose obituary was written by this pusillanimous detractor, rises in the reader's estimation and becomes the fascinating character that the writer of the account pretends he was not.[54] While certain incidents and characteristics point to Garborg as a model for the unsympathetic narrator, it would be more reasonable to assume that Hamsun had in mind the whole host of his attackers. He wrote to a friend in America: "I have not been able either to speak or to write a single word without receiving the worst abuse in Norway, Denmark, or Sweden. . . . *Morgenbladet* calls me 'the apostle of humbuggery in Norwegian literature.' "[55] The strange thing is that Hamsun was able to turn his uninspired story about Glahn into one of his most exciting novels and that it was to take the form of a hunting diary—this time written by Glahn himself.

For Hamsun to write a novel about a hunter was indeed unusual. He always claimed that he belonged to the woods rather than the city, but even though he spent long periods of his life as a tramp in Norway and America, and though in later years he led the existence of a country gentleman, he was never a sportsman, that is, he had no practical knowledge of traps, guns, fishing flies, or hunting dogs; and one might well ask where he got both this information and his inspiration. As a child Hamsun had watched English tourists fishing in North Norway, and he must have studied some of the classical accounts of Norwegian outdoor life, at least some of those contained in Asbjørnsen's folktales. In Norway there were several works describing the life of nineteenth-century outdoorsmen, such as Bernhard Herre, who resembled Glahn in being a social misfit, an unhappy lover, and a potential suicide.[56] There was Denmark's Vilhelm Dinesen (Isak Dinesen's father) who, like Hamsun, had observed the revolutionary manners of the Parisians—as well as the scenery of Wisconsin and north Norway—and described his experiences in two books, including the well known *Hunting Letters of Boganis* (1889–92).[57] Vilhelm Dinesen shared Bernhard Herre's love of the countryside and its beautiful women, but he was a more sophisticated observer of nature and less of a social misfit, since he was a progressive landowner and a member of the Danish parliament. However, like Bernhard Herre—and Glahn—he took his own life. In addition to Boganis' *Hunting Letters*—which we know Knut Hamsun read—there was in those days a whole literature of hunters' diaries, full of information for the uninitiated and of poetic passages for an accomplished writer to emulate. Even Strindberg, in his short prose collection *Flower Paintings* (1888), had a chapter called "Hunting Memoirs," in which the following passage appears: "Nature can be very charming, but when it behaves threateningly, dangerously, unfeelingly, then it is frightening. And at such times I felt that terror, from which the nature god Pan received its name panic."[58] Hamsun at the time was revising one of his old articles on Strindberg, which finally appeared in 1894, the same year as *Pan*. In it he described Strindberg as "an animal longing for the woods," a description corresponding to Glahn's "I belong to the forests and the solitude"—the last line of the novel *Pan*.

Pan is the diary of Thomas Glahn, a retired lieutenant who has just received a letter containing two green feathers, once presented by him to a young woman in north Norway. To while away his time he now (1857) sits down to write of his summer up there two years ago, playing with memories which seemingly left little impression, but which, as it soon appears, have marked him for life. A city person of good family background and education, Glahn in 1855 had rented a forest hut from a rich merchant, Ferdinand Mack of Sirilund, and was busy working on his spiritual return to Nature, when he fell in love with Mack's twenty-year-old daughter, Edvarda. The two experienced a period of intense happiness which was soon interrupted by misunderstanding and acrimony. Glahn comforted himself with another woman, Eva—"a young girl with a white woolen scarf, she had very dark hair." Later he learned that she was the wife of the local smith and Herr Mack's mistress. Edvarda, on the other hand, was seen more and more in the company of a Finnish baron, to whom she was later married. When the baron prepared his return to Finland, Glahn planned to give him a good-riddance salute by blasting a cliff and sending boulders crashing into the sea as the baron's ship was passing by. Herr Mack, however, had set Eva to work tarring a boat on the beach right beneath that part of the mountain, and she was killed by the rockfall. In the autumn, when Glahn was about to leave, Edvarda asked to keep his dog Aesop, in memory of him, but fearing that she would mistreat the dog, he shot it and then sent her the dead body. *Pan* is an unusual novel, since it is supplied with an epilogue, the short story "Glahn's Death," referred to above. Now (1859) in India, Glahn again receives a letter from Edvarda this time saying that she is a widow and free to marry him. Glahn dresses up as if for a wedding, then provokes his estranged hunting companion to shoot him.

Not since *Bjørger* (1878) had Hamsun treated the strange landscape of north Norway that was to play such a central part in his later novels. Its magnificent scenery and its provincial social life provide background and framework of the story. The picnics and balls Hamsun spoke so contemptuously of in his literary program have not been avoided here. Indeed, the plot is organized around two island picnics and two Sirilund parties—social occasions on which either Glahn or Edvarda or both fail to maintain community standards. During the first outing, Edvarda exclaims quite unabashedly "I love only Glahn." During the second, an annoyed Glahn throws Edvarda's shoe overboard. After the first Sirilund gathering, Glahn in desperation forces the lame doctor to jump like a dog over the barrel of his outstretched gun; and at the last ball, Glahn, pretending to whisper something to the baron, spits into his ear. As so often in Hamsun's novels, the climax of the romance is reached fairly soon—one third of the way through the plot—and is followed by painful and prolonged scenes of love-hate. As in *Hunger,* the development of the love story is accompanied by a seasonal movement—the transformation of the natural landscape from spring to winter—but it is more pronounced in this hunting diary. Here the progression of the seasons, and in particular the arrival of the fall with its first killing frost (the Iron Nights), pushes the pitch of Hamsun's prose to heights it never reached before or after. Finally winter arrives with its first northern lights.

The ruler of the place is Ferdinand Mack, a powerful merchant somewhat in the style of E. M. K. Zahl from Hamsun's own youth. Age (he is forty-six) has not reduced his sexual prowess nor his jealousy and hatred. When Mack's mistress Eva—the smith's wife—

gives him up for Glahn, he arranges to have her killed and burns down Glahn's hut in the woods. Mack's style—including his poise and sharp intelligence—is reminiscent of that of an Eastern potentate, and Glahn seems to respect him as a worthy antagonist. Mack's daughter Edvarda feels differently about him. No love is lost between them, though she is willing to consider the eligible suitors he brings to the place—a lame doctor and a pedantic natural scientist, who is also a baron and whom she finally marries. But as Glahn loves Edvarda, so she loves him, and since the lovers do not succeed, the book sets out to show what is wrong with one or both of them.

In Edvarda the reader recognizes a woman who is afraid to break away from the norms of society, though she is much more a true daughter of nature than her literary predecessors, Dagny Kielland and Ylajali. Glahn's image of love in this northern landscape is represented by his dream woman, Iselin, whose name combines the elements of *is* ("ice") and *lin(n)* ("soft" "mild") and whose temperament is similar to Edvarda's. Edvarda is a motherless child, and it shows in her somewhat haphazard clothing and a general helplessness that touches Glahn: "her thin arms gave her a neglected look." But she has a generous mouth; her lips are red, and the "wrinkles on her knuckles were full of kindness." Since her face and neck are described as brown, there is a certain indication of southern blood—with its overtones of passion and fickleness—that Hamsun later developed more explicitly in Teresita *(The Game of Life)* and the Mexican Mariane *(Segelfoss Town).* As an only child brought up by her father to be the local princess, she is pert, proud, generous, and impulsive, but also lacking in education and social graces, weaknesses that cause her much humiliation and which she sets out to remedy. The local doctor, a lame little man who has courted her in vain for years, describes her as being simultaneously calculating and passionate, and much given to fantasy. Edvarda, who looks and acts like a young teenager and who begins by publicly confessing her love of Glahn and ends by marrying the Finnish baron, seems to be the usual Hamsun heroine who is spoiled by social ambitions. She sits waiting for her hero, but finds that Glahn does not measure up to her dream picture.

Glahn is handsome, likeable, of good family background, well educated; and even if not learned ("I am no student"), he is able to read the minds of people around him. Socially speaking, his case is opposite to that of Edvarda. Formerly a gallant Kristiania lieutenant, he is driven by *weltschmerz* to the forests of north Norway, where he seeks an unspoiled nature and tries—unsuccessfully—to unlearn his city manners. He manages to upset glasses and feel awkward in the company of young society women, but he is not free from all traces of social polish. Whenever he hates Edvarda, he thinks of her as an uneducated fisherlass, and in the end he is not above sending for his uniform to impress the stubborn princess with his military splendor. More particularly he is unable to shed his social training in his way of treating women. It costs him nothing to seduce the goatherd girl Henriette or to become Eva's lover, but he is deeply embarrassed by Edvarda's uninhibited declaration of love, and though they later meet every night for a week, there is no direct indication of a sexual relationship. Glahn's reluctance with the "princess" may be the reason for Edvarda's erratic behavior, which finally changes their friendship into hatred. When Edvarda hears of Glahn's meetings with Eva, her love is reawakened by jealousy and she comes back wearing a white scarf, like her rival (in *Mysteries,* the frustrated Dagny suddenly had appeared in a white hat, simulating Martha Gude's white hair). But it is too late. Glahn's cruel treatment at the hands of Edvarda now makes him deaf to her moving confession of love.

Certain readers of *Hunger* accused "Andreas Tangen" of being incapable of loving; otherwise, they claimed, he would have been able to seduce Ylajali. In a letter Hamsun answered the critics: "But now once more I shall try to show that I don't have a 'cold spot.' I shall document, so to speak, that I am normal. That will take place in my next book."[59] But Nagel exhibited the same lack of enterprise as "Andreas Tangen," and so does Glahn. One reason for Glahn's failure to act might be that Hamsun has not really succeeded in creating a lieutenant of the upper classes but rather a farmer who can function erotically only with women he is able to rule. That was the view of Hamsun's Danish colleague Johannes V. Jensen, who praised Hamsun as the ultimate farmer: "Culture consists of . . . eating with a fork and being unable to distinguish one kind of grain from another. These things Hamsun studied and saw how one should set about bending a woman to one's will without at the same time breaking her. Hamsun struggled late and early to become a refined person. . . ."[60] Another reason for Glahn's hesitation is that, like Edvarda, Glahn is a proud dreamer who refuses to be satisfied with things as they are; he has many ways of compensating for his losses with Edvarda, on the prosaic level there is Henriette, the seventeen-year-old goatherd girl, or he can satisfy himself in his poetic dreams of Iselin:

> when she comes, my heart understands it all and it no longer beats, it booms. And she is naked under her dress from head to foot and I place my hand on her.
>
> Tie my shoe-lace! she says with flaming cheeks. And in a little while she whispers against my mouth, against my lips: "Oh, you are not tying my shoe-lace, you my dearest heart, you are not tying . . . not tying. . . ."
>
> But the sun dips his face into the sea and comes up again, red, refreshed, as if he had been down to drink. And the air is filled with whispers.[61]

Iselin, Glahn's vision of love as a natural force, is totally amoral. To her husband, who saw her with Glahn and accuses her, she says, " 'What did you see? I did nothing.' . . . Then her loud and happy laughter sounds through the forest and she walks away with him, exulting and sinful from head to foot. And where does she go? To the next one, a hunter in the forest."[62]

But in his difficulties Glahn is not without faithful friends. There is Eva, exploited and sacrificed by Mack and Glahn, who together cause her death—one by his hatred, the other by his negligence. In Hamsun's love triangles from the 1890s, Eva's is the most moving portrait of a "slave of love," coming closest to the heroine in Hamsun's short story by that name: "You gave all, all did you give; and it cost you no painful surrender, for you were the wild child of life itself. Yet others, who grudgingly husband even their glances, seem to have all my thoughts. Why? Ask the twelve months and the ships at sea, ask the mysterious God of the heart. . . ."[63] The peaceful and paternal tone of Glahn's relationship to Eva also characterizes his life as a woodsman. After his self-inflicted gun wound has finally healed, he experiences his first day back in the forest: "The mood of the forest suffused my senses through and through. . . . I stop, turn in all directions and, weeping, call birds, trees, stones, grass and ants by name, I look about me and name them each in turn."[64] "I love three things," Glahn tells Eva; "I love a dream of love that I once had, I love you, and I love this patch of earth," and when she asks which he loves the best, he answers "the dream."[65] He is speaking of his love of Edvarda and its projection as an ideal in his dreams of Iselin. Glahn is smitten with love, a natural force against which Eva's solicitude and the tranquillity of the forest are powerless.

Glahn, like Nagel, has been half in love with easeful death, and his comparison of its beauty with the joy of continued living is rendered more poetically in *Pan* than anywhere else in Hamsun's prose. Death is viewed as an island existence and the image, which is probably inspired by Böcklin's painting *Island of the Dead* is later repeated in Hamsun's poem "Island off the Coast." Glahn is the Pan-Narkissos, referred to in the text as "crouching so that he seemed to sit and drink out of his own belly." But in the novel the general temper is rather that of Nietzsche's Dionysian spirit, the goat-god Pan, from whom the word panic is derived.[66] Glahn's development describes a gradual unbalancing of the mind. He knows that Mack has spied on his blasting project and he has seen Eva tarring the boat at the foot of the mountain, yet he, who used to be particularly astute in reading all manner of signs, takes no heed, and the catastrophe resulting in Eva's death cannot be prevented. Actually it has been in preparation for a long time. When Glahn, for no apparent reason, throws Edvarda's shoe into the sea, shoots himself in the foot, spits the baron in the ear, and sends Edvarda a dead dog, these acts are only stations on a well-mapped way to defeat. He tells Eva: "There are times when it is a bliss to be dragged along by the hair. So distorted can the mind become. One can be dragged by the hair up hill and down dale; and if anybody asks what is happening, then one answers in ecstasy: I am being dragged along by the hair!"[67] On his last day Glahn dresses up like a bridegroom, knowing that only death can be his true bride.

In the midst of this melodrama, with the faithful maiden brutally killed, the proud mistress married off to a wizened scientist, and the hero slowly losing his mind, Hamsun's joy of life is still present. *Pan* owes its Norwegian popularity less to its tale of passion than to Glahn's eloquent declaration of his love of nature—in a manner closer to Nietzsche's than to Rousseau's. Glahn is not so much botanizing on the Île de Saint Pierre as singing his wild incantations in the style of Zarathustra: "A toast to the merciful stillness over the earth, to the stars and the crescent moon, yes, to it and to them!"[68] Hamsun's fascination with autumn, indicated already in *Hunger,* is particularly evident in *Pan.* Glahn tells Eva: "It is the third of the Iron Nights. I promise you I shall be a different man to-morrow. Let me be alone now. You will not know me in the morning. I shall laugh and kiss you, my sweetest girl. Remember I have but to-night, and then I am a different man, in just a few hours now."[69] But even if autumn hits him harder—like an alcoholic bout—during the so-called iron nights (when farmers expect the first killing frost), Glahn is always roused by nature, and his language assumes its rhythms accordingly. Instead of the long involved periods of discursive style with its many subordinate clauses (hypotaxis), coordinated sentences are favored (parataxis). Short sentences, often completely without conjunctions (asyndeton), or else studded with them (polysyndeton), characterize this kind of prose, which is reminiscent of the Bible's, particularly in such poetic books as the Song of Solomon (cf. *Hunger:* "I heard the music of the Bible in my ears"). Hamsun, like Whitman, may well have been one of "those who read the Bible for its prose," but most nature-loving readers of *Pan* have not been upset by its studied rhetoric: if it imitates the Bible's lofty style, it also copies its basic message—Praise be the Lord from whom all blessings flow!

I give thanks for the lovely night, for the hills, for the whispering of the darkness and the sea . . . it whispers within my heart. I give thanks for my life, for my breathing, for the grace of being alive to-night, for these things I give thanks from my heart! Listen in the east and listen in the west, but listen! That is the everlasting God! This stillness murmuring in my ear is the blood of all nature seething, is God weaving through the world and through me. I see a gossamer thread glistening in the fire's light, I hear the rowing of a boat in the harbour, the Northern lights arise against the northern sky. Oh, I give thanks by my immortal soul that it is I who am sitting here! . . . [70]

Victoria

"*Victoria* is nothing more than a little poetry. A writer may have some poetry he wishes to get rid of, particularly if for ten years he has written books that strike you like a fist,"[71] Hamsun assured a critic. And indeed, *Victoria* (1898)—one of the great love stories of world literature—is the sweetest of all Hamsun's novels and used to be considered a suitable confirmation present in Norway. It does have lovers who torment each other, but not unendingly and unnaturally; the atmosphere is relatively harmonious, showing Hamsun's own happiness and peace of mind after he had married and spent his honeymoon with old friends in Valdres. The book might best be termed a sentimental romance—the beautiful heroine dies from tuberculosis—and models come easily to mind: well-known works like Dumas's *La dame au camélias* (better known as Verdi's opera *La traviata*), and somewhat lesser known classics like J. P. Jacobsen's short story "Mrs. Fønss," with its moving letter at the end. But first and foremost *Victoria* is a rewriting of Hamsun's own early nouvella *Bjørger* (1878), where a poor boy (Bjørger) falls in love with a rich man's daughter who betrays him for a better match. Later she decides to go back to the hero, but then he rejects her. Whereupon she becomes ill and dies, and Bjørger, who in the meantime has become a poet, has nothing left but his art.

Johannes is the miller's only child, and for playmates he has to seek out Victoria and her brother at the Manor. Sometimes there are other youngsters visiting there such as Otto, son of a wealthy state official. A healthy boy, Johannes is not at first bothered by his own modest background. He and Victoria become natural comrades, and it is only through Otto that they are gradually made fully aware of the barriers of social class, which cannot be overcome either by Johannes's good looks and intelligence or by such heroic acts as his jumping into the sea to save a girl from drowning. Johannes does well at school and spends years in the city, where he slowly makes a name for himself as a poet. During his visits home he sees Victoria, whom he loves and who is the inspiration of his poetry, though she often appears aloof.

On one occasion, when Victoria is staying with Otto's parents in town, she meets Johannes and confesses her love for him. Thinking that the new ring on her hand does not mean she is engaged, Johannes is encouraged to approach her at a theater performance where Otto too is present, but is humiliated once more by her seeming indifference. Johannes nevertheless accepts an invitation to a banquet at the Manor, since Victoria claims she has a surprise in store for him. The banquet turns out to be an engagement party—Victoria is pledged to Otto and from now on will always wear his ring—however, she has brought along a "substitute" for Johannes, a charming young woman named Camilla Seier, who is none other than the girl Johannes had saved from drowning several years earlier. The party develops into a dramatic affair. Speeches are made and insults exchanged. Otto slaps Johannes in the face and then goes off hunting with a friend. Soon after the news is brought that he has been accidentally shot to death. Victoria's father, who had hoped to avoid bankruptcy through Otto's union with Victoria, uses the occasion of the funeral, when his whole household are absent, to set fire to the Manor (and himself), in the belief that the insurance money will save his estate for the surviving members of his family. When Johannes meets Victoria, she again confesses her love for him, but he tells her he is now engaged—to Camilla. But Camilla, who does not receive much attention from her poetry-writing fiancé, falls in love with a young civil servant, while Victoria moves more and more into the background. Victoria is said to have contracted tuberculosis, and at a party, to which Johannes too had been invited but does not come, she livens up, dances the whole evening, and then collapses. The book ends with a long letter from Victoria to Johannes in which she tells her story: how she was forced, out of loyalty to her father, to become engaged to Otto though she had always only loved Johannes. By the time Johannes receives the letter Victoria is already dead.

Once more Hamsun proceeds quickly through the overture part of his love story: Victoria and Johannes's "I love you / Don't pursue me / you can surprise me no more" are contained within the first half of the book, and what follows is the usual extended catastrophe with its alternate moods of love and hate. Like *Mysteries, Victoria* is written in the third person with a viewpoint consistently close to that of the protagonist (Johannes), except that in the final long letter the heroine is given a chance to supply *her* version of the story. This is a variation of the device in *Pan,* where an outside view of Glahn is provided in an epilogue, and both these forms can be seen as an attempt on Hamsun's part to approach his subject matter with a degree of objectivity or, as he preferred to put it, with "disinterested subjectivity."[72] Most of the minor characters in the novel are merely sketched in. Otto, like the conventional villain of popular literature, is no more than a caricature, nor is Victoria's old tutor, though he has a symbolic function: by entering a marriage of convenience, rather than living on the memories of his first great love, he represents an inverse (and bourgeois) reflection of Johannes's own situation. Furthermore, the sinister way in which this tiresome talker suddenly tells Johannes the news of Victoria's death brings to mind certain surreal characters often found in romantic works like Ibsen's *Peer Gynt* (the strange passenger, for example).[73]

Camilla, with her youth, beauty, and good family background, is characterized by her charm rather than by the humility of her predecessors, Martha and Eva; but, like the heroine of the short story "Slaves of Love," she passes the Hamsun hero's test for patient women. (In the short story Wladimiertz gives the woman a large bouquet of flowers, and when he sees her joy, adds that he really bought them for somebody else, namely, for the Yellow Lady; and she reflects "Oh, well, perhaps he did buy them for somebody else, but I got them. I got them before the one he bought them for. And he also let me thank him for them."[74] In *Victoria* Johannes tells Camilla that he has thrown away the various presents she gave him, and when she passes the test by saying meekly that she will get him another for each of the ones he has lost, he asks her there and then to marry him, since she is clearly the perfect wife for a selfish poet. But there is a limit to the kind of neglect a young, beautiful woman can suffer at the hands of an older, hard-working artist: Camilla, dancing away in her sleeveless red dress, finally loses her heart to the young and handsome Richmond, and Johannes's reaction is given in an allegory about an older man cuckolded by his young wife. Victoria writes to Johannes: "I want to ask you not to come and see me in the coffin. I suppose I shall look much the same as when I was alive only slightly paler and I shall be in my yellow dress."[75] As in *Hunger* and *Mysteries,* yellow is again Hamsun's color of the dream. We see Victoria from her tenth year. Although she is free from the snobbery that characterizes her brother Ditlef and, particularly, Otto, she is her proud father's daughter and has, from childhood on, a sense of loyalty to family and tradition which persists even after it has become a matter of life and death for her. Her attitude gives her story a touch of old-fashioned tragedy, lacking in *Mysteries* and *Pan,* and this tragedy, as well as Hamsun's sparing use of realistic detail, makes *Victoria* less a conventional novel than a tale in the tradition of oral literature.

Still, in the midst of these seemingly distant places and events there is Johannes, not an agronomist of Lappish origin or an aristocratic lieutenant-diarist, but a real writer whose psychology, if no less complex than Nagel's or Glahn's, is much more clearly mapped. Johannes's lowly background makes him an outsider to his companions from the manor and turns him into a dreamer. He wants to become a matchmaker, with hands bleeding from the sulphur (as were Strindberg's when Hamsun saw him in Paris), so that women will look up to him for his dangerous work—or he wants to be the leader of the world's bravest robber band: Victoria and her friends would fall into his hands, and he would save them only because Victoria was among them. But Johannes is more than a daydreamer: like the biblical Joseph in Egyptian politics, Johannes works hard and wins a name for himself—as a writer. The image of the artist is taken from folktale and popular literature: a poor boy, finding life in a class-ridden society difficult, decides to enter the enchanted mountain and apprentice himself to the Giant, who will reward him with half of his kingdom and the princess, who is more beautiful than any other woman in the world. Johannes's love of Victoria is his inspiration—whenever he sees it as hopeless he feels like a clock without hands or like a boy he saw in the street, whom a disease had turned into a bald little man. Love is described as a terrifying force that can reduce the most dignified man to a clown. Glahn's image of a person dragged by his hair and enjoying it is repeated in Johannes's dream of a severed head rolling along the road and whispering obscene words. Poetry is similarly denigrated. Johannes's dream of a bleeding organ playing in a distant depopulated valley is the usual romantic picture of the poet as a tormented musician, while his next image—of words changing into dancing old men, blind, deaf, dead—seems to indicate the impotence of poetry, a point Hamsun never tired of arguing, being himself cursed with the gift of words. A third section of this prolonged dream (chapter 5) finally indicates why Johannes is unable to realize his love. He sees himself diving into the ocean and finds himself approaching a gate where a big, hairy fish barks at him—behind it Victoria stands naked. An interpretation explaining the symbolism as fear of sexual involvement with the princess seems acceptable here, not only for Johannes, but for his companions among Hamsun's early heroes.

In Ibsen's last play the sculptor Rubek tells his one-time model "I was still young then, Irene. I was obsessed with the idea that if I touched you, if I desired you sensually, my mind would be profaned and I would be unable to achieve what I was striving to create."[76] Like Rubek, Johannes chooses to sacrifice sexual involvement for his ability to sculpt, in Keats's words, his "still unravished bride of quietness"—but also like Rubek, he deplores this choice. Ibsen called his play *When We Dead Awaken.* Hamsun, by using the names Victoria and Camilla Seier (*seier,* "victory"), seems to indicate that, like Ibsen's "dead" artist Rubek, Johannes is a loser.

Victoria offers the reader an opportunity to peep into the workshop of a writer like Johannes—and like Hamsun, to the extent that they share each other's writing habits. Typical of Johannes is his fertile and undisciplined imagination, which often "played crazy tricks on him, obtruding into his book irrelevant conceits which he afterwards had to strike out and throw away. This set him back considerably. A sudden noise in the stillness of the night, a carriage rumbling through the street, could break his train of thought and send him off at a tangent."[77] The result is given in the text as samples of various short scenes inspired by some general theme, such as suicide. At other times a whole chapter of a book by Johannes is quoted, or else a tale or parable is told without introduction as to its authorship, though we must assume it is Johannes or a character in one of his books, such as Monk Vendt. (We are told that Johannes is working on a "series of tales from the land of his imagination, an endless sun-red night.") Chapter 11 begins in the following manner:

> If someone should ask what love is, then it is nothing but a wind whispering among the roses and dying away. But often it is an inviolable seal that endures for life, endures till death. God has fashioned it of many kinds and seen it endure or perish. Two mothers were walking along a road talking together. One was dressed in joyful blue because her lover had returned from a journey. The other was dressed in mourning etc.

Hamsun's other heroes ("Andreas Tangen," Nagel) often tell tales, but in *Victoria* the stories are more numerous and more organically incorporated in the text. The change in the texture of the Hamsun story, after the scrupulous realism of *Hunger,* was paralleled by the development of a simplified iconography in contemporary Norwegian painting, where realistic detail gave way to simple symbolic forms. A suitable example would be Edvard Munch's *Sick Girl* (1885, referred to earlier) compared to his *Dance of Life* (1899), in which a young woman in white enters the painting from the left, while a wildly dancing woman in red takes up the middle field with her partner, followed to the extreme right by a woman in black. The women in black and white have full facial features. The man and the woman dancing have a tormented/ecstatic expression, while several pairs dancing in the background are merely sketched in.[78] A similar reduction of detail takes place in *Victoria:* we do not know the second name of either Johannes or Victoria. Their parents are referred to as, respectively, the miller and the castle master; furthermore there is the tutor, the mother in blue, the mother in black, the lord and the lady, and other allegorical designations. The subtle psychology Hamsun had called for in his literary manifesto of 1890 (see Preface) had finally given way to tale, allegory, mood, color, ornament—a lighter and more sentimental kind of literature, which Hamsun called "just a little poetry." And poetry he described at the time (1898) as "the only form of writing that is not both pretentious and inconsequential, but merely inconsequential."[79] *Victoria* lacks the power of Hamsun's other great novels from the 1890s, but it is still the quintessential Hamsun love story: with nothing really new to say, the author stated his case more simply, clearly, economically and as beautifully:

> Love was God's first word, the first thought that sailed across his mind. He said Let there be light, and there was love. And everything that he had made was very good, and nothing thereof did he wish unmade again. And Love was creation's source, creation's ruler; but all love's ways are strewn with blossoms and blood, blossoms and blood.[80]

Other Works from the 1890s

In addition to his four major novels, Hamsun during the 1890s completed three plays and three lesser known prose works (two novels and one collection of stories), which may have contributed little to his international reputation but which are nevertheless an important part of his oeuvre. In the plays, for instance, Hamsun's aristocratic radicalism is carried to an extreme, while in the two novels he uses unexpectedly a conventional realistic style, seemingly imitating certain writers of the 1880s, such as Alexander Kielland (1849–1906), while at the same time anticipating the style of his own twentieth-century social novels. *Editor Lynge* (April 1893) is a novel about the Oslo editor Olav Thommesen (1851–1941) and his paper, *Verdens Gang (Gazette),* and attempts to analyze certain conditions that determine modern news dissemination. Alexander Lynge manipulates other people to get his will, and other people manipulate him—there is for instance Dagny Hansen (Dagny Kielland of *Mysteries*) who uses her beauty and social position to secure Lynge's support of a royal decoration for her husband, and there is Endre Bondesen (he later returns in Hamsun's Kareno trilogy), an unsavory opportunist who learns his methods from the *Gazette.* Lynge's chief critic is Leo Høibro, who once liked and respected Lynge but now describes him as "one of us peasant students who was damaged by being transplanted to a foreign soil and atmosphere."[81]

Against this background of irresponsible journalism Hamsun draws up a brief love story. Leo Høibro, a young bank official of dark complexion and bright ideals, is fond of Charlotte Ihlen and wants to buy her a bicycle, even though he opposes sports for women. Since he has already lent her mother all his savings, he has to help himself to the required sum at the bank. He does so knowing that he will soon be able to pay it back. Charlotte in the meantime is seduced by Bondesen, but after seeing through this hypocrite, she returns to Høibro, who loves her as before—until she tells him that she is "no longer innocent." It appears to be more than he can take ("she could have stolen, murdered, only not this"). He considers everything to be lost and gives himself up to the police, despite the fact that he now has the money needed to redeem his unauthorized loan. We understand that Charlotte will wait for him.

By some young critics and writers *Editor Lynge* was praised for its biting irony but attacked in "Lynge's" own paper *Verdens Gang* by Arne Garborg, who called it "a literary lynching, staged for the rabble."[82] Even so, as a novel in the Kielland tradition, *Editor Lynge* is not without literary merit (which Garborg also admitted). It has sections showing indignation, keen observation, and good writing, but it lacks a unified plot, probably because the central character has been split into a Leo Høibro and an Alexander Lynge—Høibro a rather humorless Nagel, Lynge a more superficial and time-serving version of that same hero. Olav Thommesen, who had referred to Hamsun the lecturer as a charlatan, is generally taken to be the model for Lynge; but, as Garborg had pointed out, Hamsun was not excluding himself in his exposure of Høibro's curious double standards and Lynge's need to be in the news: in this respect *Editor Lynge* is a continuation of *Mysteries*'s discussion of the charlatan.

Shallow Soil, published on the last day of November 1893, continues the pattern of *Editor Lynge,* but the social satire in the background and the love story in the foreground are both better integrated and better separately—indeed, *Shallow Soil* is a good novel, even if its social protest, irony, humor, quick-witted dialogue, and inspired pictures of pulsating city life make it a book more in Kielland's than in Hamsun's style. As social satire it records the daily routine of half a dozen artists—poets, painters, journalists—kept from earning an honest living thanks to government grants, people's general goodwill, and friends in the business world whom they exploit. Their artistic output is minimal and, judging from samples in the text, poor, but they have a high opinion of their own works and rely on a corrupt press to spread their reputations. In contrast to them are two merchants, the good friends Ole Henriksen and Andreas Tidemand, hard-working and imaginative business men who are also interested in literature and the arts and willing to share some of their fortunes with the creative bohemians, who repay them with contempt for their bourgeois life-style.

The love story takes two forms. Tidemand's wife Hanka is seduced by the poet Irgens, partly because Tidemand in his eagerness to appear liberated shows too little of the firmness and authority his wife is apparently longing for. But since she is a person of quality—misguided, yes, but intelligent, proud, fair—she sees through Irgens's incredible egoism, breaks with him, and in the end is able to regain her husband's love and respect. In Ole Henriksen's case the outcome is different. Ole—even though his character is not highly individualized (like Høibro he is dark and blue-eyed)—appears more proud and introspective, and his fiancée from the country, Aagot Lynum, is both less intelligent and less critical of the poetry-writing parasites than Hanka. Irgens's seduction of Aagot is a central part of the plot, painfully decadent, but well executed. The decadence is further underscored by the presence of a somewhat unusual Peeping Tom, Aagot's old tutor Coldevin, who follows her to the wicked town and watches her degradation with the excitement of a Victorian voyeur. Coldevin, like most of Hamsun's interesting men, is developed out of Nagel. Like Nagel, he is a detective, though of a more sinister kind: not interested in exposing the crimes of old, serene-looking criminals, he shadows instead a young woman, to whom he is simultaneously conscience, father figure, and vicarious lover—a forerunner of Knut Pedersen in *The Wanderer,* and, as *raisonneur,* of Baardsen in the Segelfoss novels.

The story line is brought out in a series of scenes—the bustling life of a small capital city, the artists discussing their petty problems at the Grand Café, the poet Irgens demonstrating his seductive arts, the merchants doing their daily chores and analyzing the world market—scenes that are organized into three sections entitled "Germination," "Ripening," "Sixty-fold," with a "Prologue" and a "Finale," making in all some forty chapters. The book's title, *Ny Jord*—literally "New Soil"—seems to be taken from the Copenhagen journal *Ny Jord,* with which Hamsun was associated after his return from America, whereas the section headings bring to mind the biblical parable of the Sower. However, rather than "new soil" in the sense of "Young and unused, providing better growing conditions for the arts," as presumably is meant by the journal title, Coldevin explains the term as "new soil, anemic soil, without much growth, without fertility," which supports the English translation of the title as *Shallow Soil.* In this unique novel Hamsun seems to be reversing his argument from *Hunger,* in which a gifted artist suffers at the hands of an insensitive business community (Mr. Christie and others): in *Shallow Soil* businessmen are the heroes and artists the villains. However, it is not so much a negative attitude to the word "artist"—which can be found throughout Hamsun's writings—as an understanding of the gainfully employed, including for once the workingman, that singles out *Shallow Soil* in Hamsun's early production.

That *Shallow Soil* became the first book by Hamsun to be published in America may have been partly owing to its special endorsement by Hamsun's first biographer, Carl Morburger, who described it as "Knut Hamsun's most significant work . . . a book of exquisite lyric beauty, of masterly psychology, and finished artistic form."[83] On the other hand, with its unique advocacy of honest labor and business enterprise, *Shallow Soil* is also Hamsun's most "American" book, as its translator, C. C. Hyllested, observed: "[since it is] in some respects the most contained of Hamsun's works, it is perhaps best suited as a medium for his introduction to Anglo-Saxon readers."[84]

Knut Hamsun never tired of referring to the drama as an inferior literary form since it could not people its scenes with characters of unambiguous psychology: Hamlet had been interpreted a hundred times and each time differently. Still, because Hamsun knew himself to be a master of dialogue, he also felt challenged by such successful Norwegian dramatists as Ibsen and Gunnar Heiberg, and during his years in Paris (where he also met Strindberg) he decided to try himself as a playwright. In Hamsun's dramatic trilogy from the 1890s Ibsen motifs are evident throughout—the competing professors resemble the Tesman/Løvborg conflict in *Hedda Gabler;* the cuckolded husband and father is reminiscent of Hjalmar Ekdal in

The Wild Duck; but first and foremost the central theme of the uncompromising idealist brings to mind Ibsen's verse play *Brand.* On the other hand, the idealization of erotic love—which was alien to Ibsen's temperament—is more in keeping with Heiberg's drama, particularly with his highly stylized play *The Balcony,* which appeared only one year before the first part of Hamsun's trilogy *Ved Rikets Port* (At the gate of the kingdom, 1895). In Hamsun's play Ivar Kareno, a twenty-nine-year-old philosopher of Nietzschean persuasion, is preparing a new book for publication and hoping from the income to pay his debts and provide for himself and his wife of three years. Owing to opposition from the powerful utilitarian philosopher Professor Gylling and because Kareno, as opposed to his former friend and colleague Jerven, refuses to revise his manuscript, the book is not accepted by the publisher.[85] Worse is the circumstance that Kareno's young and sensuous wife Elina finally gives up competing with her husband's love of philosophy and goes off with the philandering journalist Endre Bondesen (from *Editor Lynge*). In the last scene of the play the bailiff arrives to seize Kareno's property.

Part 2 of the trilogy, *Livets Spil* (The game of life, 1896), takes place in north Norway. Kareno (now thirty-nine) has become a tutor for the children of a certain Mr. Oterman, a friendly and generous merchant who suddenly, after the discovery of valuable marble deposits on his land, turns into a pitiful miser. Oterman's erotic and capricious daughter, Teresita, is loved by Jens Spir, but she herself loves the innocent Kareno, until love is finally awakened in him, at which point she shifts her favors to a hunchbacked engineer. In the first play Kareno had stubbornly refused to compromise and enter the open gate leading to the kingdom of success, but in the third, *Aftenrøde* (Evening Glow, 1898), Kareno is back with his wife Elina and her illegitimate daughter, Sara. With Elina's inheritance, poverty has given way to wealth and luxury, and Kareno is seen walking around in a dressing gown, using a walking stick, and drinking tea—all supposed signs of approaching old age (he is fifty!). Bondesen, now a newspaper editor like Lynge, persuades Kareno to give up his membership in a radical youth party and join the establishment in order to beat his old rival, Jerven, at the polls. The play trilogy ends as Kareno tells his daughter a fairy tale beginning "There was once a man who would not give in. . . ."

Kareno, though clearly meant to be a hero in the Nagel-Høibro-Coldevin line, does not have a sufficiently striking personality to captivate an audience for the duration of twelve acts. In the first play he is irritatingly naive, in the second uninteresting, and in the third—where for the first time he seems to be aware of the world around him—age has turned him into a cynical compromiser without appeal. His wife, Elina, has often been praised by theater critics for her refreshing youthfulness. At first childlike in her naiveté, she can also be hard and calculating; later we see her as morally corrupted and finally as a social climber. Hamsun's sexism is nowhere more evident than here, and even though Elina could be made credible on the stage, as a heroine in a serious play many modern readers are likely to consider her an insult to womanhood. Bondesen is Hamsun's usual type of hypocrite, and Jerven an average opportunist (though the author has tried to show Jerven's self-contempt); more interesting is the telegraphist Jens Spir, cynical but genuine, a character who later returns (with variations) as Arentsen in *Rosa* and Baardsen in *Segelfoss Town.* Most interesting of all the characters in the dramatic trilogy is Teresita, motherless like Edvarda in *Pan* and Mariane in *Segelfoss Town,* but more passionate than either of them. Indeed, she is the closest Hamsun ever came to drawing the biblical Salome, a favorite subject of the symbolists. Teresita loves Kareno because "he is not of this world. When I go to meet him I look straight at him and whisper Yes, for it seems to me he is the moon that comes and wants something of me. . . .Kareno is like a green island that I come to and stay with." But when Kareno wishes to return her love, she answers "Good Lord, do you really think I loved your Lapp face and your spindly legs. Oh, no, you are no beauty. But you were so quiet, I thought you were full of something from another world, and your face did something to me. And then you disappointed me."[86] Jens Spir associates Teresita with the goddess Ishtar, known for the cruel way she treated her many lovers.

Most of Kareno's Nietzschean ideas are well known from *Mysteries, Editor Lynge,* and *Shallow Soil*—his attack upon the English (for their utilitarian philosophy), on humanism generally, and specifically on the modern sympathy for the industrial worker, "which in our day and age has replaced the rampant farmer romanticism from the middle of the century." Against such weak humanism Hamsun places the terrifying life forces—greed, love, jealousy—which may strike a person without warning, as in the case of Oterman, who changes from philanthropist to miser overnight; or Teresita's love or Kareno's old age, which bends even the unbending. In his youth he had declared a man physically and mentally unfit at fifty: "off the road, old man. I am younger than you, Your life is ended; make room for mine." Hamsun's attack on the older generation of Norwegian writers in 1891 is said to have inspired Ibsen's Ragnar Brovik (in *The Master Builder*). However, unlike Brovik, the youth in Hamsun's play is not able to bring down the old tyrannical master builder. The assassin fails in his aim, and Kareno's political victory is assured. Somehow Ibsen's open ending is more subtle: by finally defeating their master builder here and now, the young only contribute to his eternal victory.

Hamsun apparently had written his three plays in the hope not only of seeing them performed but of considerably improving his finances through theater royalties. To Bjørnson, who had not been moved by *The Game of Life,* he wrote,

> I hope you will read *The Game of Life* once more. By understanding nothing and then speaking about it you have prevented its publication in Germany. It is the most profound book I have written. I have put all my bitter brooding into it, and I can assure you I do brood quite a bit. According to your opinion it was also impossible as drama, but all who have written about it, even the detractors, feel that the opposite is the case. . . .*The Game of Life* is written in one long breath, with my soul in my throat. . . .[87]

Although the three plays have been performed at several Scandinavian theaters, it is clear that Hamsun's Norwegian readers have looked upon them as incidental to his production. Only in Russia, where the first two plays were long favorites at Stanislavski's Moscow Arts Theater, Hamsun's ambition to be played and paid was fulfilled. It was also the Russians who brought Hamsun the dramatist to New York, where Boleskavski's Laboratory Theater performed *At the Gate of the Kingdom* in 1927. It proved to be "an interesting and provocative drama, albeit one whose last two acts did not quite live up to all the implications of its first two."[88]

Chapter Three
Wanderer

It stands to reason that a writer with Hamsun's enormous zest for life must suffer more than others from approaching age, and of the many crises in his career certainly two deal directly with his pangs over his growing years—at the end of his youth around forty, and at the beginning of his old age around seventy. Hamsun married Bergljot Bech in 1898, and the following years, which should have seen him settle down to family life, found him more restless than ever. He lived a year in Finland (1899), where he lectured on "the years of fading creativity,"[1] then (1900) traveled on a state scholarship through Russia to Caucasia and Turkey, and these politically backward countries, rather than rocking his reactionary views, confirmed them and made him long for the harsh paradise of his own youth in Nordland, which he had not seen in twenty years. In order to be close to nature there, he lived in a turf hut on the hillside above his childhood home, working on his verse play *Munken Vendt* (Friar Vendt), which appeared in 1902—the same year his first child, Victoria, was born. It had been the hope of both parents that Victoria would help patch up their unhappy marriage. Hamsun at home was a tyrant and a pedant who could not tolerate his wife's slovenliness and lack of thrift. On the other hand, he was himself not only generous to a fault, but a free spender, losing once a whole fortune in a gambling casino at Ostende, which did not help either his finances or his relationship to Bergljot, since she had to bail him out. The following years found him working frantically to pay back his wife, and in one single season (1903) he published three books.[2] When, in 1905, the one-hundred-year-old union between Sweden and Norway was finally dissolved, Hamsun was politically engaged on the side of a free Norway, while at the same time he was trying to cement his own marriage union by designing and building a home for his family. But it was too late, and in 1906 he was divorced from Bergljot Bech. He spent the following years living in hotels in various parts of the country and writing novels about a wanderer in the countryside who had fled, like himself, from a wasteful café life in the cities.

Although for Hamsun his age was a particularly hard blow, his attack on "old age" (that is, the age of fifty) in the Kareno plays was repeated in Helsinki in 1900 and at the Norwegian Students' Union in Oslo in 1907, where, in a lecture entitled "Honor the Young,"[3] he ridiculed the Bible's fourth commandment. The following year he met the beautiful actress Marie Andersen, who was twenty-three years his junior and whom—after long periods filled with suspicion and jealousy (she had lived six years with an actor)—he married in 1909. As the newspapers celebrated his fiftieth birthday (the journalists thought he was born in 1860), he wrote his last play, *Livet ivold* (*In the Grip of Life*), in which he seems to be warning his actress wife against the depravity of the theater world. Two years later he completed the third volume in his *Wanderers* trilogy, "The Last Joy" (*Den siste glæde,* translated as *Look Back on Happiness*), in which he tells Marie, more directly than anywhere else in his collected work, that the only answer to the troubles of a young wife is having a child: a child is the ultimate joy.

During all those confusing years Hamsun had not been inactive. He published no less than thirteen books—a collection of poetry, three volumes of short stories, six novels, and three plays. Most of them belong to the author's lesser works, a fact some critics explain—though not altogether convincingly—as a result of his restless life: after all, *Mysteries* too was written on endless journeys and lecture tours. The many different forms Hamsun was now attempting tell us, rather, that he was searching not only for a new way to express his thoughts, but indeed for new thoughts or at least for new emphases. The shifting style of the short stories is typical of his state of mind: old and new ideas are thrown together without order; there is a mixture here of coarse naturalism and very romantic moods. His new ambition to write poetry was not only the result of recent romantic currents, for the poetic quality of his novels had actually been increasing throughout the 1890s. That he should have written a verse play like *Friar Vendt* is also not surprising: he had long wished to present his philosophy in verse form, through a kind of Hamsunian *Peer Gynt,* and his study of Ibsen's play, as well as his thoughts of visiting Nordland again, probably triggered his inspiration. His travel accounts from the East tell us of a man tired of Western civilization and dreaming of the beauty of a feudal society. The prose plays deal more directly with his two marriages. *Dronning Tamara* (Queen Tamara) argues the impossibility of a situation in which a husband is not master of his household, and *In the Grip of Life,* as mentioned above, is a warning to his young bride to forget her ambitions as an actress. His novels too are discernibly autobiographical. In *Sværmere (Dreamers)* an underdog, like Hamsun himself, manages to win a princess, but more particularly in a subplot about a minister and his untidy wife there is a rather close portrait of Hamsun's first marriage. In *Benoni,* Hamsun laughs good-humoredly at his own boorishness, while in *Rosa* he describes at length the problem of marrying—as he had—a woman with a past. Finally, in the first two volumes of *The Wanderer* the autobiographical quality is only faintly disguised. The protagonist is even called Knut Pedersen, and what he experiences is basically Hamsun's own chaotic life between the ages of forty and fifty.

What characterizes all of Hamsun's work during the first decade of the twentieth century are the moderation of his earlier high melodrama, the reintroduction of irony and humor, and the protagonist's reduced demands on life. The hero gradually gives up his Jacob's struggle with God, and like a sullen Achilles retires to his tent—which is in Hamsun's fiction the deep forest, where the hero communicates with nature. The hero is no longer an irrevocably displaced person, but rather a wanderer who, even if restless, is not alienated. The princess is replaced by a variety of more prosaic women, and even though Tamara is a heroine in the old high style, the fact that Hamsun the misogynist makes a woman the central character of his plot (and repeats it in *Rosa* and *In the Grip of Life*) represents a conciliatory gesture. As to social class, there is a similar leveling off. The protagonist is generally viewed humorously, and—whether an illegitimate son like Friar Vendt or an upstart country bumpkin like Benoni—he is a local resident rather than a visiting comet like Johan Nagel. Even the poet in *The Wanderer* has lost his former magnetism and appears under the very prosaic name of Knut Pedersen. In Hamsun's production, the years before World War I constitute a period of limbo in which he sorts out his forces before a new attack—one more consciously under the colors of Jean Jacques Rousseau.

The Wild Chorus

Hamsun wrote only one book of verse, *Det vilde kor* (The Wild Chorus, 1904). In connection with its translation into German, the author gave the following description of his attempts in this new genre: "Every poet knows that poems come to life under the stronger or weaker pressures of mood. A sound is heard humming within you, colors hit your eyes, you feel something rippling inside you. It depends on how lasting this state of mind is. I have experienced—in good moments—not being able to complete one stanza before the next was streaming in."[4]

Knut Hamsun does not belong among the great classics of Norwegian poetry. Even if he is said to have liked music, some of his verse shows that he lacked an ear for the special regularity of poetic rhythm, and though he held strong views on painting (usually mistaken ones), his visual imagery is not remarkably structured and rarely striking. As a prose writer Hamsun was the most meticulous craftsman in Norwegian literature; as a poet, on the other hand, he showed little patience for polishing his lines, as he himself admitted. But his verse is valuable, not only because it explains the thoughts of a great novelist, or because it was once able to change the course of Norwegian poetry, but because it is melodic and down-to-earth in a way that is still refreshing. Typically, of Norway's youngest generation of ballad singers, several have shown an interest in Hamsun.[5]

Central to Hamsun's poetry—as to his prose—is Love, an irresistible life force that laughs alike at mellowed men and aged virgins (cf. such titles as "Aftenrøde" [Evening red] or "Gammel Jomfru" [Old spinster]). Much of this love poetry is incidental and often not above the commonplace—the poet watching his sweetheart leaving, arriving, playing the piano—but it takes on more verve when he is made to feel the sting of her whims. He then compares her to a spider and steels his heart against her. Not surprisingly there are lines that remind the reader of Nietzsche's "don't forget the whip when you go to women," as when the poet sees himself riding on horseback, while his mistress runs naked beside him; and there are poems describing a woman's love in terms of class, the working-class girl's concern about her future, the middle-class wife's concern about what is proper, and the true Lady's indifference to everything but the few minutes of perfect love. Interesting in Hamsun's description of such perfect love are the uses of drugs. While *The Song of Songs* (chapter 7, stanza 13) merely mentions the power of the mandragora, Hamsun devotes a whole cycle ("Alrunen") to its aphrodisiac properties, while imitating, as often before, King Solomon's sensuous style. In other cases Hamsun's inspiration is the Koran rather than the Old Testament: one poem has a young Abdullah longing for the houris who await him after death. Finally there is the mythical world of Iselin. Even if she does not appear herself, as in *Pan* and the play *Friar Vendt,* her milieu—a north Norwegian feudal never-never land, with lords riding to their hunt in feathered hats and the woods echoing their hunting horns—is seen in several stanzas.

Nature is equally central to Hamsun's poetry and appears to the poet as mother image and mistress: the soughing of the trees—rendered as a lul-lul—is either a love call or a beckoning back to the womb. This latter idea is also brought out in the use of flowering bushes, lilacs, chokecherries, bridal wreath spiraea—all known for their suffocating fragrance, which helps provide a gentle passage from full life to peaceful death. In Hamsun's poetry death is attractive rather than frightening, and Böcklin, whose painting *Isle of Death* is often recognizable in certain Hamsun scenes, receives a special memorial in this collection ("Böcklins død"). Finally there are several poems that indicate a belief in reincarnation, a never-ending cycle, which likewise takes away the sting of death.

Quite different from those sentimental ideas is a streak of humor that, although very rarely to be found in Hamsun's prose from the 1890s, was so evident in his twentieth-century poetry and prose as to become a typical feature. This humor was part of a new realism, a willingness to accept commonplace situations as respectable motifs in literature, and it was seen in references to everyday things—like a farmer's tools, domestic animals, the magpie (the least aristocratic of birds; cf. Mark Twain's jay), etc.—constituting a poetic low style which ended the moonlight poetry of the 1890s and, in Hamsun's case, the high passion of his early prose. Humor also colored his poetic rhythm. Although Hamsun had no deeper feeling for prosody—some of his poems, like some of Bjørnson's, are difficult to read as verse—he was fond of experimenting with meter and could come up with pleasing new lines. Thus, by combining the typical folk ballad lines of four and three, he arrived at a proselike long line, as in Whitman's "O Captain! My Captain!" Similar lines had of course been used before both in and outside Scandinavia, but the lilting, nonchalant tone appealed to the younger generation, and was soon to receive Norwegian fame in the poetry of Hamsun's young colleague Herman Wildenvey.

Nagel's antidemocratic stand in *Mysteries* was revived in an unstanzaic poem, "Himmelbrev til Byron" (Letter to Lord Byron in heaven). In title and content it is somewhat reminiscent of Ibsen's "Balloon Letter" from 1869—in which the author deplored both Germany's preoccupation with military expansion and its neglect of beauty—but Hamsun's poem is less philosophic and more indignant. Those whom Ibsen later (1885) claimed to be our only hope for the future—women and working men—were targets for Hamsun's quite intemperate attacks. Byron was invoked not only because he was a poet, but because he was a "lord, a leader, a man among dissemblers." Naturally, in the many postwar attempts to explain Hamsun's support of Nazi Germany, "Letter to Lord Byron in Heaven" became a very central document. In some ways related to the Byron letter is a powerful poem dedicated to Bjørnson on his seventieth birthday (1902). Bjørnson was singled out as the "great master, watchman, leader," but equally important to his personality was his general compassion, viewed by Hamsun as a feminine quality. Particularly impressive was Hamsun's ability to evoke Bjørnson's image in terms of Norwegian scenery and industry, in the mountains, woods, wheatfields, and fisheries—all everyday details that add up to an unsurpassed portrait of Norwegian literature's most active personality. Hamsun became disenchanted with Bjørnson during the years immediately preceding the Union crisis of 1905, when Bjørnson, then an old man, pursued a policy of appeasement. That disenchantment was reflected in the Byron letter, in which the poet deplored the loss of idealism among the older generation and referred to the Danish poet Drachmann as Byron's only worthy successor in the north. However, when Bjørnson died in 1910, Hamsun wrote a second memorial poem which, together with the first, remains the outstanding characterization of Bjørnstjerne Bjørnson.

When Hamsun introduces onomatopoeia or unusual names (Ture, Alvilde, Margaret Mort, Sorosi), he sometimes achieves special melodic effects. Innovative is also his use of *stev,* a special Norwegian dance rhythm which Hamsun used in his best known poem, "Skjærgårdsø" ("Island off the Coast"), with the beginning lines

"Now glides the boat to / the coastal island / A blue sea island / A verdant strand." Hamsun, who did not accept the Christian view of an afterlife, nor the Viking belief in everlasting fame (cf. his poem "Om hundrede år er alting glemt" [A hundred years and all's forgotten]), often expressed an interest in the concept of reincarnation in Eastern religions. In the poem a festive island picnic—a childhood memory from Nordland which occurs again and again in Hamsun's novels—is fused with the serenity of a final parting, as in Böcklin's painting *Isle of the Dead,* into a pantheistic dream picture of exquisite beauty and simplicity:

> My heart becomes like
> A magic garden
> Its flowers the same as
> The island's now.
> They speak together
> And whisper strangely
> Like children meeting
> And smile and bow.[6]

Drama

Knut Hamsun in 1910 described his play *Friar Vendt* (1902) as "the first part of a trilogy in which I wanted to show the three attitudes to God—rebellion, resignation, and living faith. I am through with 'Rebellion'—it is not even an attitude. I am still not weak enough for 'Resignation,' nor toothless enough to provide 'Faith.' It'll come with the years—as to all of us."[7]

The eight-act play records the life of Friar Vendt—a former student of theology and now a wandering free spirit, hunter, lover, and jailbird (sentenced for crimes he has not committed)—between the ages twenty-five and fifty. More particularly the play tells the story of his relationship to various women: the Lappish girl Inger, the servant Bliss (and, toward the end of the play, to her illegitimate daughter, Alexa), and finally to Iselin, a rich man's daughter, who is the mistress of several noblemen, such as Dundas and Sven Herlufsen, and the wife of Sir Diderik. In act 1 Friar Vendt returns to his home in north Norway, where the merchant Sir Diderik and Lady Iselin rule, finds a treasure but is unjustly sentenced for theft, and spends several years in prison. In act 6 he returns home for the second time; he is now a rich man who wants to buy the estate of his previous overlords, but through his arrogant behavior he provokes the anger of Lady Iselin, who has him punished in a rather unusual manner: he is tied for four days to a tree in the forest until grass germinates in his cupped hands, which have been filled with soil and seeds. In the last act of the play Friar Vendt has given his money to the local church, even though he had spent his days fighting its slave morality, and lives out the remaining part of his life in the house of the village cobbler. His hands are withered after the tortures he endured in the forest and he finally dies from a fall on a slippery road, just as Sir Diderik launches his new ship, named after his wife Iselin. But Lady Iselin, who is upstairs in Sir Diderik's manor when she receives the news of Friar Vendt's death, steps through an open window to her own death in the sea deep below.

Hamsun, knowing full well that the play would not work on the stage in this form, tried to make a shortened version of it for the German theater, but he gave up, claiming in the end that he did not understand the basic principles of drama. And certainly by the standards of the person he tried to emulate—Henrik Ibsen—Hamsun was no master builder. His borrowing from Ibsen's *Peer Gynt* is evident throughout, even in verse form—four-footed iambs with alternating feminine and masculine rhymes and frequent use of dactylic (trisylabic) rhymes. But while Ibsen's play with its emphasis on sin and atonement was essentially a Christian work, Hamsun had nothing but contempt for authors sitting in judgment over themselves. Friar Vendt, despite the cruel treatment he receives, is able to accept his fate in a spirit of stoicism. He is a rebel against a harsh God as well as against the upper classes with their arrogance and miscarriage of justice, yet he seems to be at peace with his surroundings. As in *Peer Gynt,* there is a romantic mixture of times, places, and milieus, but the play lacks Ibsen's powerful and unifying troll and animal symbolism. Of typical Hamsun features we find the exposure of greedy Lapps, old and impotent husbands, ignorant and socially ambitious women, the long-suffering rejected lover, grotesque incidents, and finally a close view of Hamsun's strange Iselin circle. Iselin, the north Norwegian nymph, is surrounded by fairy-tale characters, all of whom are known from Hamsun's *Pan.* But while their treatment in *Pan* has the timelessness of myth, the plot of *Friar Vendt* belongs to a period in the latter part of the Norwegian-Danish Union (that is, the 1700s), and makes Iselin less the wanton wood nymph of *Pan* and, as a tragic figure, more subdued and human than, say, Edvarda.

The play contains a number of songs, most of which are sung by Sven Herlufsen and some of which are included in *The Wild Chorus,* as well as several "quotable" passages of great beauty, most of them spoken by Friar Vendt. Finally there is an eighteenth-century kind of humor, known from the poems of Johan Herman Wessel or the plays of Ludvig Holberg. This mixture of swagger, sentimentality, and humor placed in a primitivistic setting makes the play very different from *Peer Gynt,* with its loftier ideal. On the other hand, *Friar Vendt* is perhaps more genuinely Norwegian as a contribution to Norway's *bonderokokko* ("rustic rococo")—a literary parallel to the many paintings with lords and ladies in floral patterns covering the interiors of Norwegian farm houses.

If *Friar Vendt* is too long and unwieldy for the stage, *Queen Tamara* has a number of advantages over the earlier play—it is short (three acts instead of eight), in prose, with an action consisting of simple and colorful episodes (women dancing, military attacks, diplomatic envoys, erotic scenes), and the general romantic attraction of distant time (ca. 1200) and space (Caucasia). The play, however, is even more arcane than *Friar Vendt* and has never been revived on the Norwegian stage after its 1904 premier in one of the National Theater's most ambitious stagings, which included music by Johan Halvorsen. The play's setting is a direct result of Hamsun's oriental journey in 1901; the plot concerns Tamara, queen of Georgia 1184–1212, and her marital difficulties. Queen Tamara's Christian forces are engaged in a religious war against the Mohammedans in neighboring Tovin. The Mohammedan Khan is captured, but Tamara's heir, George, falls into the hands of the enemy and is not released until Tamara's husband, Georgij, offers to take the place of his son. The Tovinians are willing to return Prince Georgij for the dead body of their leader; however, Tamara's religious adviser insists that the Khan be given a Christian burial, and Prince Georgij, who sees himself being sacrificed for the religious fervor of his wife, assumes power over the Tovinians and leads them in a victorious attack upon Georgia.

Queen Tamara, the title character, is a pious, generous, and mild ruler whose erotic instincts are awakened, first by her prisoner, the young and handsome Khan of Tovin, and when he is dead, by her husband's desperate attack upon her castle, through which he hopes to regain her love: "It was just as in Tiflis [that is, where she first fell passionately in love with her husband]" is her way of describing her renewed emotion. The play is also prefaced by the poem "Alrunen" (The Mandragora), to which the Khan refers in his conversation with Tamara.

Hamsun seems to admire the Moslem views on *purdah* as well as the heady erotic language of the Old Testament, but apart from the possible attractions of oriental scenes and sentiments, the main interest in *Queen Tamara* lies in the fact that it expresses more directly than any other work by Hamsun the hero's need to bend a woman to his will. Beyond this more obvious exposition of a well-known Hamsun theme, the play is another classical illustration of Freud's Oedipus theories—it is Prince Georgij's mother fixation that prevents him from establishing anything but a superficial erotic contact with the many women in his life. It is therefore natural that in an early treatment of Hamsun's work by the Norwegian psychiatrist and psychoanalyst Trygve Braatøy, *Queen Tamara* receives a prominent place.[8]

Livet ivold (*In the Grip of Life,* 1910) is a play about a former cabaret singer, Juliane, who is married to a wealthy merchant, Old Gihle, whom she refers to as "Dad." Juliane's most recent lover, the antique dealer Alexander Blumenschøn, has left her for a Miss Norman, to whom he has become engaged, and has plans to travel to South America with an old acquaintance, Per Bast, a rancher and engineer in Argentina. Juliane Gihle, referring to her age and career, keeps saying that things are going downhill, that she, who used to be the escort of princes (hence her nickname "Royal Juliane"), will end up with a black man for her lover—and this is what happens in the course of the play. Juliane has persuaded her husband to buy a country estate so that she can meet her lovers there, but Blumenschøn will not give up his plans for a South American journey. Per Bast dies during the first day of his visit with Juliane and leaves her his servant, an eighteen-year-old black man who is welcomed by Juliane in the last scene of the play.

Impossible things happen throughout. Per Bast is bitten by a cobra; another friend of Juliane's shoots himself to death; and a diamond-studded oriental tobacco pipe, known as a narghile, plays an important part in the plot, somewhat like that of the pistols in *Hedda Gabler,* which Hamsun's play resembles superficially with its collection of curiously selfish people. There is Old Gihle, with all signs of a second childhood upon him, yet with the half-charming selfishness of a child. In Alexander Blumenschøn Hamsun has created a person with absolutely no redeeming characteristics: he is pusilanimous, pathologically jealous, and insufferably arrogant—Hamsun in his own worst moments—but also niggardly, ungenerous, and proud of his forebears from Switzerland (a country for which Hamsun harbored a special hatred). Bast seemingly is a caricature of the returning Norwegian-American, complete with automobile and pistols in his pockets. He never removes his hat and carries a flower bouquet as one carries a broom. His attitude toward black people is that of the Southern planter (which was also Hamsun's attitude), but he is otherwise magnanimous and gallant, with a real appetite for life. Hamsun must have identified with him to the extent of making him a "Yankee" whose childhood home was in north Norway. Juliane is endowed with the inconsistencies of a great heroine—she is generous and warmhearted, except in the field of love, where she does not willingly suffer competition and exposes Blumenschøn's fiancée to Bast's cobra. She is also curiously unconcerned about Bast's death.

In the Grip of Life is a play about old age and innocence. Young Fanny Norman is the only untainted person. All others have a relationship to the past, typified by Fredriksen, once a famous and handsome artist, now a miserable alcoholic café musician, who plays his last waltz for losers like himself, so that they can go down, as he says, under full sail. The play treats the problem of making the transition to old age, and while Bast knows how to do it gracefully, only Juliane's development is portrayed with great artistic insight and understanding. The play is effective first and foremost because of its witty language, but the characters are too bizarre, too caricatured to give it a lasting place in theater repertories. Still, it is Hamsun's most successful play and has been performed several times in Norway and abroad. During its performance by the Moscow Arts Theater in New York in 1923 the play was referred to as a "conversation character comedy." "Those who understood Russian," it was said, "were frequently moved to laughter."[9]

Hamsun's Short Stories

The short stories are contained in three collections, *Siesta* from 1897, *Kratskog* (Brushwood) from 1903, and *Stridende liv* (Struggling life) from 1905. Since most of them had appeared in newspapers and magazines between 1896 and 1905, the publication dates for the collections can be quite deceiving: many of the later stories bear the stamp of being early literary attempts that Hamsun had put aside for a decade or more. The stories span twenty years of Hamsun's colorful life, and since they are often directly based on his personal experiences in various parts of the world, biographers will find them valuable. Furthermore, because the stories illustrate various stages in Hamsun's early writing career—from faintly disguised autobiography to fiction, from a subjective to a more objective style—the literary historian will study them with equal interest.

Among Hamsun's nonfictional short stories are a number of travel accounts from his journeys in the East. "Under halvmånen" (Under the half moon) from *Struggling Life,* originally published in *Aftenposten* two years earlier, are probably leftovers from his travel book *I æventyrland* (In a Wondrous Land, 1903, analyzed below) and, like it, the story displays Hamsun's love of the Asiatic peace of mind and his aversion to Anglo-Saxons, socialists, and modern emancipated women. Similarly the account of Hamsun's French years (1893–96) in "Litt Paris" (A little of Paris) contains, among its humorous sketches of daily life in the French capital, attacks on the enlightened attitude toward sex among the frivolous women of Paris. Hamsun's very sparse accounts of his childhood years ("Blandt dyr" [Among animals] from *Struggling Life*) are unsentimental but charming, while the stories of his youth and early manhood are related to a number of sketches by Mark Twain, in which the author presents himself in various ridiculous situations. Hamsun's own sketches may involve a young woman whom he pursues throughout southern Sweden, only to find she is already married, or an aborted lecture tour to Drammen, or a curious horse he is saddled with at a Norwegian stagecoach station, or simply an amorous fly that keeps disturbing him at his writing desk. Among Hamsun's short stories are also to be found his most extensive accounts of his life in America, particularly of his experience among the colorful hired hands on the North Dakota bonanza farms. These stories ("Zachæus," "Rædsel" ["Fear"], "På prærien" ["On the Prairie"] from *Brushwood,* and "Vagabonds dager" [Vagabond days] from *Struggling Life*) are also told with humorous detachment, though they may involve the explosive sentiments of love and hatred between rivals. In some of the stories from America humor is mixed with the shock effects of French naturalism. "Kvindeseir" ("Feminine Victory," *Struggling Life*), formed as a memory of Hamsun's conductor days in Chicago, tells of a young man who plans to throw himself in front of a streetcar in the hope of scaring his estranged wife into caring for him again. He has paid the conductor (Hamsun) to make sure he will stop in time; but the man's wife, riding on that particular streetcar to a meeting with her lover, has already given a small fortune to the driver, who speeds ahead, with tragic consequences. Another story, "På bankene" (On the banks), describing life on a fishing smack off Newfoundland, shows how the presence of the captain's wife, a singularly ugly and unsympathetic woman, provides sexual dreams for the whole crew. Equally naturalistic is "Livets røst" ("Call of Life"), about a gentleman who meets and makes love to a young society woman. On leaving her house he discovers in an adjoining room the corpse of an old man whom he later identifies as her deceased husband. The young widow apparently could not wait until after the funeral to satisfy her sexual desires.

The same naturalism, but tinged with a new individualism and mysticism is characteristic of "Damen fra Tivoli" (The lady from the amusement park), about a pathological woman who tries to share with the narrator her *idée fixe,* that her baby has been buried alive. If this story is reminiscent of Poe, "Hemmelig ve" (Secret sorrow, from *Siesta*), about a diabolic double whom the narrator encounters on three continents, is more fantastically Hofmannesque. Somewhat similar, though more in the tradition of Russian naturalism, is the story "En ærkeskjælm" (An arch scoundrel, from *Brushwood*), about a poor girl who is accused of stealing and ends up by becoming a prostitute. The girl, however, is less interesting than the strange character who tells her sentimental story to the naive narrator. More realistic and detached are the two love stories "Alexander and Leonarda" and "På Blåmandsø" ("On the Island"), both from *Struggling Life,* which the narrator reports to have heard in his youth. The realistic dress only covers a rather stereotypic theme in Hamsun's production—that of love and social incompatibility. Similar typical Hamsun themes—a woman's *faux pas* and attempted return to her lover, or a simple girl's hopeless love—are given allegorical or rhetorical expression in the two stories "Ringen" ("The Ring") and "Kjærlighetens slaver" ("Slaves of Love") from *Brushwood.* Finally an objective detachment, with humor, characterizes two stories told in the third person, "Jul i Åsen" (Christmas

Eve at the forest croft) and "Reiersen av 'Sydstjærnen' " (Captain Reiersen of the *South Star*), both from *Siesta.*

The short stories represent a very broad register of basic Hamsun themes, and it is possible to view several of them, with regard to both form and content, as precursors of later novels by Hamsun. "The Ring" could easily be counted among the incidental allegories of *Victoria.* "Småbyliv" (Small town life, from *Brushwood*) is clearly an early sketch for what thirty years later became the novel *Women at the Pump,* just as "Udi søden sommer" (During one sweet summer, *Struggling Life*), with its satirical treatment of a mountain resort, points to the novels *Look Back On Happiness* (1912) and *Chapter the Last* (1923). The humorous use of unconventional syntax and curious vocabulary in "Christmas Eve at the Forest Croft" is a first example of the new low style Hamsun experimented with in the novels *Dreamers* (1903) and, more particularly, *Benoni* and *Rosa* (1908), and which hc used in all his novels after 1913. With its description of a happy farm life, "Christmas Eve at the Forest Croft" also anticipates *Growth of the Soil.* Finally the stories from America are taken up again in Hamsun's last book, *On Overgrown Paths.*[10]

Hamsun's short stories are of lesser interest and importance than his novels. He is a good teller of tales, with a wonderful sense of dialogue and colorful situations, but he is not concerned with the special combination of economy and intellectual point that characterizes the modern short story. Except for the more objective travel accounts, the style of these largely autobiographical tales is either darkly romantic as in Poe or humorous as in Mark Twain, or it contains a mixture of both modes—as in the macabre Chicago story "Feminine Victory." The only story that resembles more directly the tone of Hamsun's great novels from the 1890s is "Slaves of Love." Its diary form has the emotional intensity of works like *Pan* and *Victoria,* and it is interesting in that it presents not only a woman's point of view, but more particularly that of the secondary woman character—the mother/madonna, rather than the princess—in Hamsun's love triangles. Just as Edvarda *(Pan)* is permitted to tell her love story in *Rosa* (see the analysis below), so her rival Eva is given a similar opportunity in "Slaves of Love."

What is generally striking about a majority of Hamsun's short stories is their clear connection with the naturalism of the 1880s, which inspired his first attempts in modern literature, before he lifted his irrational romantic protagonist out of a drab everyday to a more central position in a colorful setting. Therefore, from the point of view of his typical work from the nineties, most of the stories—like the novels *Editor Lynge* and *Shallow Soil*—represent a regression in Hamsun's development.

I æventyrland (In a wondrous land, 1903), Hamsun's account of his journey through Russia and Caucasia, belongs to the kind of nonfictional literature with which Hamsun opened and ended his authorship—his early diatribe against America (1889) and, toward the end of his life, the painful memoir of his stay at the Psychiatric Clinic in Oslo, *På gjengrodde stier* (*On Overgrown Paths,* 1947). The description of his Eastern journey, if less naive, is less entertaining than the book about America, and it does not move us like *On Overgrown Paths;* after all, in *In a Wondrous Land* Hamsun the narrator is not the interesting and pathetic subject he later became. Even so, these chapters about rather trivial people and events, which in his humorous presentation become strange and sometimes exciting, constitute a valuable mosaic of Hamsun's romantic ideas of the Eastern life-style. He is confused and impressed by the wonders of Moscow and the Caucasian mountains and states with bitter irony that he would like to retire there, since he does not have sufficient culture to utilize his present position in the West. One chapter in the book is devoted to Russian literature, more particularly to Dostoevski, whom Hamsun admired above all other writers but censored for his hysterical Slavophilia, but also to Tolstoi, whose moralizing tendencies are deplored through several pages.

Throughout the book there are references to the rigid Eastern class system, to the master, who still knows the ancient art of commanding, and the servants, whose ability to suffer seems unlimited—even the sight of a maltreated horse triggers this kind of sentiment in the author. To people in the Levant—and Hamsun approved of their Islamic wisdom—happiness means accepting life as it is. Afterward all will be better. While the men of the East are praised for their pride and stoicism, the peddlers among them—the Armenians, Greeks, and, particularly, the Jews—are ridiculed and despised, but, as can be expected in Hamsun, there are inconsistencies. The English, typically, are chastized for their imperturbable equanimity, which is called not stoicism, but plain impoliteness. The serenity of the Eastern paradise is contrasted with the enterprise of the West, first and foremost that of the Yankee, who always appears with the derogatory epithet "roaring," referring here as in *The Cultural Life of Modern America* (1889) to the rat race of industrialized nations. As a tourist prying into the private lives of an idealized Oriental people, Hamsun naturally cannot deny his own Western life-style, and even his literary style is Western, more particularly the American style of Mark Twain in his *Innocents Abroad.* In both works the humor is largely based on situations where the narrator experiences communication problems of all kinds, not understanding and not being understood in a strange land. *In a Wondrous Land,* then, provides a useful illustration of Hamsun's literary anatomy. On the one hand, we see his interest in strange people, places, and activities, and his comical manner of presenting his finds; and, on the other hand, a basic pessimism and longing for the peace and contentment of the past.

Dreamers, Benoni, Rosa

The humor and sentimentality that characterize Hamsun's short stories also color his six novels written during the first decade of the twentieth century, and indeed in such a way that the *Wanderer* trilogy is more sentimental, while the three novels *Sværmere* (*Dreamers,* 1903), *Benoni,* and *Rosa* (both 1908) are humorous regional novels of a kind that was new but later proved to be a continuing genre in Hamsun's production. Introducing this series of comical stories from north Norway is the novel *Dreamers,* Hamsun's shortest and, though not one of his great books, probably his most consistently humorous.

The action takes place at Rosengaard, where Herr Mack lives, brother of the more famous Ferdinand Mack of Sirilund (of *Pan, Benoni, Rosa*) and like him an enterprising merchant and the most powerful man in his district. The novel treats a short period in the life of Ove Rolandsen, the local telegraph operator, a jovial man, big, strong, musically gifted, and an inventor who hopes one day not only to see his special type of fish glue patented but to marry his fiancée, a talkative and short-tempered maid from the city of Bergen. The story develops somewhat in the style of a Norwegian folktale: like its hero the Ashlad who, thanks to his persistence and good humor, finally wins the princess and half the kingdom, so Rolandsen in the end wins Herr Mack's daughter, Elise, and becomes the business partner of his new father-in-law. Not only this simple plot, but a new set of characters indicate Hamsun's turn toward a new low style. Like *Pan, Dreamers* deals with a summer in north Norway, but there is less emphasis on the lovesick Byronic hero roaming around in the bright summer night, more on working men and everyday life. The characters are ordinary people with the kind of curious biblical names found only in north Norway: trusty Levion, whose sister is the village prostitute; Enok, the religious hypocrite and petty thief who carries his head in a bandage *à la* van Gogh, ostensibly because of his earache, but actually because Levion tore off Enok's ear when he was stealing fish from Levion's net.

The civil servants—from now on they will be staple characters in Hamsun's new kind of society—are represented by the over-zealous minister (who sides mistakenly with Enok against Levion) and his scatter-brained and romantic wife. Herr Mack is less sinister than his brother at Sirilund (who, after all, arranged to have Eva killed), but just as ridiculous in his attempts to keep up appearances. However, he is also generous and not without some traces of the style and integrity Hamsun liked to associate with the upper classes. Rolandsen is Hamsun's new artist type—outgoing, singing, drinking, loving the girls (he has already two illegitimate children), but also working at his invention and, for all his easygoing ways and little defeats, still a proud man. In Rolandsen and his relationship to Elise Mack there is even a little left of the arrogance and pathos between Hamsun's earlier lovers—now hurting each other with surprising malice, now endlessly forgiving.

The language is consistently comical in this book. There is the helpless high style of Miss Van Loos, Rolandsen's fiancée—resembling that of Pernille in Holberg's eighteenth-century comedy of manners—and Rolandsen's more typical Hamsun style, in which he uses a curious mixture of hyperbole and understatement. As in the folktale and the picaresque novel, fantastic things keep happening: Herr Mack is burglarized and offers the thief a substantial reward for giving himself up—an invitation Rolandsen, who needs money, cannot pass up (the real thief is Enok), with endless complications.

Dreamers is important mainly as an introduction to a new style in Hamsun's production. In itself it is lightweight, more like an eighteenth-century opera libretto than anything else Hamsun has written. It has colorful action and racy dialogue, but little food for thought. *Benoni* (1908), though its humor is even more baroque, is a better book. In it we are back to the Sirilund of the earlier novel *Pan,* though the tone seems closer to the Rosengaard milieu of *Dreamers.* There is also a connection between Rolandsen of that novel and Benoni: both are referred to as "a hell of a guy," both are favored by Lady Luck—Rolandsen inventing his fish glue and marrying Mack's daughter Elise; Benoni making his renowned herring catch, acquiring a silver mine, and becoming Mack's partner in business, and, in the following novel, marrying Rosa, who is not his partner's daughter but at least his goddaughter. Once again, the story has the quality of myth—that of the Ashlad who wins the princess and half the kingdom or, in more modern terms, that of the faithful servant who saves his master's business, as in Alexander Kielland's novel *Skipper Worse* (1882).

In *Benoni* Hamsun creates a whole little town with a number of more or less individualized characters, artisans of all kinds, merchants, servants and servant girls, often with curious names and nicknames. Benoni, the central character after whom the novel is named, is an upstart of a different type from Rolandsen (who was, after all, a well-educated young man). Benoni is a homespun north Norwegian with a tremendous appetite for life and success. He begins as a mail carrier and ends as a partner in business to no lesser person than Mack. Benoni, a big strong man, with an intelligent and friendly face, is also a child in most things. He (like Hamsun himself) writes his name with a special flourish, keeps pigeons for show, and adds to his house a veranda with windows of colored glass—something that no one up north has seen before. He overdresses and lacks taste and sensitivity. However, Hamsun must have admired the rough *élan* in him and has portrayed him as having at least some dignity, in comparison with the only real nobleman in the book, Sir Hugh Trevelyan, the first of Hamsun's grotesque portraits of an Englishman.

Mack is powerful and dangerous as in *Pan,* but his promiscuity, which there cost Eva her life, is put into comic relief here: he exercises his *jus primæ noctis* on all the young women in the neighborhood, who rub his body as he relaxes in his remarkable waterbed and who, after they get pregnant and are married off to some artisan in Mack's service, still go on loving the old master. But Hamsun has also added dignity and friendliness to Mack's qualities and seems to be saying that, if these northern provinces need a separate king, they can get none better than Mack. While Benoni is presented as sheer health, Nikolai is the symbol of a corrupted young man; the city has destroyed this farm boy, who becomes conceited and artificial and in the end a caricature of his former self. He is full of Hamsun's own sarcastic wisdom, and claims, like Ibsen in *Love's Comedy,* that marriage destroys love, that no love is worth anything except the one that is stolen, etc. Another type is the lighthouse-keeper Schøning, somewhat related to the old tutor in *Victoria.* The relationship between him and his wife is like that of the minister in *Dreamers:* an endless, boring togetherness. But while Nikolai can still formulate clever ironic remarks, Schøning's sarcasm explodes in convulsions. His only hope is that some young person—even a simpleton like Benoni—will one day find the joy he experienced as a young traveler around the world.

In this novel, even more than in *Dreamers,* Hamsun seems inspired by a special kind of popular literature, but what is serious there is here seen in an ironic light. It is as if Hamsun is making fun of his naive dreams and his artificial language in *Bjørger.* The average reader identifies with Benoni and enjoys his success, yet feels superior to him culturally; hence the great popularity of Benoni as a television film in Norway. The language is perhaps the most striking feature in this book. Some indications of the new low style are evident in *Dreamers,* but are more developed in *Benoni.* Basically the pattern is one of applying a word mistakenly in its original and literal meaning (describing, for example, a woman as impregnable instead of sterile). Also included in this more folksy style are grotesque descriptions of the kind Hamsun usually reserved for his short stories, such as a detailed account of the killing of a pig.

Though more substantial than *Dreamers, Benoni* is still not a great novel, but one marking, like *Dreamers,* a change in Hamsun's production to the humor-filled tales of northern Norway, which, when given shape and purpose, as in *Growth of the Soil* and *Wayfarers,* result in great literature. *Benoni* also contains the beginning of a social theory: when Benoni is successful, he enjoys respect, but he is ridiculed whenever he is down—as opposed to Mack, who retains respect, because of his real "royalty."

In plot *Rosa* is simply a continuation of *Benoni.* The milieu is exactly the same—Sirilund—as are the main characters Mack, Benoni, and all the lesser personalities that make up Mack's large household. The plot carries the story of Benoni to a happy ending. Benoni meets Rosa and becomes engaged to her. However, her first love, Nikolai Arentsen, now a lawyer, returns and regains her love, with the result that Rosa breaks her relationship with Benoni and marries Arentsen. But Nikolai gradually has less success in business. He takes to drink, is finally asked by Mack (Rosa's godfather) to leave the place and is later paid to have his marriage to Rosa annulled. Benoni now slowly regains Rosa's affection. First she is his housekeeper, then his wife and the mother of his child. Still, the relationship is not happy because Rosa is not sure Nikolai is really dead, as Mack and Benoni have told her. Not until Nikolai returns in person and then commits suicide, does Rosa give up her sentimental love dreams and settle down to a reasonably happy relationship with Benoni and her child. To this continuation of Benoni's story is added a subplot, namely, the story of Edvarda from *Pan,* who also cannot forget her great love, Lieutenant Glahn, but who, unlike the chaste Rosa, tries to achieve the old passion in her fleeting relationships with a number of new lovers, including Benoni, Gilbert the Lapp, and, strangely enough, the twenty-five-year-old Friar Vendt (who, according to the play about him, should be close to a hundred years old). Like the "princess" she is, she finally marries another nobleman, this time not a Finn, but an Englishman, Sir Hugh Trevelyan.

The strangest thing about *Rosa,* however, is not the presence of well known characters like Edvarda and Friar Vendt, but that of the pale, acne-marked young student, Parelius, who gives the story its special form. Like *Pan, Rosa* is the memoir of a person who has spent some time in north Norway and now reminisces in order to while away the time: he is thirty-eight, and all of this happened fifteen years ago, when he was twenty-three. Parelius resembles none of Hamsun's earlier heroes, even though, like many of them, he deserves the name of voyeur. He is more of an uninitiated passive lover-observer, as well as being religious and seemingly humble, all of which brings to mind Morten Winge, the hero of Steen Steensen Blicher's famous short story *Diary of a Parish Clerk.* Parelius tries to learn erotic strategy from his friend Friar Vendt (Hamsun's own wisdom: "make her jealous with someone inferior; then she is bound to come back to you") but is still a hopeless lover. On the other hand, he plays the piano and paints landscapes, activities that give Hamsun the opportunity to include in this otherwise rather boisterous novel a number of beautiful observations of nature, making *Rosa* a much more poetic book than *Benoni.* Compared to *Pan,* however, with its sustained dithyrambic mood, the poetry of *Rosa* is tempered in various ways, most particularly by the author's sarcasm in his description of old age (a graphic rendering of the slow dying of two of Mack's old servants)—the worst in all of Hamsun's work. *Rosa* is interesting not only as a continuation of *Benoni,* but also for its added treatment of a central character like Edvarda. Together the two books with their characters Benoni and Parelius make up an early variant of a much more famous Hamsun pair: August and Edevart of *Wayfarers.*

The Wanderer and *Look Back on Happiness*

The Wanderer books—not really a trilogy—are made up of *The Wanderer,* which is the English title for the two novels *Under høststjernen* (*Under the Autumn Star,* 1906) and *En vandrer spiller med sordin,* (*On Muted Strings,* 1909), and a lesser known novel translated into English as *Look Back on Happiness* (*Den siste glæde,* 1912). The books have in common a first-person narration by a very special protagonist: the wandering author himself, who watches the gradual downfall—and in the last novel the final salvation—of a woman he loves. Otherwise the novels vary in tone: it is as if the once carefree wanderer slowly becomes an aggressive missionary and, in the last volume, a modern-day Jeremiah.

Many critics have described *The Wanderer* (that is, the first two novels) as being set in Hamsun's childhood district of Nordland. Though it is difficult to determine the locale, it can safely be said that the action does not take place in the north, but rather in the countryside around Oslo, and the small town figuring in the second volume is most likely Kongsberg. The protagonist, who calls himself by Hamsun's original name of Knut Pedersen, has left the city to wander and work in the country. He first does plumbing at a rectory, where the minister's young and buxom daughter, Elisabeth, for a while catches his attention. Later he arrives at Captain Falkenberg's estate, where he does farm work of various kinds and falls in love with the captain's beautiful wife, Lovise. With growing dismay he watches her involvement with an unworthy lover, her worsening neuroses, and finally her death by drowning. This kind of old-fashioned melodrama serves not only as a simple plot line, but, more importantly, as an accompaniment to the real story of Knut Pedersen's own crisis over his vanishing youth but lingering appetite for all of Nature's wonders: after *Pan,* Hamsun wrote nothing more beautiful about the changing moods of the Norwegian landscape. Otherwise *The Wanderer* differs from *Pan* in having more characters of a comical cut: the minister's wife who lures the wanderer into her bed on several occasions, poor little Olga who is innocent, optimistic, and charmingly uncoordinated—and, on the other hand, Ragnhild, Lovise's servant, who spies on her master and mistress as if in an eighteenth-century comedy. There is the burned-out worker Grindhusen with his terrible table manners, and his younger and much more cheerful colleague Falkberget, who impresses the farmers' daughters with his remarkable singing voice and ability to tune pianos. All of these characters reduce the kind of high melodrama that was basic to *Pan* and make *The Wanderer* more sentimental than truly tragic, as would befit its theme of old age.

Elisabeth, who is no more than an introduction to Lovise, is younger, more prosaic, and without the lability of temperament that characterizes the older woman. Lovise Falkenberg is described as extremely fair, friendly, and erect like a pillar—the pillar being used to convey the sense of purity that Hamsun always associated with the empire or regency style. The fascination of this woman for all who meet her has to do not only with her beauty and kindness of heart, but with her passionate glance, which makes men believe themselves to be loved by her. Though she respects and loves her husband, she is not satisfied in her marriage; the couple soon try to relieve their boredom with wild parties, and Lovise, after her first *faux pas,* is never able to regain her old balance. Captain Falkenberg is described as an attractive person, intelligent, determined, fair in all his dealing, and, in coping with his wife's infidelity, at the same time proud and understanding. The difference between their affairs is that, while the captain has not behaved improperly vis-à-vis Elisabeth, Lovise has been, in her own words, "as if married" to her young engineer friend. The captain is willing to accept this fact, but the news that she is pregnant makes it impossible for him to love her as before, and she goes back to her unwilling lover and to her death.

Knut Pedersen, the main character of the novel, identifies with the captain, whose story, after all, resembles Hamsun's own—infidelity, wild parties, repeated attempts to patch up a relationship—and he suggests what is wrong with the marriage: that the captain is too military, too proud, too gallant, too forgiving; and as for his wife, she has a grand piano, but no children, that is, she has nothing to save her from the boredom that inevitably enters marriages among the leisure classes. However, this kind of didacticism is not strong enough to break the feeling of something resembling tragedy or at least of the inevitable, and this is brought out in the way all the servants see the gradual estrangement of master and mistress without being able to do anything about it. Among them is Knut Pedersen himself, who is also deeply in love with Lovise Falkenberg and watches her behavior day and night with the painful excitement of the voyeur. In all of this Hamsun tried to re-create what he considered to be beautiful about the old feudal society, which was its sense of fate and loyalty.

As so often in Hamsun's work fate is simply old age, a disease that eventually overcomes everyone. There is Grindhusen, once a red-headed devil with the women, now only a shadow of his old self and very different from his young and feisty comrade Falkberget. But even Falkberget is under the laws of change. In the second novel he is a married man jealously guarding his wife, Emma, against the attention of his old vagabond friend Knut Pedersen. Hamsun, however, seems to be looking for a remedy against old age. For the first time the reader is told that being a mother will help a woman. For a man who is creative (Knut Pedersen is the inventor of a mechanical saw for lumbermen) and depends for his success on the ups and downs of love and inspiration, there is a hint—also for the first time—that agriculture may hold promise. Hamsun still had not given up ridiculing the farmer for his primitive looks and behavior, but there is in the second *Wanderer* novel the thoughtful, genuine, hardworking farm hand Nils, an altogether idealized character who shows what direction Hamsun's Rousseauan philosophy would take him in the future.

Basically, the two novels deal with a neurotic city dweller who seeks a healthy sojourn in the country. But with Hamsun's negative attitude toward old age, health for him did not so much mean peace of mind as a reawakening of the instincts. He used an expression from a well-known folktale (by Grimm) about a boy who has set out "to learn to shudder in his shoes," which means to experience once again the basic emotions—anger, fear, jealousy, love. In describing his attempt to learn that shuddering, Hamsun was remarkably realistic: most of the scenes in these two novels strike the reader as experienced life. What is more difficult to accept—that is, on a realistic level—is the narrator's double identity as vagabond and famous author. Hamsun's old ambition suddenly to appear on the scene as an unknown entity and then disappear as mysteriously as he arrived was acceptable in the case of Nagel *(Mysteries),* because he was not, on the one hand, a wandering workman, nor was he, on the other, a writer who had made a name for himself. In the first of the *Wanderer* novels, Lovise and her husband both address Pedersen with the polite pronoun *De,* knowing that he is really not a worker, but in the second novel they use the familiar *du,* as though they had forgotten his real identity. Hamsun must have been aware that this kind of pretense would not work in the long run: in his next novel the narrator is simply Knut Hamsun, tourist, rather than the vagabonding jack-of-all-trades Knut Pedersen.

The second part of *The Wanderer* (that is, *On Muted Strings*) contains both an introduction and an epilogue, in which the author explains what the narrator has tried to show. *Look Back on Happiness* does not havc these pedantic appendages, but a didactic tone that suffuses the whole novel. It is still a book about the wanderer who observes nature—even to the extent of describing it in poems which are interspersed throughout the text. But just as there is less peace and more thunder in these impressions of nature, so too there is less of Hamsun's art and more of his intemperate journalism in *Look Back On Happiness,* making it, possibly, his least successful novel. It was the last of all Hamsun's books to be translated into English (1940) before World War II, and one can understand why.

Look Back on Happiness takes place in north Norway, where Hamsun had settled in 1911, after an absence of eleven years. The narrator for a while lives in a turf hut (as did Hamsun himself in 1900). His ambition this time is not "learning to shudder in his shoes," but doing something about what he calls his "red-hot irons" (they are sometimes less than hot), which he hopes to hammer into poetry of some sort. He moves from his turf hut to a mountain sanatorium, where he meets a number of people, who are not humorous as in *Benoni, Rosa,* and *The Wanderer,* but ridiculous and repulsive—local people who are petty thieves, pedantic school masters, pompous lawyers, hysterical sportsmen, and unsavory English tourists—as uncharming a lot as has ever appeared in a Hamsun novel. The "heroine" is a schoolteacher, Ingeborg Torsen, who confesses to having been corrupted by what little education she has enjoyed. She is tall, beautiful, and intelligent, but already twenty-seven years of age and "still not married," and the narrator deplores such an unnatural situation. He is clearly in love with her, though more as a father than a prospective husband; he watches and analyzes her confusion and is finally able to guide her into a healthy way of life. Ingeborg Torsen had first gone off with a brutal local Don Juan, then with an effeminate actor. Finally she meets Nikolai, big, burly, ugly, taciturn, and persistent, whom she marries, moving to his home in north Norway, where they bring up their children. The Norwegian title of the novel—literally "The Last Joy"—is variously interpreted in the book. At one point the narrator describes that joy as being able to sit alone in the dark, but for Ingeborg—and the author seems to agree with her—it is to have children. She is already gray and has lost a front tooth, but she is happy and enterprising. And Nikolai, her husband, though he is really a carpenter and could have taken over his mother's guest house, has decided to give up tourism and become instead a full-fledged farmer.

In a newspaper article one year earlier (1910)[11] Hamsun had complained about the lack of ministers in Nordland. Young theologians refused to spend time in that land beyond the Arctic Circle, which Hamsun referred to as a fairy-tale land and one particularly good for contemplation—actually good for anything except tourism. In the book Hamsun inveighed against the spirit of Switzerland, which he saw entering Norway, and against the English, who visited the country as sports fishermen and mountain climbers. The author characterized Switzerland as a nation of ungifted people (and, adding insult to injury, claimed that Böcklin, whom he loved, was somehow not Swiss!). The English are described as old, rude, arrogant, decadent, and kept from pederasty only by their fear of young Germany. But even more insulting to the reader than these caricatures of whole nations is his attack upon women. The novel is not only written in the first person but has a single addressee—a "You," described as "the new spirit of Norway." More particularly, however, this "You"—usually referred to as "Little You"—seems to be Hamsun's second wife. Just as *The Wanderer* was inspired by Hamsun's first marriage, so *Look Back on Happiness* was an "old" (fifty-three) man's warning to the actress Marie Andersen, who, like Ingeborg in the novel, is only twenty-seven. The author's case against Miss Torsen was Hamsun's case against his wife and against education for women, whom, it seems, finishing a Norwegian high school can destroy for life. Even Miss Torsen's well-meant attendance at a cookery school is too much for her conservative admirer, and when she makes a good meal at the end of the book, it is said to be in spite of, rather than because of, her training in domestic science.

After the charm of *The Wanderer,* with its sentimental admission of certain frailties brought on by advanced years, in *Look Back On Happiness* Hamsun launches one of his harshest attacks on old age as a period of stagnation and egoism, but at the same time he persisted in claiming that, though he was old, he could see intuitively into the future. Even if one were to grant that Hamsun, like his mentors Rousseau and Strindberg, had foreseen the ills of industrial society, the strident tone of this novel points to an author both misguided and uninspired. Toward the end of the book Miss Torsen has several very tiring monologues that, rather than characterizing her prosaic mind, show a writer who was no longer in full command of his art, and, judging from Hamsun's letters to Marie, those sections must have been added after the original novel had reached the proof stage.[12] Only Hamsun's anger was unabated: *Look Back on Happiness* showed him still fighting his neurasthenia—and he did so until he settled down and became, like Nils or Nikolai, a real farmer.

Chapter Four

The Urban Experience and the Soil

Knut Hamsun's early Rousseauism—which he picked up during his Minneapolis days by reading August Strindberg—amounted to little more than a general suspicion of city culture and a longing for unspoiled nature.[1] Hamsun was impressed first and foremost by the intensity of Strindberg's attack on modern civilization, but he did not then share the Swede's cultural pessimism and would not have condemned the arts as Rousseau did in his *Lettre à d'Alembert,* nor would he at first have understood Rousseau's enthusiasm for the simple virtues of primitive mountain farmers. In *Mysteries* Hamsun describes such people as "nothing but lice, peasant cheese, and Luther's catechism," claiming furthermore that "Ola Nordistuen" (his name for the typical Norwegian farmer) had been put on this earth to fertilize the soil; "it is Ola Nordistuen that Napoleon tramples under his horse's hoofs, that just about sums up Ola Nordistuen."[2] Twenty-five years later Hamsun headed his article "Bonde" (Farmer) with the warning "Take your daughter home from the city,"[3] and a Danish woman writer who had turned to him for advice was told: "You and I should not live on poetry and emptiness; we should play a part as human beings, marry and have children, build homes and till the soil."[4] Hamsun's journey into middle age was accompanied by an expansion of his old love of nature into including both a systematic condemnation of city life and a corresponding praise of rustic simplicity. It was a development full of inconsistencies, but one probably inspired by some sort of rationalization that farming could be viewed as poetry made respectable and was therefore a solution to his own perennial problem—that he loved what he most despised: the city with its many forms of "emptiness," including literature and the theater.

Despite Hamsun's extensive contact with city life—as a homeless wanderer in New York, Moscow, Paris, or a fugitive crossing his tracks endlessly in Kristiania—the urban experience in his life and writings is one-sided and superficial. There is little mention and no understanding of what has made the city an attractive place for millions of ordinary immigrants from the countryside—the communal spirit that has resulted in a variety of public works and institutions, from city parks to hospitals. In *Hunger* the city is either the capital of culture—which is why Hamsun's hero goes there—or else a stronghold of arrogance and heartlessness—which is why he leaves. In *Shallow Soil,* interestingly enough, that attitude is reversed: the artist colony is a nest of nasty swindlers, whereas the business men are honorable citizens—actually early forerunners of Hamsun's idealized farmer. But mainly the city is seen as an inimical entity, and the small town—as in the short story "Småbyliv" (Small town life) or in such novels as *Mysteries* and *The Wanderer* (volume 2)—does not fare much better: if, in the city, a supercilious bourgeoisie looks down on the artist as a country bumpkin, in the small town he is viewed with envy and suspicion. Admittedly the trading posts of the Mack brothers are described with humor and sympathy, but this is probably so because the author was more intimately acquainted with the life-style there.

In 1908 Hamsun published one of his most important essays, entitled "Bondekulturen" (Farmer civilization)[5] and provoked by a similarly entitled article in *Den ny Verden* (The new world), the most recent book by a young Danish friend and colleague, Johannes V. Jensen. Jensen gave his concept of farmer a rather broad definition; Frank Norris and Theodore Roosevelt both appear to have something of the farmer in them; Bjørnson *is* a farmer, and Hamsun the farmer *in excelsis.* Unfortunately, said Jensen, Hamsun was caught by the false enticements of city culture, for he wanted above all to become a gentleman, but "in order to attract attention he decked himself with eccentricity, in order to prove his genius he pretended to be insane."[6] This was so because Hamsun did not understand the farmer. Jensen wrote: "The most highly valued literary treasures have come to us from anonymous commoners. . . . Modern civilization from Newton and George Stephenson to Darwin and Edison derives in its entirety from the nature-bound imagination of farmers. There is no reason to fear that the farmer should not be modern or lack culture." Against that praise of farm culture, Hamsun in his essay described the development of the artist as a movement away from nature, from primitive origins or popular cultures. If by farming Jensen had meant rustic art and literature, Hamsun was not impressed by its accomplishments: "You [Jensen] could write a more wonderful medieval ballad than Scandinavia has ever seen." If on the other hand farm culture was taken to mean the practical achievements of everyday life, then Hamsun preferred to call it by its right name, materialism, and he did not consider such materialism a suitable subject for modern literature. Whoever had used it in America only imitated the European naturalistic writers of the 1880s. Hamsun, in his final answer to Jensen, seems to say that only by "going to the city" where he had "eliminated the farmer in him," had he (Hamsun) been able to produce art.

At that point there was no agreement between the two writers, though Hamsun soon adopted Jensen's view. The very stature he was prepared to give the farm hand Nils in his novel from the following year indicated his new direction, and by the end of World War I that development was complete. Hamsun shared Jensen's admiration of Bjørnson, and indeed of Bjørnson as a commuting farmer, fighting his battles in the cities and then retreating to his stronghold in the country—to his family and his farm Aulestad. In his poem to Bjørnson in 1902 Hamsun mentions the Aulestad balcony from which that master poet and orator addressed his people—"when Cities sometimes joined your attackers with boos and with roar / the Country backed you the more,"[7] and during Hamsun's fugitive years he envied Bjørnson's sense of security. In 1911 he himself bought and moved to a farm, although it was not until 1918, when he acquired Nørholm, that he took up gentleman farming in the style of Bjørnson. It was then that Hamsun's new gospel of the soil received its final form. In five novels published between 1913 and 1923 he presented his views of the city in various images, the first of which—a magpie nest (in Norwegian folklore a symbol of untidiness or disorder)—still shows a connection with the charmingly primitive trading posts of northern Norway.

In *Markens grøde* (*Growth of the Soil,* 1917) Hamsun for once seems to address the idea of city welfare—adult education, professional training, medical care—but ironically in the book all these blessings are enjoyed only by a convict, and the question is asked whether, since this is a prison, we should still not prefer the old-fashioned freedom of the countryside. In *Konerne ved vandposten,* (*The Women at the Pump,* 1920) the central image is that of an anthill—a primitive, structured society where every one is busy with his or her project and where everybody crawls ruthlessly over everyone else. Finally, in *Siste kapitel* (*Chapter the Last,* 1923), the city is represented as a sanatorium, where inmates are either patients or crooks, and the development of Hamsun's misanthropy since *Segelfoss by* (*Segelfoss Town,* 1915) is seen in the difference between the magpie, which steals shining objects, and Mrs. Ruben of *Chapter the Last,* who kills her husband to get another diamond ring. There is another person in this novel who kills to have his way, Daniel—but he is a farmer and a hero.

Whether or not farming is Hamsun's way of making poetry respectable, it is certainly his way of making materialism attractive. Among Hamsun's protagonists many are, like Nagel, reckless and generous; others are creative gamblers (Rolandsen, Benoni), but real materialism seems to be acceptable only in the farmer, where it is essential and constructive, rather than self-serving. Geissler in *Growth of the Soil* tells the young farmer Sivert: "You be content! You've everything to live on, everything to live for, everything to believe in; being born and bringing forth, you are needful on earth. 'Tis not all that are so, but you are so; needful on earth. 'Tis you that maintain life."[8] The idea of the farmer serving not first and foremost himself, but some higher general will comes out in a motif Hamsun pursued with considerable persistence throughout his career: the unfaithful wife and, particularly, the husband's problem in accepting a child that is the fruit of adultery. In Hamsun's first positive portrait of a farmer, Nils in *The Wanderer,* volume 2 (1909), it is indicated that Nils's girl friend has committed a *faux pas,* from which she never regained her former balance—possibly because both parties exhibited the Hamsun hero's usual pride. While it is true that Inger of *Growth of the Soil* (1917) is not always a model of virtue, Hamsun allowed her husband Isak to sire his own children, but Aksel—of the same novel—accepts a bastard child as his own because he needs its mother (Barbro) to help him run the farm. In *Women at the Pump* (1920), Oliver's children have different fathers, and Hamsun lets them grow up to become promising young men and women. Finally in *Chapter the Last* (1923), Daniel understands that another man is the father of Julius, yet he accepts him as his son: Julius one day will take over the farm and be needful on earth, like his stepfather. Hamsun changed his attitude as he began observing the problem from the point of view not of the offended father, but of the illegitimate child. Geissler of *Growth of the Soil* reminds the judge that Leonardo da Vinci and Erasmus of Rotterdam were both born out of wedlock.[9]

In the years of general disillusionment during and after World War I two Norwegian Nobel Prize winners—Knut Hamsun and Sigrid Undset—turned against Ibsen's uncommitted individualism (Nora's "I have a right to do with my life what I will"). Undset found her answers in Christianity and her faithful-wife ideal. Hamsun was not concerned about Christianity except in its most general sense as a religion, and though he supported women's emancipation no more than Undset, his new gospel of the soil was mildly progressive in at least providing an outlet for a woman's energies beyond that of mere child rearing: a woman on a tractor (he had seen them in North Dakota) was his new ideal! The patronizing tone of much of Hamsun's journalism makes it less than persuasive, but luckily for him he had the ability, like Rousseau, to present his ideas in fictional form, where they are subtly argued in an attractive context, and where the ideas themselves have been modified so as to become more complex and more humane. Hamsun, of course, differed from Rousseau in several basic ways—in temperament, in political philosophy—but where he discusses town and country, his writings reflect very closely the spirit of the French master:

> Men are not made to be crowded together in ant-hills, but scattered over the earth to till it. The more they are massed together, the more corrupt they become. Disease and vice are the sure results of overcrowded cities. . . . Man's breath is fatal to his fellows. . . . Men are devoured by our towns. In a few generations the race dies out or becomes degenerate; it needs renewal, and it is always renewed from the country. Send your children out to renew themselves . . . send them to regain in the open field the strength lost in the foul air of our crowded cities.[10]

Children of the Age

If, in *Benoni* and *Rosa,* Hamsun had been an extravagant teller of tales of success, in *Børn av tiden* (*Children of the Age,* 1913) and its sequel, *Segelfoss Town,* he is more an "objective" historian, describing the economic and social development of a north Norwegian district during the last quarter of the nineteenth century. In the latter novels Hamsun adopts a genre that he had earlier ridiculed as lacking in psychology—the social novel of the 1880s, particularly the kind practiced by Alexander Kielland, whose elegant depiction of his ancestors' business fortunes won him a permanent place in Norwegian literature. The name of another forerunner that comes to mind is Bjørnstjerne Bjørnson in his novel *Det flager i byen og på havnen* (*The Heritage of the Kurts,* 1884), where, in the introduction, an old document (invented for the purpose) is quoted as historical background for the plot development in the following chapters.

Hamsun's novel opens in a somewhat similar fashion, by his first quoting oral traditions and local history, and then proceeding to chronicle the sudden industrialization of Segelfoss, originally a feudal community, presently ruled by Lieutenant Willatz Holmsen III. The lieutenant lives at Segelfoss Manor with his German wife, Adelheid, and a son, Willatz Holmsen IV. If the couple's marriage is not what one would normally call happy, the reason, as so often in Hamsun's works, lies in the extraordinary pride of the two partners and its attendant communication problems, rather than in a lack of mutual respect. Lieutenant Holmsen is not only a wealthy husband but one unusually generous. He has built a beautiful church to be used by the whole district, only to honor his wife and their newborn son, and it is painful to him that financial considerations later prevent him from also providing an organ for the building.

To this area there one day comes a stranger, Tobias Holmengraa, originally from the district, but most recently a prosperous business man in Mexico. He impresses the proud lieutenant and his equally proud wife with his modesty and quiet charm, and when he mentions his hopes of finding a retreat to restore his failing health, they agree to sell him a piece of land, which in the end turns out to be considerable in size. Rather than building a retreat, however, Mr. Holmengraa proceeds to develop a prosperous mill industry, employing a large number of local workmen and bringing a number of professional people to the region, including a general dealer, a doctor, and an attorney at law.

With the sale money Lieutenant Holmsen is able for some time to continue the extravagant life-style of his forebears. He keeps a large household, provides higher education for a gifted farm boy, and sends his own son to an expensive boarding school in England. However, since Holmsen does not produce anything himself and cannot locate the legendary hidden treasure of his grandfather, he becomes increasingly indebted to Mr. Holmengraa. The latter nevertheless remains on good terms with the lieutenant and, particularly, with Mrs. Adelheid, who appreciates his gallantry and generosity. The Holmsen marriage is neither better nor worse than before. Adelheid Holmsen, who is artistically gifted, spends her time singing, writing, and painting, and her attempt to establish a more cordial or even erotic relationship with her husband fails as in the past. She finally follows her son Willatz IV to Germany, where he is to receive his musical education, and there she dies in an "accident" (drowning herself, like Lovise Falkenberg of *The Wanderer*). Life at Segelfoss continues much as before, except that the lieutenant now understands that he is insolvent and that his estate is actually owned by Mr. Holmengraa. To reduce his household expenses, he closes the manor and moves into a couple of rooms in the old brick works. He is also thinking of sending some of his prized possessions—paintings and silverware—to the antique dealers in Trondheim, when he suddenly discovers the old family treasure. Although fatally ill, he arranges to have his son settle all outstanding debts with Holmengraa and pays the price of a new organ for Segelfoss church.

The last detail is not without special significance: like most of Hamsun's major protagonists, Lieutenant Holmsen sets his house in order before departing from this life, and, indeed, he is a major, if not the major *hero* in all of Hamsun's work. This is so despite the fact that he is presented in many situations as quite laughable. Although he may treat the local doctor and the minister with the utmost contempt, when he chooses to overlook the warning shouts of a blasting gang, he is nearly thrown from his horse. But he returns to the surprised workmen and orders them to repeat the experiment until the horse is under control. That kind of extreme pride and arrogance, bordering on insanity, which earlier times often associated with the Spanish nobility (cf. Ludvig Holberg's play *Don Ranudo*), and which our democratic age finds not a little ridiculous, Hamsun had accepted with something like admiration. Throughout his authorship he had called for a great leader, and, though he did not pretend that Lieutenant Holmsen was a man of international format, in his time and place and circumstances he was as close to the ideal as Hamsun could hope to make him. He is only a lieutenant, yet people greet him "as though he were a general." Hamsun's idea (and experience) of the absolute power of Eastern potentates—including their power over women—colored his miniature portrait of Lieutenant Holmsen, whom he refers to as an Arab in looks and behavior. Holmsen seems to be naive in the ways of the world, not because he is stupid, but because he looks upon all everyday money transactions with contempt. He is a learned man, a philosopher, and though his views are mostly expressed in action and brief statements, where we find him engaged in discussion—as with his old friend Fredrik Coldevin—he expresses what we know to be Hamsun's views on the hierarchy of classes in society, including his contempt of civil servants, that is, men who have worked their way downward, after being originally respectable peasants.

Lieutenant Holmsen's problem with his wife is that, while he wants her to be proud and aristocratic, he would also like her, on occasion, to be sweet and gentle. But because he is too proud not to take no for an answer, he has to satisfy himself with the assurance that her sharp tongue at least reveals her jealousy (and hence her love), a jealousy that he himself causes by inviting to his room various good-looking servant maids, who read to him or play games with him in the evening. However, unlike Hamsun's other pashas, such as Mack of Sirilund, Lieutenant Holmsen is also philosophic in his ability to withstand the temptations of the flesh. Adelheid Holmsen has little to offer her husband except her nobility. She is neither beautiful nor rich, but she is blessed with a remarkable singing voice, and her artistic gifts are a great comfort to her in her loveless marriage. She has also been blessed with a child, whom, unfortunately, she sees slowly growing away from her and become a man. Rather moving in this marriage—as in Ibsen's *Master Builder*—is the special kind of spiritual love shared by the spouses. Adelheid late in life admonishes her son to work hard at his career and make a name for himself, so that in this way he will be able to gladden the heart of his old father; and the lieutenant not only permits, but even begs his son to begin using his middle name of Mortiz, because it would have made his mother happy.

Since Adelheid is a woman, she is, in Hamsun's eyes, a weaker vessel than her husband. Typically, as with Eve in the biblical story of the serpent in Paradise, it is she who concludes the tempting deal with Mr. Holmengraa and thereby causes a fall in the fortunes of the Segelfoss people. Even so, the decision is not an easy matter. The old landowner Coldevin, who advised against selling the land, does not realize that his own estate is kept from bankruptcy only through the liberal subsidies of his merchant son, Fredrik: times are ripe for the kind of tragic social and economic transition the novel sets out to describe; even the most romantic reader will realize that Lieutenent Holmsen's style is that of a bygone age. The problems of transition are presented in a discussion between the lieutenant and his friend, the practical man of the world Fredrik Coldevin. According to Holmsen (and Hamsun) it takes several generations of wealth to make a true gentleman: the first stage—that of the ambitious upstart, a servant, a farmer's son—is represented here by the general dealer, Peter Jensen; the second stage is represented by Tobias Holmengraa; and the third by the lieutenant himself. Typically, the lieutenant has no difficulty in dealing with either his workers or Mr. Holmengraa—to the lieutenant the former represent Nature, the latter a beginning culture, which means self-knowledge and self-control, rather than education. Fredrik Coldevin, for all his joviality and pretended common touch, is more of a snob than the lieutenant. He has more difficulty accepting his daughter's marriage to a coastal skipper than does her godfather, the lieutenant, to whom a husband of the civil servant class is a still worse proposition, since such a person would have left Nature behind him without attaining culture. Those who have studied books and believe they know life's secret are the really arrogant people. The lieutenant may ride around the district on his horse, like some lord protector, but he rides with a bowed head: "I am never done with gazing at the earth, at the grass and the stones; no I am never done with the grass and the stones."[11]

In the Segelfoss novels, the picaresque qualities of *Benoni* and *Rosa* have been fused with the melodrama of *The Wanderer,* but the style is more detached and there is less concern with a single protagonist and more with several parallel developments, through which plots are varied with subplots. The central conflict—between conservation and the forces of change, as embodied in the major characters of the lieutenant and Mr. Holmengraa—is present in the cases of Old Coldevin versus the lieutenant, the lieutenant versus Fredrik Coldevin, and, on a lower social level, of Bertel in Sagvik versus Lars Manuelsen, and that of their sons, Gottfred versus Julius. However, Hamsun's use of theme and variations is less musical than painterly, more as in a Breughel canvas, with characters, events, and styles for all seasons. There is Holmsen's imperial manner, Holmengraa's unassuming ways, Fredrik Coldevin's facetious small talk, and all the local peasants and their promiscuous women (with names that are in themselves humorous: Florina, Palæstina, Daverdana) speaking their delightful form of (Hamsun's) Nordland dialect. On the other hand, there are several grotesque portraits of civil servants such as Dr. Muus. Finally there is a new type, Baardsen, a broad-shouldered, musically gifted, and alcoholic telegraph operator, somewhat like Rolandsen of *Dreamers,* though Baardsen is more clearly the author's spokesman—a person who has seen through life's temptations but does not have sufficient character to withstand them. Baardsen supports Holmsen's elitist view of society, a view that has many parallels in Norwegian literature, from the Eddic poem "Rigsthula" down to Ibsen's *Enemy of the People.* It is strange that Hamsun, himself of the lower classes and living in a country that had abandoned nobility as early as 1818, should deplore the loss of lords and ladies. But equally strange is that he should come to agree with Matthew Arnold's rhetorical question of "whether upon the whole earth there is anything so unintelligent, so unapt to perceive how the world is really going, as an ordinary young Englishman of our upper class."[12] Hamsun's next novel tells something about the ambivalence he still felt with regard to class and the English.

Segelfoss Town

The second of the two novels about Segelfoss (1915) opens with Theodore's festive preparations for the visit of a distinguished commercial traveler. He is so secretive about it that Lars Manuelsen and Ole Johan spend hours wondering what a flag flown at full staff might mean. The economic wisdom of Theodore's father, the general dealer, was limited to parsimony and forced saving. His son, however, wants to invest in the future and make money. He advertises, for instance, in the local paper *Segelfoss Times,* now in its seventh year and edited by an aggressive union man (but owned by no less a person than attorney Rasch). A sign that Segelfoss is finally a town in its own right is the sudden visit of a traveling theater group, which approaches Theodore about using his store for a stage, much to the annoyance of the town's two members of the cultured middle class, Mr. Rasch and Dr. Muus. Theodore, however, has received expert help from his former enemy, the telegraph operator Baardsen, who, it appears, was once an unsuccessful playwright. Baardsen falls in love with one of the actresses, even though he does not attend the group's performance and has nothing but contempt for the acting profession as such. Mr. Holmengraa is lonely after the deaths of Lieutenant Holmsen and his wife, Adelheid (although he does entertain Rasch and Dr. Muus on occasion), and seems to have problems with his workers, who have become lazy and disrespectful. In his attempt to improve this situation, he enjoys the support of Willatz Holmsen IV, now a well-known composer, who has recently returned home to Segelfoss Manor, where he tries to uphold the feudal ideals of his imperious father. Two special events provide some excitement for the town's inhabitants, attorney Rasch's garden party and Theodore Jensen's even more spectacular island picnic, with wine, dancing, and fire works. Willatz Holmsen's friend Anton Coldevin has arrived for this latter occasion and pursues Mr. Holmengraa's daughter, Mariane, so vigorously that she stabs him with a fork. Theodore also tries to win Mariane's favors with small gifts from his store but has more luck in his fight with lawyer Rasch, who represents Theodore's sisters in a family feud over ownership of the store. Theodore outmaneuvers them all and establishes his own flourishing business.

Lars Manuelsen—father of Holmengraa's mistress Daverdana and of Julius the tavern keeper, as well as of the Reverend Lassen—finds a key in the nest of a pair of magpies, and, as the whole town goes off to attend Mr. Rasch's garden party, lets himself into Mr. Holmengraa's storehouse. Because of the improved fare at Julius's hotel, rumors spread that the food is stolen, and the Reverend Lassen has to leave his church politics in the south and move home to clear up the affair personally. Important events quickly begin to happen. The theater group returns, and at a wild party Baardsen is accidentally stabbed by his friend Clara. Feisty Peter Jensen, whom a stroke has left bedridden for years while it strengthened his resolve to survive all relatives, gives up and dies just as Mr. Holmengraa's business activities come to an abrupt end. As the creditors move in on Holmengraa, his only two faithful workers begin to build a fireproof bunker which he does not, however, need to use. He leaves the district the way he came, in a spirit of mystery and magic. He is fetched by his Mexican son Felix, captain of a big ship, on which Mariane also departs. Willatz Holmsen, Mariane's sweetheart since childhood, had finally experienced the kind of inspiration that produces masterpieces. Reassured by that victory he had proposed, and Mariane is happy to sail south, with her father and brother, to meet her future husband.[13] The book ends where it began, with its two most curious characters, Lars Manuelsen and Ole Johan, snooping around once more. This time they find Baardsen, who has been missing for days, lying dead in Mr. Holmengraa's bunker.

When Mr. Holmengraa first arrived in the district he was described as an unhealthy-looking, pot-bellied man on spindly legs. He also spoke about his poor health and during a meal would almost imperceptibly slip a pill or two into his mouth. After the land purchase he surprises the Holmsens by looking thin and wiry, and he is not above explaining the situation himself: the common people of north Norway are impressed by corpulence and ostentation. That is why on his arrival he dressed as he did, with several jackets, one outside the other, even on a hot day. His aim is to get his way, and he chooses his means accordingly; his apparent modesty, for instance, had the desired effect on the Holmsens, as did also his generosity, his will to assist the lieutenant, and his gift of a horse to Willatz IV. But Mr. Holmengraa is something different from and something more than a confidence man. His relationship to his children is that of a close friend (as opposed to Mack's relationship to his daughter Edvarda), and the warmth and dignity of his personality is equally evident in his intercourse with conventional bourgeois people like Mr. Rasch and Dr. Muus. On the other hand, he cannot completely hide his lowly background: the sailor suddenly comes to light. He sometimes boasts a little (if in his usually low-keyed manner) and he chases the women, particularly after Adelheid's death—which makes the reader wonder whether in all those years there was an intimate relationship between them, or whether his admiration for the lady of Segelfoss was enough to keep him from the escapades of his sailor days. His sexual exploits eventually become his undoing; his workers feel that he is no better than they and treat him accordingly. The text shows us that, because of his farmer/sailor background, there is in Holmengraa a crippling sense of inferiority. Unlike Lieutenant Holmsen he is no commander and he knows it: "When nature produces masters, she does not always produce the right kind."[14]

Holmengraa's contrast in *Segelfoss Town,* Willatz Holmsen IV, has the firmness of his father, though it sems to come less naturally to him. The lieutenant, with his constantly bowed head, was not a spectacular man, but he did not need to build up his sense of security in some artificial manner, as Willatz does, by mixing with the lords at Harrow and keeping physically fit with dumbbells and other sports equipment of the kind Hamsun associated with English public school education, which he both hated and admired. The ambivalence in Hamsun's attitude is well illustrated by an incident in which Willatz, to the pleasure of the author and presumably that of many readers, knocks out a truly obnoxious worker; the text however, describes the happy blow as "brutal" and "English." Whenever Willatz is uncertain of himself, it is as an artist—he recognizes that inspiration is a divine gift, and when it is withheld feels inferior, yet too proud to accept Mariane's love. Mariane is one of Hamsun's most attractive minor women characters. As with many of his temperamental heroines (Edvarda, Teresita), he makes her at the same time exotic (Spanish, Indian) and Norwegian. The text uses the Norwegian term *kjekk* ("spirited," "sporty"), and though in a misogynist like Hamsun the word may not always be positive (since it could be interpreted as "bold," even "brash"), the reader feels it is so here. Impulsive, intelligent, and charmingly childlike, Mariane is not spoiled by education (always Hamsun's greatest worry) but remains true to her nature.

Segelfoss Town offers an improved insight into Hamsun's preoccupation with class, since his historical stages can be seen in clearer perspective, complete with beginning and end. The upstart Peter Jensen, whose only goal in life is hoarding, produces a son, Theodore, with higher ambitions. He sees the value of popularity and social prestige and is willing to pay a price for it, though none too high: his embroidered handkerchiefs are still a limited extravagance compared to the generosity of Tobias Holmengraa (of the following stage), who buys Willatz IV a horse and wants to present Mrs. Adelheid with a grand piano. However, as the reader is told, it takes generations of wealth to produce a gentleman and free spender like Lieutenant Holmsen, whose philanthropy is both truly royal and seemingly selfless. Willatz Holmsen IV has inherited some of his father's instincts, but there is something in his nature that points to a certain decadence: clearly the Holmsen family had reached its apex with the lieutenant.

The novel also shows the complete development of a typical civil servant—the farm boy Lars, whose education was paid for by the lieutenant. In keeping with Willatz's definition of the civil servant as "a person who does not belong anywhere, whose roots trail behind him,"[15] Lars Lassen leaves his native Nordland to spend his days where the action is, in a cultural center known as Kristiania.

Lassen is described as a man with no redeeming character feature: he is primitive and calculating like his father, Lars Manuelsen, and, unlike his more attractive brother, Julius, completely humorless. Several details in his biography—the title of his scholarly publications, his interest in antiques, and his promotion of Norway's minority language, *nynorsk*—points to Bishop Anton Christian Bang as a model for this unflattering portrait of a plebeian cleric. The novel furthermore gives the first Hamsun portrait of an industrial worker. The faithful servant, a Bertel or a Martin, is well known from earlier novels, as—with certain modifications—is the lazy hypocrite Lars Manuelsen. Konrad and Aksel, however, who teach their fellow workers the importance of striking as a weapon against an unpliant employer, are entirely new creations. They ride to their jobs on bicycles (Hamsun's hatred of the bicycle goes back to the early 1890s) and waste their hard-earned money on cheap consumer goods from Theodore's store. The author tells us that, since it is so important for the young to learn being modern, the teaching of what was formerly known as character is neglected, and that sad development seems to cut across class lines: Anton Coldevin, of good family background, is not above giving up Mariane as soon as he hears of her father's bankruptcy.

Two special issues are taken up by Hamsun in *Segelfoss Town*. The first is the language *nynorsk (maal),* which he claims is not understood by the people of the north. He writes of Lars Lassen's preaching that "it was a cheerful and simple sermon, a part of it was in *maal,* but the rest was quite intelligible."[16] Hamsun's lack of respect for *nynorsk* (which is actually what most people in Nordland speak) has to do with its connotation of being the "farmers' language," but probably also with the author's conviction that the accepted norm of a country's national language should always be the result of culture and refinement. In other areas he feared that refinement might remove a person too far from the natural. Young Willatz's English mannerisms are a step in the wrong direction, and the visiting actors and actresses illustrate the artificial life-style of theater dilettantes. Typically, after Clara has accidentally stabbed her friend Baardsen, she sends a telegram to the big newspapers to describe her own part in the drama and indicate Baardsen's suicidal tendencies: what counts for this performer is sensation of whatever kind (Hamsun's attacks upon the theater, like his personal struggles with his actress wife, seem endless).

Exposing the ills of city culture is a major concern in all of Hamsun's work, from his first to his last novel, but not until the second Segelfoss book was there an attempt to create a complete view of a whole town. It had to be a miniature town that could fit into the pages of a single novel, and even so, the overall picture was too diversified to receive the kind of focus a first-person narrative could have offered (say, that of Kongsberg, seen through the eyes of Knut Pedersen in *The Wanderer*). But Hamsun's ambition seemed to be to move in a new direction—toward a novel that, as it were, told itself. There was still a long way to go to the sophisticated method of *Wayfarers,* for the irony was too obvious to conceal the author's personal view of the characters and opinions of, say, Mr. Rasch and Dr. Muus. On the other hand, the author's own spokesmen were not spared: Old Coldevin does indeed sound senile; Lieutenant Holmsen acts like a maniac. Holmengraa is pitiful in his helplessness, and Baardsen, probably the character closest to the author's heart, is little more than a philosophizing bum. This was the sort of impartiality that Hamsun was able to apply even to his antagonists, because, as he once said of his characters, they were all taken from within himself: Holmengraa's admiration of the nobility, Dr. Muus's longing for the south, Lassen's tampering with his name, Willatz's morbid jealousy—all were typical examples of the author's own weaknesses and account for his humanity, which keeps disarming even those of his readers who disagree with his philosophy. The finest expression of that overall tolerance is found in the humorous chapter about the magpie—one of many aspects making *Segelfoss Town* a better book than *Children of the Age.* The magpie is not only an apt symbol for the Lars Manuelsen family, but with its mixture of roguishness and healthy self-preservation a suitable emblem for *Segelfoss Town* and indeed for city dwellers anywhere.

Growth of the Soil

Called "the least characteristic novel that Hamsun ever wrote,"[17] *Markens grøde* (*Growth of the Soil,* 1917) is, of course, very different from any one of Hamsun's four major novels from the 1890s. The label, however, can be accepted only with the added understanding that *Growth of the Soil* still shares many of the features of Hamsun's other seventeen novels and that it is still a work of superior quality. The book's popular appeal has not helped its standing among certain critics—it has even been claimed that Hamsun wrote it specifically to win the Nobel Prize, a statement showing not only a deficient understanding of the novel, but of Hamsun's work generally.[18] On the other hand, the common epithet "Hamsun's greatest novel" is also inappropriate: the book is strongly polemical, and the literary achievement of part 1 is not sustained in part 2 of the novel. Nevertheless, *Growth of the Soil* belongs to Hamsun's great works; after *Pan,* it contains Hamsun's special rhetoric at its most consistently high level and is, as H. G. Wells said, "saturated with wisdom, and humor and tenderness."[19]

The story is of Isak, "a lumbering barge of a man" who looks for homesteading land in north Norway. He needs a woman to help him at his new settlement, mentions it to the Lapps that walk past his place, and soon Inger arrives from the nearest parish. She is not much to look at with her harelip (neither is Isak, for that matter), but she is a good worker, and what is more, she owns a cow. Isak gradually gets himself a horse, and Inger has her first child, Eleseus. An old woman, Oline, comes to look after the little homestead while Isak and Inger walk down to the parish to get properly married and have their child christened. They have a second boy, Sivert, and a third child is on the way when a Lapp arrives with a hare, which Inger sees—a frightening experience to her, because she knows that a hare is also what her mother saw before she had Inger. Now the bailiff himself, a certain Geissler, arrives. He surveys Isak's extensive acreage of government land and proposes a reasonable price. Before leaving he gives the new farm its name of Sellanraa, and, noticing some peculiar rocks Isak has found up in the mountains, indicates they may contain copper. Inger now has her third child, a girl with a harelip like herself, and thinking of what she has had to suffer because of her blemish, she kills the baby. Old Oline arrives at Sellanraa a little late for the birth of this third child but soon enough to practice her evil ways. She finds the little grave and spreads the news—assisted by Inger herself, who needs to confess her problems. After weeks and months of waiting, Inger, who is pregnant again, is finally taken to prison by the new bailiff Heyerdahl. (Geissler in the meantime has been fired.) Isak during the coming years has to rely on the "cursed old hag" Oline to help him with the animals and the children. A telegraph line is being constructed across Isak's new property, and the engineer in charge of the construction wants Isak to take over the job as a lineman.

He refuses and, in what little spare time he has, tries instead to teach and entertain his two little children. Geissler returns to Sellanraa one day to buy up Isak's copper mountains and, more important to Isak, to tell him the news that Inger has served her time and will come home with her five-year-old daughter, Leopoldine. Isak is not altogether happy with what Inger has learned during her six years in prison—reading, writing, and dress-making. She likes to have people around her, she even dances with the telegraph workers, and she wants Eleseus to accept the engineer's offer of an office job in town. It turns out to be a very costly decision for the parents: Eleseus spends money on useless things and Inger has to help him as best she can. When Isak discovers her one day taking some of his "copper" money, he loses his patience and chastizes her, an event that appears to be a turning point—to the good—in their married life.

Isak and Inger keep extending their pasturing land, and new people move into the area—Brede Olsen, formerly the bailiff's assistant and not much of a farmer, and Aksel Strøm, a hard worker, at whose farmstead Brede's daughter, Barbro, becomes a maid, after having spent some time in the city of Bergen. Geissler arrives one day with a following of rich-looking foreigners. He sells the copper mountain to his wife's relatives and at the same time forces them to pay Isak a considerable sum for the right to mine the area. For part of his money Isak buys himself a marvel of a mowing machine. Barbro has a child, which she kills; there is even an indication that during her time in Bergen she had also killed a baby. She leaves Aksel, who has no choice but to hire old Oline, and while he waits for her to arrive, the tree he is felling falls on him. None of his limbs seem to be broken, but he is unable to free himself and spends seven hours in the snow and frost. Brede Olsen, now a lineman for the telegraph company, comes by and pretends not to see his unfortunate neighbor, but luckily Oline arrives to help free Aksel. By that time however, Brede returns, and the two of them quarrel over which of them has saved Aksel's life. Brede later sells his land to Fredrik Strøm, another hard-working farmer.

As a result of Geissler's mining project, industrial workers invade the area; even Mr. Aronsen sets up a store, but it is all ephemeral: the company needs to explore a different part of the mountain, which Geissler has bought from the government and is now unwilling to sell. In the meantime, Oline, snooping around as always, discovers a second dead baby, and soon a case is brought against Barbro (and against Aksel as her possible accomplice). Mrs. Heyerdahl, the bailiff's wife, acting as a witness in the case, delivers a moving speech that helps sway the jury so that Barbro is acquitted, and Mrs. Heyerdahl keeps her promise to take Barbro on as a maid in her house. For Eleseus, who has become more and more lost in town, Isak purchases Mr. Aronsen's store, and Eleseus then travels around the country buying up goods, while his store manager, Andresen, spends most of his time cultivating the land with the help of Eleseus's healthy and lively brother Sivert. Barbro, by spending her nights with the young men of the district, loses her job with Mrs. Heyerdahl and returns to Aksel. They get married, and though it is soon evident that Barbro is again in an advanced state of pregnancy, Aksel does not seem to mind: the important thing for him is to get someone to help him on the farm. Eleseus, seeing that he cannot get any more help from his parents who have spent all of their copper fortune on him, decides to leave for America, a land from which he never returns. On the other hand, Isak has the comfort of seeing that by this time ten families have followed his example and homesteaded in the wilderness. The book ends with the three young doughty farmers, Sivert, Fredrik Strøm, and Andresen, picking up all the useless goods in Eleseus's store and selling them for a good profit to the mining people down on the coast. Having rid the settlement of those last traces of industry and commerce, they return to their farms by early morning, just as Isak begins a new working day. And then it is evening:

Nothing growing there? All things growing there; men and beasts and fruit of the soil. Isak is sowing his grain. The evening sunlight falls on the grain that flashes out in an arc from his hand, and falls like a dropping of gold to the ground. Here comes Sivert to the harrowing; after that the roller, and then the harrow again. Forest and field look on. All is majesty and power—a sequence and purpose of things.[20]

Growth of the Soil resembles *Benoni* in not being a "character novel": its protagonists are not psychologically interesting. Because they are primitive, yet not without a certain stature, one could perhaps apply the old romantic term "noble savages" to them, but their nobility is not of the conventional heroic kind—theirs is not the ability to face death fearlessly in battle, but rather the "heroic" ability to be jammed into the snow-covered ground under a fallen tree for seven hours and yet survive in good shape. They have the health and the manners of animals—Isak's rasping voice, rough looks, and tremendous strength and Inger's bloody fight with old Oline all show this clearly. They are "lonely folk, ugly to look at, but a blessing for each other." In writing about marital problems among the Norwegians, nineteenth-century authors such as Bjørnson and Ibsen often emphasized the lack of communication between spouses. In *Growth of the Soil* a similar lack of communication is seen as a positive feature: while Brede Olsen is a chatterbox, good people like Isak are men of very few words. Furthermore, Isak's secretive manner helps increase Inger's interest in what he is up to and ends by kindling her admiration of all the remarkable things he can think up—which Isak is again sufficiently childlike to appreciate.

As usual Hamsun is prejudiced against women, whom he considers to be more promiscuous than men; however, when Isak is faithful to his wife, he is so, the reader is told, because he is less exposed to temptations. Isak is not altogether free from a healthy vanity: he loves to hear Inger praise him, pretends he can read, dresses up in his bright red flannel shirt, and even rubs in a little tansy for good scent. In Inger's case there are special reasons for her escapades. Because of her disfigured face she did not enjoy a normal girl's courting adventures but had to wait until more mature years before she could pull up her skirts and dance with the miners. Although the author seems to laugh—with the miners—at the "old woman," he understands her perfectly well. All of this is natural. What is not natural is her social ambition, the way she is impressed with city life and bookish learning. In her insistence that her oldest son "become something," Inger is partly to blame for Eleseus's tragedy. Even so, Inger and Isak's relationship is close to ideal. It is a dollhouse idyll, less like Ibsen's play, more like the Norwegian fairy tale about Gudbrand of the Hillside and his wife, who never stopped marveling at the backward ingenuity of her husband.

In the Sellanraa boys, Isak's strength and Inger's weaknesses seem to be reproduced. Sivert has his father's integrity and robust health, and a deep, almost poetic, sense of belonging to Nature—which we see when, as a child, he looks deeply into the billygoat's eyes and, later, when he watches the mating ducks in spring. But above all he has humor, and that coupled with his physical strength and easygoing manner makes him an attractive boy; typically, Geissler befriends him right from the beginning. Eleseus, on the other hand, is more reflective and more romantically inclined. He finds physical labor on the farm unfulfilling and longs for something different without knowing really what it is. He tries city life and, later, America, and in the process he loses whatever comes naturally to a farm boy, physical strength and sound sexual instincts. Even though Eleseus is shown to be quite ridiculous in his corruption, there is also something tragic about his character. He is basically a person of good will, only he has lost his orientation. But he goes off to America and never returns.

The relationship between Isak and Inger is repeated on a somewhat less idyllic level in the case of Aksel and Barbro. Aksel is a hard-working man, but he is not a child of luck, nor does he seem generally happy like Isak; rather he feels he is being taken advantage of (which he is). He has less humor than Isak and, above all, less generosity, though he shares Isak's naive religion. Isak, for instance, puts up with Oline's crookedness in the hope that his meekness will get Inger out of prison, and Aksel, similarly, keeps his promise to God not to report Brede for failing to save his life (when the tree falls on him). If, in the reader's sympathy, Aksel has been placed considerably below Isak, Barbro is even further removed from Inger. Their cases are parallel: both women are accused of murdering a child, but Inger, whose crime is easier to excuse, is sentenced, while Barbro, a callous murderer, is acquitted. Yet, even for Barbro there are excuses: she may have profited from her intelligence and beauty, but she is also a hard-working woman, and since her corruption comes from her upbringing and her life in the cities, it is indicated that even for her—if she stays with Aksel in the country—there is hope. More than any other person in the book Barbro illustrates the author's major thesis that Nature is capable of healing all wounds. Around these more central men and women are a group of rather grotesque characters, either second-class citizens like the Lapps, or poverty-stricken Oline, or else a straightforward good-for-nothing like Brede Olsen. This last type is known from most of Hamsun's novels after *Dreamers* (from Enok to Lars Manuelsen). Such a person's unusual life force is fired by envy, which makes him a malicious and dangerous enemy, yet also easy to please, and, for all his petty criminality, he is treated with much more humor and sympathy than, say, Mrs. Heyerdahl.

The only character in the novel who is psychologically interesting is the deposed bailiff, Geissler. Very clearly he is the author's spokesman, even to the extent of being supplied with the same birth place as Hamsun—Garmo in Gudbrandsdal. Basically, Geissler is a resentful person. He bears a grudge against the villagers who had him disbarred, and they in turn may be right when they claim that he has tried to ruin his home town: he has given them industry and a new way of life, and when that industry leaves they are lost. On the other hand, although he punishes the villagers, like some God in disguise he blesses the work of the settlers: he obtains land for Isak at a reasonable price, teaches him irrigation, helps Inger out of prison, withholds information about Barbro that could have sent her to jail, and gives Isak a mechanical hayrake and Aksel a mowing machine. The author has taken care not to idealize him: Geissler drinks like Baardsen, he shows off like Holmengraa, and he is a big talker and seemingly a very poor listener, yet he sees through everybody and everything. He refers to his son—a sharp business man—as "the lightning that's nothing in itself, a flash of barrenness; he can act. He's the modern type, a man of our time,"[21] but he calls himself the fog—fog can be confusing to townspeople, but is beneficial to the soil. He also says of himself that he is a man who knows the right thing to do, but does not do it, a paradox that illustrates Hamsun's personal dilemma as a man who despised art and literature yet could not stop producing it.

Growth of the Soil was written during World War I, while bombs were dropped on women and children in many parts of continental Europe, and Geissler's message to Sivert is Hamsun's to his readers: "Look, Nature's there, for you and yours to have and enjoy. Man and Nature don't bombard each other, but go together."[22] But more particularly *Growth of the Soil* was shaped as an artistic response to a newspaper discussion of how to treat unmarried mothers who had murdered their newborn babies.[23] Rather than Hamsun's shrill journalism ("Hang them both, hang the mother and the father too!"), what we have here is a fairly low-keyed "Yes, I see the problem, but . . . ," in which seeing the problem makes up part 1 of the novel, and part 2 is made up of the *but.* When Oline hears that in prison Inger has learned reading, writing, and dress-making, she wants to be thanked for having reported Inger to the police in the first place. The novel describes the city as a prison: the city is where Inger's prison is and where she acquires the prisoner's syndrome, a blind acceptance of conventionality and aimless materialism which also leads to Barbro's corruption and Eleseus's undoing. What is needed to correct such a situation, according to the novel, is not the leniency asked by today's humane laws: Mrs. Heyerdahl's speech, though wonderfully well made from arguments Hamsun had picked up from his antagonists, is deeply ironic. The book instead emphasizes discipline within the family—the parents' attitude toward their children, and, typically of Hamsun, a husband's right over his wife. When Isak chastizes Inger, it is said to be a beneficial experience for Inger and a turning point in her life. But there is also the discipline of Nature, the discipline required in a farmer's daily struggle to feed his family and his animals. In contrast to the materialism that led to the war Hamsun was writing about, there is also a materialism that is attractive because it is constructive and satisfies a basic need to create: this is the settler's slow building up of his estate. In that respect Isak is distantly related to the artistic heroes of Hamsun's earlier novels. In trying to bridge the gap between the city (of *Segelfoss Town*) and wild nature (of *Pan*)—or between Nature, Art, and the acquisitive instinct—Hamsun at last had come up with a viable compromise—the family farm.

It has been said that Hamsun achieved the happiness of Isak and Inger at the expense of their consciousness—which is natural enough, since it is well known that "he that increaseth knowledge increaseth sorrow."[24] Geissler knows that. Perhaps so even does Eleseus in his brightest moments. Hamsun, like Ibsen in the *Wild Duck,* was writing about ordinary people, and Dr. Relling's variation of Ecclesiastes that "whoever takes the life lie away from average man, also takes his happiness away," is probably also shared by Geissler, who, like Dr. Relling, helps create a happy household of settlers in the wilderness. Hamsun, however, was less pessimistic than Ibsen (or than Camus in *The Myth of Sisyphus*): Geissler does not look upon the life of his settlers as meaningless, rather he believes in some sort of evolutionary system: "Listen to me, Sivert: you be content! You've everything to live on, everything to believe in; being born and bringing forth, you are the needful on earth. . . . Generation to generation, breeding ever anew; and when you die, the new stock goes on. That's the meaning of eternal life."[25]

Like his mentor, Nietzsche, Hamsun had no use for conventional Christianity, for Kierkegaard's insistence that we are all guilty, or Ibsen's that living means fighting the trolls in our heart and brain.

Such Christianity is seen humorously as the result of a bad conscience or of the weakness of age. There is a central scene in which Isak, under the influence of one of Inger's religious spells, claims to have seen the Holy Ghost or, as he later believes, the Devil. Typically, Isak is tired after a long day in the woods and sits down in the snow to rest, when the apparition moves in on him. He wonders whether his guilt might not be his all too great love of the land, and an uncanny sensation stays with him for quite some time. But, as the winter wears on, things begin to look brighter for both husband and wife. Inger is actually the first to lay aside her depression, and the reason she can is that she is expecting a child again. The book, however, does not reject religion as such. There is, as always in Hamsun, the joy of being alive and of experiencing the wonders of the surrounding world, described in very beautiful language: "North of Sellanraa there was a little tarn, a mere puddle, no bigger than an aquarium. There lived some tiny baby fish that never grew bigger, lived and died there and were no use at all—*Herregud!* no use on earth. One evening Inger stood there listening for the cowbells; all was dead about her, she heard nothing, and then came a song from the tarn. A little, little song, hardly there at all, almost lost. It was the tiny fishes' song."[26] Unlike Hjalmar and Gina Ekdal (in Ibsen's *The Wild Duck*), Isak and Inger are conscious of nature's wonders and secrets. They are also conscious of their own insignificance, yet, like the little fishes, they sing.

In their simplicity Isak and Inger mark the culturally lowest level so far of Hamsun's heroes, and the style describing their looks, behavior, and conversations is commensurately simple—a low style, but with excellent dialogue, remarkably modest in its use of dialect and relying for its comic effect mostly on understatement or exaggeration: "Now was his time—he could do it now: reach out with his hands and alter the shape of Oline considerably with but one good grip. . . ."[27] Despite such use of hyperbole it is still a low style of greater dignity than that of *Benoni,* and—as in the passage about the little fishes—it is sometimes paired with highly poetic language. Indeed, *Growth of the Soil* has some of the dithyrambic mood of a first-person novel like *Pan*—some of the rhetorical style Hamsun had brought with him from America, with short sentences, repetition, questions and answers. This is the opening of the book: "The long, long road over the moors and up into the forest—who trod it into being first of all? Man, a human being, the first that came here. . . ." And this is from the last page: "Isak, the Margrave. . . . A tiller of the ground, body and soul; a worker on the land without respite. A ghost risen out of the past to point the future, a man from the earliest days of cultivation, a settler in the wilds, nine hundred years old, and, withal, a man of the day."

Because of its association with the Nobel Prize, *Growth of the Soil* may well be Hamsun's best known book; it is also the one most often referred to when critics speak of Hamsun's fascist ideas, his *Blut und Boden* mysticism. True, in *Growth of the Soil* there is a tone of masculinity and anti-intellectualism, as well as an emphasis on discipline, but there is no idealization of race, and even the picture of farm life is viewed with a humor that is alien to the Nazi spirit. Hamsun the artist indeed differed from Hamsun the journalist, whose outpourings are difficult to defend against accusations of fascist thinking.

Even so, *Growth of the Soil* is not a completely successful novel. If the idea was to have part 2 repeat in minor what part 1 had played in a major key, the effect is not altogether satisfactory. In Hamsun's early love stories the protracted recrimination scenes are more intense than the first sweet meetings, but Barbro's and Eleseus's tragedies, however important to a total picture of the book, do not move the reader—possibly because they lack the author's sympathy. There are a number of Scandinavian writers whose novels take up Hamsun's typical theme of pioneer settlement. Tarjei Vesaas in *The Great Cycle* (1933) concentrates his efforts on the conflict between town and country in a character who in some ways resembles Eleseus, yet is much more deeply experienced. Another writer, O. E. Rølvaag, treats the husband-wife conflict more seriously, and the Icelandic novelist H. K. Laxness takes up the relationship between the settler and society—the land office, and banks, the unions—in considerable detail.[28] These writers may have felt they could improve upon Hamsun in the realism of their novels. For even though Hamsun did not exclude realistic details in his plot and characterization, the way all difficulties are reduced to trifles by a mighty life force shows that he is dealing with myth rather than experienced reality. The size of Isak's land and the rapid development of his prosperity point to an American (160 acres) rather than a Norwegian settlement, or at least to the conditions of a prosperous gentleman-farmer like Hamsun himself at Skogheim.

The novel, then, does not give an actual picture of a Norwegian settler, but rather Hamsun's dream of one, and as such it is comparable to similar books of earlier times, for example, *Robinson Crusoe.* Still, a myth may be what Hamsun felt the age needed, and in that view he was joined by other intellectuals of his day, including H. G. Wells, who wrote of *Growth of the Soil:* "I am not usually lavish with my praise, but indeed the book impresses me as among the very greatest novels I have ever read."[29]

The Women at the Pump

For Norwegians in general and particularly for Norwegians from north Norway such as Hamsun, the so-called Bodø Case was long a source of resentment against the English: in 1821 British smugglers, who had been duly arrested in the Nordland port of Bodø, secured an indemnity of £18,000 on the strength of forged documents; the full truth came to light twelve years later, by which time the forger was the police inspector for Glasgow![30] Many critics have mentioned the Bodø Case as one source of Hamsun's lifelong Anglophobia. As a young man, Hamsun also loved to recite Ibsen's poem "Terje Vigen"—about a poor Norwegian ship's pilot who, during the Napoleonic Wars, was captured by a British man-of-war and spent years in an English prison.[31] In *Konerne ved vandposten* (*Women at the Pump,* 1920), the postmaster declares that "the Englishman enslaves one people after another, takes their independence from them, castrates them, makes them fat and placid. Then one day the Englishman says: Let us now be righteous according to the Scriptures. And so he gives the eunuchs something he calls self-government."[32] In the novel a couple of Englishmen rob the post office of a small Norwegian port and get away with it, and the central character is a eunuch, who grows fat and placid. To that extent *The Women at the Pump* demonstrates Hamsun's deep depression after the Germans lost World War I—which the postmaster calls "the Englishman's war"—and it explains how a beautiful account like *Growth of the Soil* could be followed by such an ugly picture of Norwegian small-town life.[33]

The place is not unlike Segelfoss, except that instead of Holmengraa, there are a number of small ship owners—all of them consuls—and instead of industrial workers, a group of fishermen, sailors, and artisans, with their wives and children. Consul Johnsen, like Mack in the *Benoni* and *Rosa* novels, has a great number of his illegitimate children about the town, all easy to track because of their unusual brown eyes. The central character is Oliver Andersen, a lively blue-eyed sailor who suffers an accident at sea, which leaves him, after weeks in an Italian hospital, one-legged and emasculated, and his life story henceforth is one of trying to overcome his physical defects and his depression. He does a little fishing, eventually gets a job as a custodian in a warehouse, marries his first sweetheart, Petra (after she has become pregnant by Consul Johnsen's son), and has several children. The appearance of the children does not upset him until there is a variation in the color of their eyes: two blue-eyed babies, sired by the local lawyer, suddenly cause Oliver confusion and jealousy. Whatever Oliver loses in prestige in the small town because of his physique, he tries to restore with the help of his intelligence, and he has extraordinary luck on several occasions, particularly when he is rowing around the skerries looking for driftwood. Once he is able to salvage a storm-tossed ship that has been left by its crew; at another time, when he is stealing eider down, he discovers letters, some of them full of money, in among the feathers of the eider ducks' nests. After a robbery of the post office a couple of years earlier, the thieves, who were members of an English crew, had thrown all empty or uninteresting envelopes over board, and the eiders had picked them up and used them for their nests: a story sufficiently fantastic for the narrator to need assure the reader that "Oliver never rejected adventure, and adventure had not yet rejected him!"[34] Apart from the robbery not much happens in the town. Consul Johnsen suffers a near bankruptcy and his son has to marry the daughter of one of the lesser consuls. The only two religious people in town, the postmaster and the blacksmith Carlsen, end up completely heartbroken because of their children (all implicated in the post office robbery), while Oliver's offspring (or, rather, his wife's) grow up to become important men in the town—Frank, a philologist, is made headmaster of the local high school, and Abel takes over the forge after smith Carlsen (he also, as the reader is told three years later in *Chapter the Last,* ends up as mayor).

Good people in this coastal community are few and far between. Double-Consul Johnsen is described as "a good-natured creature without seriousness or constancy, but *primus inter pares,* a major town dignitary."[35] There is the doctor, a little brighter than, but equally as unsympathetic as, Dr. Muus in *Segelfoss Town,* and the lawyer is like Mr. Rasch of that novel. Furthermore there is Frank, a variant of the Reverend Lassen in *Segelfoss Town,* except that this time Hamsun is ridiculing, not the upstart theologian, but the philologist—another person corrupted by learning. Similarly there is Fia Johnsen, a rich man's daughter who wants to be an artist and succeeds only in crippling her natural instincts, to the extent that she looks at a man and a milestone with the same eye. However, in among these members of Hamsun's new vanity fair, there is a small number of genuine people: Jørgen, the slow-witted fisherman; Mattis, the cabinetmaker, similarly slow-witted but endowed with a terrible temper; Olaus, the town drunk, with his total lack of reverence; and Oliver's son Abel—who resembles Sivert in *Growth of the Soil.* Very special in character is the postmaster. Like Geissler in *Growth of the Soil,* he is the author's spokesman. In this instance he is religious, but not conventionally Christian. He seems to be a firm believer in the transmigration of souls and tires his listeners with his endless philosophic talk. He is a mild-mannered, seemingly happy man, yet, as we find in his conversations with the insufferably arrogant doctor, he can be both logical and sharp-tongued. Although his perpetual insistence upon the importance of offspring—Geissler's "eternal life"—is placed in an ironic light, since his son, the Englishman, is the one who robs the post office, the postmaster's statements still support the novel's general thesis—its attack upon the English, on workers, and on education and democracy.

Oliver is a unique character. He resembles the postmaster in being at least a relatively happy person and far surpasses him in the treatment of his "offspring." To his children Oliver is a comrade and a friend rather than an authority figure, and the scenes between him and Abel are most charming passages, of which, incidentally, there are a fair number in this otherwise dark book. On the other hand, he is clearly related to the Midget of Hamsun's *Mysteries* and, through the Midget, to no less a person than Nagel himself, but a Nagel stripped of all his stature and brilliance. Indeed, Oliver is the ugliest portrait ever of Hamsun's "artist" hero. At first Oliver is described as "an ordinary, blue-eyed working-class lad, but a sturdy fellow and a daredevil, with a widowed mother. He is below middle height, but compactly built, used to resemble pictures of Napoleon, but now he has grown a beard and struck out on his own."[36] After his fall from the ship's mast Oliver is still able to function in the community. He is referred to as not only a work of art, but as something smashed but still ticking away, a Napoleon at Saint Helena, a crushed insect warrior still crawling around an anthill of a town. He is described as repulsive to the townpeople at the dance hall, and even to his wife, Petra, who has had two children with the unappetizing lawyer Fredriksen. It is even indicated that Oliver is responsible for the accident that kills his sharp-tongued colleague Olaus. But Hamsun has no difficulty turning the argument around; he gives Oliver more intelligence than Ibsen gave his Hjalmar Ekdal, and he makes Oliver artistic, at least to the extent that he knows the value of luck and inspiration—he salvages a ship, and he finds money in the eiders' nest, because he, and he alone, has the necessary sense of right time and right place: "All these folks here, what are they? Nonentities, a class, banal smalltown bigwigs in starched linen. Oliver is something special. Here, where everybody is much of a muchness, he is bound to be regarded as unique. A child of misfortune, if you like, chewed and spat out by life, left high and dry, but possessed of an undying instinct for survival."[37] This is a left-handed compliment, perhaps, but a compliment: few other people in this book receive one.

Chapter the Last

Hamsun's 1923 novel, *Siste kapitel* (*Chapter the Last,* 1923), brings to mind not only Thomas Mann's *The Magic Mountain* (1924), but even more another Hamsun novel, *Look Back on Happiness,* from 1912. Hamsun's earlier novel takes place at the mountain resort Torahus, the latter similarly at a mountain sanatorium, Toretind, and the action of both novels is much the same: the slow transformation of a neurotic woman of city background into a happy mother and farm wife. It is as if Hamsun agreed that the 1912 novel needed improvement, and, indeed, if some kind of rewriting was his purpose, he has succeeded: *Chapter the Last* is almost totally free of the didacticism that mars the earlier book, and even if it has some slow-moving passages, the main plot around the character of Julie d'Espard and her relationship to a young man named Daniel is developed with considerable suspense and finesse.

Daniel's father had to give up his farm in the parish, and Daniel consequently had to give up his sweetheart, Helen, who instead married the bailiff. Daniel was left with nothing but a mountain pasture, which, however, he developed single-handedly into a croft of some considerable promise and which he did not want to sell, even though there were city people who wished to buy it to build a resort there. Another farmer sold them the land, and soon Daniel had a large sanatorium as his neighbor in the woods. The novel deals mainly with life among the patients at that sanatorium, most of them "mis-shapen in one way or another, some with leanness, others with fat, deformed barrels on legs, overworked schoolmistresses and clerks with the long, thin limbs of insects."[38] There is the obese Mrs. Ruben, whose main interest in life is jewelry and who kills her husband in order to pay for a new diamond ring. There is a Mr. Magnus, usually referred to as "the Suicide," whose wife has left him for another man (with whom she has a child), and who dares not kill either his wife or himself, because, as he says, "suicide may bring disgrace upon murder." There is a consumptive Finnish nobleman by the name of Fleming, and a secretary from Oslo, a Miss Julie d'Espard, who has not only a French name with a faint resonance of Rousseau's Julie d'Étange, but also some knowledge of French language and literature. Among the somewhat less permanent guests is a Dr. Oliver (actually the older son of Oliver Andersen from *The Women at the Pump*), not only himself a bore of a schoolmaster, but one provoking the author to the longest and least interesting monologues in the book.

Against a background of typical scenes—the discussions and actions of these patients and guests—Hamsun has spun the following plot: Mr. Fleming has found out that visits to Daniel's mountain farm are good for his health and begins going there with Miss d'Espard. The two of them meet in Daniel's haybarn, and after some time Miss d'Espard notices that she is pregnant. Mr. Fleming in the meantime has been found out; he is no "Fleming" at all (the name of an authentic Finnish noble family), but only a farmer's son—a Mr. Axelson, who has worked in a bank and, after he developed tuberculosis, embezzled funds so that he could go away to be cured. He is able to escape the Norwegian police and get back to Finland, where, it seems, he pays back what he owes the bank by selling the farm left him by his deceased mother. Miss d'Espard now takes up with Daniel, who—she feels—could be quite a gentleman if he were given a good wash. He could also be the father she needs for her child. They plan to get married in the parish church, but there are various obstacles. One day Miss d'Espard is accidentally bitten by an adder and gives birth to a child, and she pretends that it has come much too early and hopes thereby to hide the fact that Daniel is not its father. Everything could have turned out well, but at this point Mr. Fleming returns. Miss d'Espard's love is reawakened, and she tries to get Daniel to release her from her promise, but his reputation—which as a farmer's son he is very proud of—cannot suffer another blow (that is, after Helen left him for the bailiff), and he tells Julie in so many words that he will not let her go. He surprises Mr. Fleming and Miss d'Espard on several occasions in the woods, gives them a final warning—which they do not heed—and finally takes his gun and shoots the "count" dead. He lives like an outlaw in the mountains for several days but in the end surrenders and accepts his sentence, which turns out to be relatively mild: he is not broken. Instead, he gives his housekeeper directions for running the farm while he is away and goes to serve his seven years of hard labor.

A kind of subplot is provided by the story of the Suicide. His wife comes to the sanatorium; they are reconciled, and he stays with her in her room until she falls asleep. He then locks her room from the outside (this is apparently before the introduction of Linus Yale's lock). During the night the whole sanatorium burns down, and Mrs. Magnus is unable to get out of her room. Now that he is free to commit suicide, Mr. Magnus does not have the courage, and luckily, Miss d'Espard is there to remind him of his wife's daughter who will now need his care, and he sets off for town. Miss d'Espard herself settles down at the mountain farm to wait for Daniel—seven years is a long time, but the reader is led to believe she will manage.

"Things could have turned out differently, but didn't": the novel has several instances of such forecasting—a technique Hamsun had used already in *Mysteries*. However, rather than listening to an old-fashioned teller of tales, the reader is dealing with a communal central intelligence, with the whole parish, as it were ("this happened when we were all much younger")—a method Hamsun later perfected in a novel like *Wayfarers*. On the other hand, the reader is not in doubt as to where the author stands: actions and characters are commented upon throughout, so that the book's value system is clear enough.

The characters fall into two major groups, people who refuse to see themselves as others see them—like Dr. Oliver and the Suicide and his comrade Moss—and people who are more or less consciously swindlers of different varieties and degrees—like Robertsen, the sanatorium director; Mr. Bertelsen, the rich timber merchant; Miss Ellingsen, the telegraph operator with her head full of garbled detective stories; and, first and foremost, Mr. Fleming and Miss Julie d'Espard. Mr. Fleming is a farm boy passing for a count and winning the respect of his inmates through his pleasant manners, fine clothing, and diamond ring. It is interesting to see that he understands both Daniel's pride and his concern about what people in the parish might say, and it is Fleming's own stubborn pride that provokes Daniel to shoot him. Julie d'Espard is the illegitimate daughter of a French bigamist. By her references to Akerselven, where she played as a child, it is evident that she must have grown up in the slum quarters of Oslo's East End district. That she is no stranger to deviant behavior is further shown by her artful lying, whether to Daniel or to the sheriff. Like Ingeborg Torsen of *Look Back on Happiness,* Julie d'Espard is attracted both to the strong, brutal, or primitive man (Solum/Daniel) and to the considerate, weak, or decadent (the actor/Fleming). As with Ingeborg Torsen, the author has Julie lose a front tooth during pregnancy; furthermore, after her child is born he makes her flat-chested and shaped for a life of labor rather than glamour. She is not as innocent and not as neurotic as Ingeborg Torsen; rather she is friendlier and more charming, and if she seems an even less likely farm wife, the author nonetheless maintains that she has always been good at imitating new life-styles and will become an ideal mate for Daniel.

A strange case is that of the Suicide, a difficult man with no experience in, or understanding of, the ways of sex. His wife goes off with her first love, and unlike Isak, who suddenly one day taught Inger a valuable lesson, the Suicide does not know how to handle this situation, though at the doctor's (and Nietzsche's) suggestion, he decides to try the whip. But when she comes back to him and asks his forgiveness, the Suicide, like most Hamsun heroes, finds it very hard to keep up his front of stern aloofness. Unfortunately, as in *Bjørger* and *Victoria,* their reconciliation is followed by the woman's death. The Suicide is also remarkable for his strange comradeship with the leper Moss. High intelligence, pathological suspicion, and an ability to hurt are qualities that draw the two together in some sort of grotesque, yet also moving, relationship. Finally the Suicide is special in that he sometimes takes on the role of the author's spokesman, particularly in certain attacks upon Dr. Oliver and his useless book-learning.

Dr. Oliver is not consciously a swindler, although in his dogged belief in the general usefulness of foreign language knowledge, as also in his personal conceit, he is one of the most pedantic and least sympathetic (as well as least realistic) characters in the book. His favoring Switzerland, women's liberation, and special education for the handicapped shows how consistent Hamsun is in his antipathy toward him. Still, this man, so thoroughly corrupted by learning, has two fine boys, and both are healthy, natural, and full of fun.

The novel is about a sanatorium, and the sanatorium is Hamsun's symbol of a sick society, where no one is cured and where many die—often of unnatural causes. Mr. Ruben is literally scared to death; one woman is killed by a bull; another, who is caught peeping, falls to her death; Mr. Fleming is shot; and Mrs. Magnus is burned to death. The flag is often at half mast there. On one occasion, when Dr. Øyen himself falls through a hole in the ice and contracts pneumonia, the flag becomes stuck half way up, and the whole mast is hurriedly taken down. But it is to no avail: three days later the doctor is dead.

Class plays a major role at this sanatorium. A princess (Mylady), a count (Mr. Fleming), and a learned man (Dr. Oliver) attract people to the place and make it prosper. But Mylady is no lady, Mr. Fleming is no count, and Dr. Oliver, for all his university degrees, is an ignorant man. A kind of nobility is found instead in the farmer Daniel, who is, as Holberg said of Norwegian farmers, a nobleman in miniature. The sanatorium is not a philanthropic institution, but strictly a business enterprise. Mrs. Ruben, who lives for her diamond rings and is willing to kill her husband to get one more, is only an extreme example of the cupidity that characterizes most of the inmates. Typically, like the gold that leads to the destruction of the world in the Old Norse *Edda,* it is one of Mrs. Ruben's rings that causes the final conflagration: at a drunken party, some of the guests search with burning candles for the ring, which has fallen to the floor. Though greed and intelligence is what characterizes most of the sanatorium inmates, Hamsun is not an anti-intellectual who blesses the poor in spirit. What he does claim is that intellectualism often corrupts, as in the case of Oliver Andersen's two sons, of whom one (Abel) has all the sense, the other (Dr. Oliver) all the learning. Like the postmaster in *The Women at the Pump,* the Suicide is an intellectual, but he does not know how to sire children, just as the postmaster does not know how to bring them up: intellect, too, can be senseless when it goes against Nature.

It is sometimes said of *Chapter the Last* that it is Hamsun's darkest novel, and there is no denying that Hamsun has reduced his ideals considerably since the 1890s. But the novel is not altogether pessimistic. If it shows the sickness of the town/sanatorium, where even small accidents lead up to "the last chapter," that is, to death, it also shows once more the ability of Nature to turn bitter defeats into victories. In 1898, when Kareno finally accepted his wife's illegitimate daughter into his home, it was seen by Hamsun as a sign of his depravity. In 1923 Daniel does not care whether or not he is the father of Julius, for the boy is going to be a farmer and inherit Daniel's land—for Daniel that is all that counts. And the Suicide accepts his wife's daughter, now as a symbol of life, of something worth living for. Ibsen's play *The Wild Duck* has an alcoholic and cynical doctor preaching the people's need for a "Life Lie." Hamsun preaches the same, though he is less sinister and less pompous about it. He describes how spring arrives at the mountain home of Julie and Daniel and little Julius, "like a marvellous idea, hasty and wild, suddenly thrown out," which inspires Julie to tell Daniel that his son was born many weeks too early.

And Hamsun adds: "Family life made up of lies? Oh, yes—a lie may contain beautiful truths. If Life did not make the lie necessary it would not exist."[39] This is a long way from Rousseau's Émile in his emotional farewell to Paris "with all your noise and smoke and dirt, where the women have ceased to believe in honor and the men in virtue. We are in search of love, happiness, innocence, the further we go from Paris the better."[40] Hamsun would have smiled at words like honor, virtue, and innocence, and if his message was still from Rousseau, it was a Rousseau seasoned with some of Ibsen's skepticism.

Chapter Five

Vagabond

Even if the military operations of World War I did not directly affect the Scandinavian countries, the war naturally influenced the daily lives as well as the art and literature of their peoples and dispelled once and for all the optimism that had resulted from the economic and social progress of recent decades. In Norway the major writers called for a return to old values: Hamsun emphasized the pagan strength of a life in close contact with nature, Sigrid Undset preached old-fashioned Christian discipline, while Norway's third great novelist, Olav Duun, saw salvation in a new union of Christian and pagan values of the kind that had earlier inspired Bjørnson.[1] For most of the young writers who began their careers in the shadow of the war—they are sometimes referred to as "the generation that was to stumble in the start"[2]—there were no acceptable old values. They looked instead for new religions and sometimes found what they looked for in communism, like Hamsun's admirer Nordahl Grieg, or in Freud's psychoanalysis, like another admirer, Sigurd Hoel.[3]

Hamsun, though he was past sixty, shared the confusion of the young. He had been confused and depressed by the German military defeat and by the problems of the young Weimar Republic, but he was strongly antisocialist and anti-English, and those basic sentiments were his principal guides to European politics between Versailles and Munich. In 1932 he supported the work of a Norwegian anti-Bolshevik committee; in 1934 he defended for the first time Hitler's Germany; in 1935 he attacked the German pacifist Carl von Ossietzky, and in 1936 he wrote for the first time in support of Quisling.[4] In the fields of literature and the arts he seemed less reactionary. In his 1928 article about America he had described the American novel as "the most refreshing and most original in the world, a renaissance and an example for Europe,"[5] and he admired and supported economically many of the young poets in Norway.

Much of Hamsun's disorientation during the 1920s resulted from tensions in his private life. His deep depression over the war and Germany's defeat was generally compounded by his concern over aging and a feeling that he would no longer be able to create. Negative reviews of his books also affected him more than before. He who had always tried to pretend that what people wrote about his life and works did not concern him in the least now suddenly found himself deeply hurt by adverse journalism and even tried to have old friends intervene on his behalf.[6] As mentioned above, he was also involved in several court cases relating to his "copyrighted" name, all of which tended to destroy his peace of mind and sidetrack and diminish his creative powers. His inspiration was also affected by his work on the farm, which, because of his marital troubles, had turned out to be no lasting blessing. Hamsun continued to practice his double standards, by praising life on the farm as salutary and idyllic, yet feeling constantly the call of the cities, which he visited several times each year, while his wife—a former actress who was envious of his exciting life and full of misgivings about his female friendships—had to stay home.

Hamsun realized that what was lacking in his present life was first and foremost his old ability to create, though he was not aware that his lack of productivity was caused by some form of *angst.* In the early spring of 1926 he subjected himself—as one of the first patients in Norway—to psychoanalysis.[7] Living for several months in Oslo, he was soon able to report to Marie at Nørholm that telling his dreams and having them explained to him seemed beneficial. He spoke about learning to dance (Marie first, then he) and going more often to the movies: "We have been too lonely at Nørholm, which is not good for either of us. . . .The expense [of an extra maid] would be balanced by a brighter disposition in both you and me, so that I would be able to work."[8] For some time his old doubts and bad dreams continued: "It was terrible, you sang bawdy songs, offered yourself to other men and when I wept, told me, 'If you can find another, you just take her.' "[9] Nevertheless, Hamsun seemed to undergo a gradual improvement, and he could finally write: "I am definitely different from what I was, and that I ascribe to the fact that I have mixed a little with people and been twice to the theater."[10] When he returned to Nørholm in the summer, he was able to complete the first part of *Wayfarers* in a couple of months. To people who had advised him to travel and gain new impressions and inspiration, he had said he could write only of what he knew well; and at last memories of his childhood years mixed suddenly and easily with daily events at Nørholm to furnish fact and fiction for the longest and most colorful plotline in his entire production. But all was not well. After completing his last novel, *The Ring is Closed* (1936), he tried in vain to find inspiration by traveling abroad.

There also came about a more lasting rupture in his relationship to Marie, and he lived by himself for one whole year at an inexpensive hotel in Oslo. It seemed as though he, finally deceived by his muse, and she, similarly deceived by her husband, found agreement only in politics. She became the first member of the Nazi party in their home community, and he was soon to begin writing the political articles that led to his conviction but also indirectly to his last moving work, *On Overgrown Paths* (1949)—and to her equally moving account of their life together, *The Rainbow* (1953). Readers of either book will find themselves wondering where in all this beauty, humor, and pathos one is to look for truth—in or between the lines—and this question also arises in reading the novels of Hamsun's old age. Despite his use of the popular picaresque style of the fable, the absence of simple answers in these books gives them some of the mystery that colored Hamsun's best work of the 1890s.

The August trilogy and *The Ring is Closed* are the result of a personal and domestic crisis, much like Hamsun's books before World War I. His restlessness then found expression in two series of novels—one humorous, about the upstart capitalist Benoni, and one melancholy, about the poet-artisan Pedersen. In the August trilogy the two styles are fused, but Hamsun's age tempered not only the folksy comedy and sentimental poetry of the earlier works, but also the strong convictions that inspired *Growth of the Soil.* Instead, the new novel has wisdom and irony, and rather than the term *Wanderer*—so laden with lofty romantic associations—*Vagabond* is used to describe its hero.

The August Trilogy

The trilogy over the lives of the vagabond August and his friends consists of the novels *Landstrykere* (*Wayfarers,* 1927), *August* (1930), and *Men Livet lever* (*The Road Leads On,* 1933). After Hamsun's long silence his regular readers were eager to see the new novel, Hamsun's first with the recently established Norwegian publishing company

Gyldendal, in which he was a major shareholder. The company advertised *Wayfarers* well, and in the three months before Christmas—when Norwegians buy their books—it was able to print and sell 30,000 copies, the largest edition ever of a Scandinavian book in the year of its appearance.[11] It was the longest book Hamsun ever wrote, and some readers complained about its length, not knowing that what they had worked their way through was only one third of what was to be the author's most massive novel.

Wayfarers tells the story of Edevart Andersen (born in the 1850s),[12] a big, strong farm boy from Polden in north Norway. He is slow at school and a little naive, but as he watches two mountebanks who are on a visit to the north with their barrel organ, he begins discovering that out in the big world most things are not what they seem. Edevart befriends the sailor August, two years older than himself, who had already seen most parts of the planet Earth, and with him begins buying up hides in their home district and selling them at a fair north in Lofoten. They make money and lose it again, a pattern they continue to follow throughout their lives. Returning to poor, stagnant Polden they have the idea of clearing new drying grounds for codfish, which immediately results in business: a wealthy bachelor skipper by the name of Skaaro arrives with a shipload of fish for drying. Although he has some success with the beautiful and proud Ane Maria, whose husband is rich but unexciting, Skaaro apparently is not sufficiently hot in his pursuit of her, and out of spite and frustration she lures him to a grizzly death by drowning in a bog. August and Edevart then sail with Skaaro's ship south to Bergen, settle with the skipper's heirs, and make a nice sum of money for themselves. But more important is the fact that on his trip south, at a place called Doppen, Edevart meets and falls in love with a young mother, Lovise Magrete, whose husband is serving time in prison for assault. A moving relationship develops between them, but when the husband returns, Edevard retreats to the neighboring town, where he gradually obtains a good position with a merchant named Knoff.

Lovise Magrete and her husband want to leave for America. They approach Edevart for help in buying two tickets, and full of despair he gives Lovise Magrete all he owns. He later spends a relatively happy time as a peddler up and down the countryside of north Norway and finally meets his old friend August, who has recently held a lowly job as a farm hand. Back in Polden with August,

Edevart has become strangely passive, while August, always full of energy, helps the young farmer Ezra increase his farm land in an ingenious manner. The two of them scare Polden's inhabitants by shouting from the bog where Skaaro drowned. People hurriedly set out to find Skaaro and remove him to hallowed ground and in the process manage to drain the whole bog, which is soon Ezra's finest farm land.

At this point Lovise Magrete returns from America without her husband. Edevart and she relive their first wonderful days at Doppen, but like so many returned emigrants Lovise Magrete has lost her peace of mind. She soon quarrels with Edevart and then sails for America a second time. Edevart languishes at home until a letter arrives from Lovise Magrete in America. Joakim lectures his older brother on the danger of losing one's roots, but Polden holds no attraction for Edevart the vagabond, and he too leaves for America.

The action of volume 2, called *August,* begins twenty years later. A balding middle-aged (forty-seven-year-old) man arrives on a ketch loaded with canned foods and other merchandise, and it gradually becomes apparent that it is August come back to Polden to stay. He is as active as he used to be, planning this time to start a herring meal factory as well as a bank and a post office, and he begins buying up farm land and building expensive homes, which he sells to wealthy fishing merchants from out-of-town. When Edevart and Lovise Magrete arrive, it appears that all their time in America has left them no richer than they were when they sailed away twenty years ago. It has been Edevart's hope that they would now remain in Polden, but Lovise Magrete once more returns to her children in the United States, while he stays behind, taking on menial odd jobs, but becoming generally more and more lethargic. August, on the other hand, continues with ever new projects, arranges for Ane Maria (now back from prison after the Skaaro murder) to adopt two boys, tries to interest Polden's few remaining land owners in Christmas-tree farming, and begins a small tobacco plantation. An envious neighbor destroys the plants, and August stabs him in anger and leaves the district to escape the police. However, not only is August not indicted, but notice arrives soon afterward that he has won a large sum of money in an international lottery. Edevart sets out in an open boat in the hope of reaching his old comrade before he leaves the country, but he is caught in a storm and dies at sea.

As in Hamsun's other trilogy *(The Wanderer),* the locale of the third volume is different from that of the preceding two: the action takes place back at Segelfoss, now ruled by a third generation of Jensens: Theodore's son, Gordon Tidemand, who is married to the daughter of Edevart and August's old employer, Knoff. August is central also in this novel. He earns his living as an indispensable jack-of-all-trades in the service of Consul Tidemand and gives good advice to all who listen to him. Throughout most of the story he works as a foreman on a road the consul wishes to have built to his cabin in the mountains. August is now around seventy and at first appears rather subdued; however, his old extravagance has not altogether left him, and when Edevart's sister, Pauline, finally arrives from Polden with his old bank holdings, he not only takes up sheep farming in a big way, but begins running after the young Cornelia as well, even though the local witch, Åse, warns him on several occasions. The other people in the novel provide a variety of subplots. There is Gordon's mother, a merry widow who keeps her old gypsy lover (actually Gordon's natural father) as a member of the household until she finally marries the druggist Holm. There is Holm's friend Mrs. Hagen, who is married to the postmaster but likes the druggist and always enjoys a frivolous banter with him. When Holm marries Gordon's mother, Mrs. Hagen takes to drink and finally commits suicide. On the day before Michaelmas, as August is driving his thousand sheep down a steep mountain road, the herd is scared by the sudden appearance of Consul Tidemand's automobile. Because the only escape route for the sheep is blocked by Åse, they jump off the road and over a 900 foot precipice—with the old salt August borne along in their midst. In the words of the subsequent "Ballad of August," "An ocean of sheep was the sailor's death."

Hamsun's usual view of the stages in human development—innocence, corruption, old age—can also be applied to the trilogy, though more than the protagonists' ages (August at twenty-seven, forty-seven, and sixty-seven) separate its three parts. Volume 1 is the best, not only because it is the first and hence free from the repetitions that sometimes mar the following volumes, but also because its heroes Edevart and August are young and either innocent or refreshing. Volume 2 singles out for special treatment August's tall tales and colorful business projects, which are at first exciting, though in the end just as tiring to some readers as Edevart's endless lethargy. The third volume differs from the other two in having passages of a certain historical interest—nostalgic descriptions of old-time country life—in which the narrator is both poet and social anthropologist. Furthermore, the action of the last novel is generally enlivened by the addition of new characters from the civil-servant class (a class lacking in volumes 1–2). There are, however, also unfortunate scenes, in which Hamsun's humor seems curiously forced (chapter 21). Even so, the August trilogy is a remarkable work from a seventy-year-old novelist. It brings together many basic Hamsun motifs and character types, and at the same time presents the old in a new light: the plot is weightier than that of *Benoni;* Edevart is a more realistic version of Glahn, and August is a more complex Oliver, etc.

The narrative technique of the trilogy is not new, but still special in Hamsun's production. There is for instance the author's use of forecasting. "He did not come back—for a long time"—the sentence which ends *Wayfarers*—is a conventional way of bringing the narrator out from his hiding place, as the only person who knows the future. A different and very rare way of forecasting in Hamsun's work is illustrated by the following passage: "Neither he (Norem) nor his family knew that the tiny white speck on the end of his tongue betokened any danger. It meant death. But they did not know that."[13] In one of his letters to Marie after he had seen a play in Oslo, Hamsun wrote, "I do not doubt for a moment that I could do it better. I also understand that there must be suspense, which I have never cared about before."[14] The ominous words about Norem's tongue may be an attempt to create a new kind of suspense, but suspense as such had of course not been missing in Hamsun's earlier work, in which he particularly used the idea of fate slowly catching up to its victim. Nagel was warned by the Chinese woman; Oterman (Kareno trilogy), by a man referred to as "Justice." In *Pan,* Glahn saw that someone had inspected his drill holes, but "no suspicion awoke in me. And I began to hammer on my drill, never dreaming what madness I was doing."[15] In the August trilogy the absence of drill holes (which should have held the iron fence facing the precipice) is emphasized and repeated, thus provoking a sense of fate with much less subtlety—Hamsun even needs a local witch, Åse, to help bring August's life full circle—but there is still suspense in the forecast: "a spirit of mute resistance seemed to lurk in those undrilled holes!"[16]

Apart from such cases, where prognostications in the text suddenly make us feel his presence, the narrator is especially unobtrusive in the August trilogy. Indeed, if Hamsun's first-person novels were grouped at one end of a spectrum, *Wayfarers* would probably be at the opposite end as the novel in which the teller is best hidden behind his story, almost as in a play, in which the action "tells itself." A certain quality of play rather than novel is also present in the use of brief "stage directions" used as introductions to scenes and chapters—"At Indrebygden," "At Polden Again," "At the Store," "Friday," etc.—as well as in the use of name plus adverb and colon rather than the conventional "He said/asked." The following are examples: "August, evasively: 'Well, we can always talk about that,' " and "Edevart, cravenly and mollifyingly: 'It was scandalous, was it? I didn't read it.' "[17] Another way of hiding behind the story is for the narrator to pretend a certain general statement is said by someone else. The following is a description of the pastor's wife *(The Road Leads On)*: "a charming little woman, still pretty, still girlish, ready to blush on the slightest provocation. [It is wrong to say so, but it is right nevertheless:] Her face and her personality were strongly dove-like. She was quiet and retiring in manner, but she had a pair of bright little eyes which never missed a thing."[18] The effect of the coy "It is wrong to say so," etc. is to suspect that some person other than and inferior to the narrator—perhaps one of Polden's own inhabitants—is giving the characterization. Such scenes have led critics indefensibly to claim that the author is not responsible for any of the opinions in the book.

Several statements, said by no one in particular, could be the opinions of people in Polden—that it is a blessing to have children, that the woman called the Old Mother was worse (that is, more erotic) than the young, even that August is to be praised or damned. On the other hand, when it is said that the consul was inferior because of his mixed race and that schoolteachers knew nothing but were nonetheless (politically) radical, that a clerk is a "budding Norwegian bureaucrat," and that August is lacking in depth, then any reader acquainted with Hamsun's works will know that the author is not far away. What may seem confusing, however, is the fact that in the August trilogy what are clearly the author's opinions often contradict each other. Still, what Nordahl Grieg called Hamsun's grandiose inconsistencies[19] is in this case rather his refined dialectical method, whereby prosecution and defense drag on endlessly, with no verdict in sight. As often pointed out above, the difference is between Hamsun's one-dimensional journalism and his art, and defies the attempt of all critics who have generalized merely on the basis of single "opinions" in his work.[20]

Hamsun was proud that in the course of his writing career he had created several hundred characters, "all of them out of myself,"[21] and the August trilogy with its more than sixty named men and women has contributed substantially to that gallery of people. The characters are determined by their settings. There is the typical north Norwegian farm and fishing community (Polden), with the wealthy seine owner(s) at the top, then fishermen and small holders of varying prosperity, down to poverty-stricken families, whose members live from odd jobs and petty thievery. The trading post (Sirilund) is differently populated, with a big merchant surrounded by the workers and artisans of all kinds who are in his service. The small town (Segelfoss) is again different, with shipping and industry and a professional class—a consul, a doctor, a lawyer, a postmaster, a newspaper editor, etc.—all of them known from Hamsun's earlier work. In the trilogy about the vagabonds there is also a country fair with its itinerant merchants and entertainers, including the old watch-selling Jew, Papst, a unique character in Hamsun's work and one often used in discussions of Hamsun's possible anti-Semitism.[22]

When the two first meet, Papst sells Edevart a good watch and chain. Some time later, when they again meet, Pabst hires Edevart to sell watches too, but since they are of poor quality, Edevart earns the reputation of being a swindler and quits. When they next meet after several years Papst offers to clean Edevart's watch and later returns it in shining condition, almost as if it were a new watch. That same evening Pabst is robbed and Edevart, who happens to be nearby, chases and fights with the robber. Papst is grateful and, rummaging in one of his pockets, says "I have something for you. Here is your watch. You shall have it back again." Papst, then, had not cleaned and returned Edevart's good old watch but had given him a worthless new one. Those who would defend Hamsun against the charge of anti-Semitism still get the last word. Next year Edevart receives a letter containing one hundred dollars: Papst had died and remembered his young friend in his will. The narrator furthermore seems to agree with the following obituary from a local paper: "Papst was not always as obvious as he seemed; at times he could be quite a different person from the usual swindler. In Karmsund, for example, he gave away a very expensive silver watch for nothing to a lad he'd scarcely seen before; and when this occasioned great surprise, Papst explained that the lad came of good people and that he had a good heart." Despite its somewhat caricatured features the portrait of Papst, which is distantly related to that of Geissler, is one of many examples of Hamsun's dialectical method: praising and condemning he ends up with something beyond a mere type, something more like a human being.

Of minor characters in the trilogy some are interesting mostly because of their unusual psychology, others mainly because of the ideas they represent. To the former category belongs a group of women who are frustrated in love, such as the stately woman Åse, half Gypsy, half Lapp, with beautiful face and body—and magical powers. One evening she stops Solmund and his horse. What do you want, he asks. I want you to have me, she answers. Never, he says, and get out of my way. Not long after, Solmund's young wife becomes a widow, when both her husband and his horse disappear into the Segelfoss Falls. If Åse is part of the book's "anthropology," Karolus's wife Ane Maria, illustrates its psychology. She is a beautiful, intelligent, and proud woman, and the way she lures Captain Skaaro to his death in the bog is the most intense single scene in the novel. Afterward, when she confesses her crime, she gives as her motive not the fact that he pursued her, but that he did not pursue her long enough. Unlike Inger in *Growth of the Soil* who has her periodic religious spells, Ane Maria gets through her penitence once and for all in prison and manages still to retain her pride. After she has adopted her two boys, she loses all interest in men, and the narrator comments "So it must have been children she had really felt the need of, all her days. She had been intended for motherhood, but had been cheated."[23] The narrator is especially fond of this character, probably because she is spiritually related to Hamsun's greatest hero, Willatz Holmsen, who did not bend in adversity. In the course of the novel Ane Maria loses everything—her farm, her wealth, her youth, and her foster children—and then begins all over again by clearing a little patch of rough ground, which was all she had left of her former expanse of pasture: "Each morning she walked past that moor of Ezra's where once upon a time she had let a skipper from Hardanger go to his death—the memory of this no longer affected her. Were she to meet that skipper again this very day, she would pass him without feeling the slightest twinge of conscience."[24]

Two other minor characters are central to the novel, Paulina, Edevart's youngest sister, and Lydia Jensen, Gordon Tidemand's mother, usually referred to as the Old Mother. They are in many ways opposites, Paulina being the typical old spinster, referred to as "dry and unnatural" and "a flower of steel" (August's expression). She is admirable first and foremost because of her untiring sense of justice. After August has ruined Polden with his many projects, she remains the keeper of the bank safe, refuses to pay August what he needs to complete the factory, and in this way is able to return to every shareholder his original down payment intact. Paulina generally takes August for the windbag he is, but, like her big brother Edevart, whom she never ceases to look up to, she cannot help liking August for his kind heart. Of the many memorable characters in the book, Lydia Jensen is the most charming. In his praise of older women Hamsun had earlier drawn a minister's wife in *The Wanderer* who was sexier than the young and totally free from the social ambition that plagues so many of his other woman characters. Lydia Jensen is a much fuller portrait. Bright, efficient, humorous, kindly, and already a grandmother, she still loves life, enjoys her wine at parties—though without losing her charm and dignity—keeps her old Gypsy lover constantly busy, and ends by marrying the somewhat younger Mr. Holm. She confides in August that the bridal night might very well result in a child! "How beautiful the world seems!" she says. "I shall never leave it if I can do anything to prevent it!"[25]

Characters like Ezra and Joakim are important more for what they have to say than what they are. Ezra is described as coming from poor people. He is hired at twelve as a cook on Edevart's boat. Later he marries Edevart's sister Hosea, becomes a farmer, and finally the biggest taxpayer in Polden. He is probably the closest duplication anywhere in Hamsun's work of Isak Sellanraa, without, however, Isak's naiveté and simple charm. As a child, when Ezra climbed the mast of Edevart's ship, and as a young man, when he scared people by shouting from the bog in which Captain Skaaro had drowned, he had a sense of humor, which has since worn off. He becomes more and more a slave to his land: the expression "greedy for soil," which Pedersen applied to an unsympathetic man in *Look Back on Happiness,* is used several times of Ezra. He has no patience with August's plans and forgets that August was the person who suggested that they drain the bog and that Ezra build a large barn. Ezra speaks with the arrogant and categorical voice used in Hamsun's journalism. His development is drawn by a master of realism, but when the narrator tries to show us Ezra's idyllic life with his wife, that they are frugal and industrious *and* have lots of fun together, the picture is not quite convincing. There is also their son who, like Eleseus in *Growth of the Soil,* reacts against his father's preoccupation with the soil and chooses to live his life in the city. Somewhat like Ezra, but much more understanding of August, is Joakim, an old bachelor, who lost his sweetheart to America years ago. Polden's only intellectual, he reads newspapers and studies new methods for increasing food production. Hamsun showed some special identification with Geissler *(Growth of the Soil)* by giving him his own birthplace of Garmo, and in the trilogy Hamsun gives Joakim his own birthday (4 August). As a young man Joakim too had his fling when he went out with the seine and made a fabulous herring catch, the sudden wealth from which almost destroyed Polden. Later he settled on his farm and became a wise man—unlike his older brother Edevart, whose life promised so much and ended so sadly.

Edevart is the major protagonist of *Wayfarers.* Distantly related to such different men as Glahn and Daniel Utby and more closely to Abel Brodersen, he is still unique and clearly among Hamsun's ten or twelve greatest characters. Edevart is handsome and strong, with a fiery temper. The last may have to do with his slowness. Ragna, the neighbor's daughter, laughs at him in school and he develops into a resentful type who sees that things are wrong and need to be put right. He is the oldest child and looks after his brother and sisters, which also helps develop him into a little lord protector. At thirteen he attacks a mountebank who pretends to beat up his partner in business. Later he helps Ragna extort money from a man she claims to be the father of her child. He reports his good friend August to the doctor for spreading venereal disease in the district and gets involved in a fight with the man who has tried to rob Papst. Even in Edevart's last year, when he seems to care about nothing, the possibility of punishing Kristofer for his vandalism to August's tobacco plantation sends a spark of life into him. This wish to set the world straight gives Edevart an air of innocence which combines with his good looks to make him attractive to motherly women. We hear repeatedly of his illegitimate offspring, and it is indicated that Ragna's handsome children are also Edevart's. The girls laughed at him in school, but later, when he has them at his beck and call, he no longer enjoys their company. Edevart's success with women is also caused by his economic and social standing. He has learned from August not to place his light under a bushel, and since he does not invest his money in impossible deals, he could have become a prosperous man. However, what August wastes on fantastic projects, Edevart wastes on a particular woman, indeed, he is smitten with love like Hamsun's early heroes, even if the novel's low style tends to conceal its old-fashioned tragic theme.

Edevart's never-dying love of Lovise Magrete has to do with his dream of innocence. He likes to think of her—going barefoot and wearing her thin skirt—on the little croft Doppen where she brings up her children, tends her sheep, and spins and weaves materials of the finest design and quality. She is also the perfect lover, mother and mistress in one. After his first great love experience—although he has to leave Lovise Magrete to her rightful husband—Edevart's fortunes continue to grow, and he reaches the climax of his career as skipper of Knoff's sloop *Hermine.* Even after Lovise Magrete leaves for America Edevart is not broken; the vagabond spirit has entered his blood, and he enjoys the chance of prosperity and adventure offered by his new life as a peddler. It is after Lovise Magrete's second departure for America that he becomes a different man. For a short time they have experienced their first ecstasy once more, but Lovise Magrete is changed, and he loses her again. Lovise Magrete this time is looking not only for her lost husband, but for the excitement of America's cities. Edevart's pathetic loneliness and despair after Lovise Magrete has left Doppen is the beginning of his final decline. At Polden he is passive and restless, and though at one point it looks as though he might put down his roots for good, a letter from Lovise Magrete is all it takes for him to leave. After his long stay in America he is entirely changed, gradually spending most of his free time dreaming in a grove of aspens: "The silence crowds into his ears like two small wads of cotton and it seems as though he has forgotten something, and it seems, too, as though the clock has stopped. So oddly desolate, a forlorn landscape. Edevart, a towering figure of a man, a handsome fellow, serene from apathy alone."[26] Edevart was drawn to Lovise Magrete of Doppen as to a revelation of ultimate virtue and purity, but he saw this idyll through the eyes of his own youthful innocence, which gave Hamsun an opportunity to reemphasize the importance of first love. The tragedy of the situation is that, however much it seems otherwise to Edevart, not he but Haakon is Lovise Magrete's first love. Haakon Doppen must have looked like a Scandinavian Gypsy; he is described as having "curly hair, hooked nose, wild eyes, large mouth . . . ," and Edevart admits that "perhaps by foreign showy standards he might be thought handsome."[27] Try as she may, Lovise Magrete is unable to forget her husband, and for Edevart that means a lifelong fight, in which he finally has to give in, even to the point of being chivalrous to a man he has every reason to despise.

When Lovise Magrete leaves for America the last time, Edevart rows out in his boat to say good-bye, but he arrives after the steamer is already standing out to sea. The symbolic scene resembles Pedersen's expression in *The Wanderer* of "coming too late to the woods where the berries grow."[28] The pale cast of thought, though, is not Edevart's domain.[29] Unlike Glahn or Johannes or Pedersen he can put neither his dreams nor his sense of being cheated into poetry; for him there is only alienation, and he becomes an easy prey to the disillusionment and death wish that characterize one kind of vagabond. The other kind—to which August belongs—is driven by the spirit of adventure that is lacking in Edevart. Typically, after all Edevart's time at Doppen, he had not been to see its magnificent waterfall before he was asked to show it to the returning Americans. His imagination is as limited as Ezra's and he could have become like him, had it not been for August and Lovise Magrete.

August's literary ancestors come easily to mind; in Norway they were particularly the many legendary sailors whose stories of foreign adventure had attracted willing listeners since Viking times and had sometimes even appeared in print.[30] In Hamsun's own work August is directly related to Benoni and Oliver but also more distantly to Student Tangen of *Hunger* (in his storytelling), to Knut Pedersen of *The Wanderer* (in his technical know-how), and to Isak of *Growth of the Soil* (in his optimism and enterprise). In Norway, August may well turn out to be the most lasting of Hamsun's literary figures. The trilogy about him occupies one fifth of Hamsun's literary production; his life is not only more completely illuminated than that of any other Hamsun characters, but also commented on by Edevart, his friend, and by Edevart's sister and brother, Paulina and Joakim as well as by Ezra and others. August has never known his parents;

he is therefore tied to no one, which gives him greater freedom, while making him at the same time more insecure. It is important for August to win the respect of his fellowmen, and he shows his powers in various ways, by playing the accordion, making mystical signs, or, sometimes, by drawing his pistol, and, above all, by being a great promoter who works to improve conditions in his home parish. Some of his ideas are worthless—the shooting range, the savings bank, the tobacco plantation, the herring-meal factory. Others result in great and good works, notably the draining of Ezra's marsh.

The August trilogy is a novel about emigration and industry—about the spirit of America—and August above all others in the novel is the embodiment of that spirit. Technically he is a Norwegian, a *nordlending,* and an American only insofar as he represents the style and philosophy that Hamsun and most of his Norwegian readers associated with the New World. Joakim calls him an American, and at Edevart's question of whether he intends to return to America, August replies: "Ay, you needn't think I won't!. . . That's the only place in the world for a man like me!"[31] August has a number of qualities that, while they are common among ordinary men in all countries, are often singled out as being typically American. There is, for instance, his belief in all manufactured goods, synthetic products of all types (including LSD and the Pill!),[32] and everything that is large. August's gold teeth, his propaganda for canned foods, verandas with colored glass, red mail boxes, door bells, his Christmas-tree farm, and giant sheep ranch are expressions of an imagination that could well be Norwegian. But when August carries out his dreams, he is driven by a pioneer instinct that is better termed American. Thus the people of Polden have some difficulty understanding how August, who is such a wonderful liar, can also be a hard worker. American is also August's violence: people are known to carry guns in other civilized countries, but he is a man who shoots or stabs without warning. His vehemence is frightening even to friends. Somewhat reminiscent of the gangster spirit is even August's religion, a religion without repentance, though not without the fear of retribution: like Ibsen's Master Builder, who cannot stand climbing his own towers, August of the Seven Seas loses all his courage in small open boats. His religion is a mixture of superstition and practical sense: one never knows what secret signs can do. August crosses himself before all dangerous and important enterprises and sows his tobacco with his head bared. The Catholic confession he looks upon merely as mental hygiene, and his rebaptism in Segelfoss River is only part of a scheme to outdo a rival lover. American above all is August's unusual energy. His projects, however, are not based upon sound thinking and thorough investigations, but are the results of sudden inspiration. August's activity resembles a nervous disorder, like that "restless racing around" which Hamsun associated with America.

Time and again August is described as being sterile, which no doubt means that nothing of what he does is constructive, just as the development he symbolizes leads only to nothingness. However, August is not only sterile and useless, but a danger for all people with whom he comes into contact. From the girl with the lion mane he had received "a reminder," a "disease of two and a half years' duration." The doctor keeps him quarantined at Polden, but at Segelfoss he courts the young Cornelia with his disgusting old man's love, which is really what destroys him in the end: the witch warns him, and when he persists, she plunges him into the abyss. August's disease is an image of the world's disease. Hamsun enumerates the symptoms: August is not only a liar but ruthless and unreliable; he has no weight; he is without depth; he drags his roots behind him; and Hamsun concludes, "This single individual had it in his power to corrupt both town and countryside."[33] However, this harsh judgment of August is contradicted elsewhere: August is "unselfish, and conscientious as an ant," "thin and easily satisfied," "full of enterprise, faithful, well liked by everyone," "innocent of malice, born with a friendly nature," "happy and grateful when things went well"; and, in summing up, "Here he stands in his old age and, in the language of Gordon's accountancy, his assets exceed his liabilities."[34]

That Hamsun qualified his verdict so radically when he was dealing with the very "emissary of the times, of the spirit of modernity" was due to a number of factors, one being his psychoanalytic treatment, which seems to have improved his relationship to mankind in general. Moreover, his work with the article "Festina Lente" brought back to him memories of his vagabond days in America and resulted in a new theme in his novels: good companionship. Probably the most attractive quality about August is his readiness to take a turn whenever it is asked of him. Joakim said of him, "In one thing he was human and August himself: he was kind and unselfish; he gave everything away even to the shirt on his back and he went his way not one øre to the good."[35] Such helpfulness was typical of Americans, and Hamsun mentioned it in his *St. Louis Post-Dispatch* article ("Festina Lente"). Also likeable, if in a different way, is August's "American" lying. In the last instance his telling of tall tales is what saves him. August's disease leads him to death, but he himself lives on in the "Ballad of August," and he is the only Hamsun hero to have such an apotheosis. As a storyteller August is an artist, and it cannot be said of him that he hides his talent; on the contrary, even in the midst of his lies and unreliable ways he is faithful to himself. Really August is Hamsun's Peer Gynt. Hamsun had attempted to shape him before in *Friar Vendt,* but at that time Hamsun lacked the dignity and humility that are necessary for the person who has to sit in judgment over his self. August is tried and sentenced over and over again throughout the three volumes. Apparently it is of the greatest importance to the poet that this gad-about receive full justice. And although August has little reason to feel happy about the final verdict "he was ignorant and therefore innocent,"[36] he would be pleased with the judge's wonderful humor and understanding, with the spirit of humanity that colors the whole case against him.

Lovise Magrete, because she is a woman and therefore in Hamsun's opinion more likely to be misled, illustrates better than any other character in the book the ill effects of emigration. Not since Aagot of *Shallow Soil* had Hamsun shown a more complete corruption of an innocent soul, though the changes in Lovise Magrete are of course less drastic. Aagot began by being impressed by Kristiania artists and ended as a prostitute. Lovise Magrete's development is different—from having been innocent and natural she becomes artificial as her value system is breached and contaminated by social ambition. August's and Edevart's cases are again different: August was born a vagabond, Edevart becomes one, though things familiar from his childhood can always speak to his heart. In contrast, Lovise Magrete, who had lived in happy isolation in her little paradise, comes to view her old life with patronizing sentimentality, and she spends her time with the shop lads in the Knoff store, where she hopes to introduce her and Edevart's daughter to the Knoffs and, through them, to society.

Unlike Edevart, Lovise Magrete is corrupted, not only by the competitive spirit and social mobility of American society, but by the false puritanism Hamsun had already attacked in *The Cultural Life of Modern America*. Edevart "observed the manner in which she had stepped into the loom, with her legs together to make it look refined—she who without any shame had just promised him a torrid night. She had acquired artificiality; she had learned affection."[37] He remembers her as wholesome and beautiful, though he later claims their first night together was wrong, since she was still married to Haakon. And his concern is inspired not so much by a belief in the sanctity of the marriage vow, as by his (and Hamsun's) almost religious feeling concerning the meaning of first love, which makes Edevart and Lovise Magrete equally tragic cases. It is not only Edevart who looks in vain for something that was. Behind Lovise Magrete's peaceless flight across the United States lies a dream of which she is not aware: the memory of her first husband as she first knew him.

Of the three volumes in the trilogy the first is the best, partially because in it the author handles his argument most skillfully; in volumes 2 and 3 his concern seemed to be bringing the story of August to a logical conclusion. The theme throughout is the vagabond—the vagabond in life and the vagabond in love. Healthy erotic relationships are mentioned—Ezra and Hosea, Gordon Tidemand and Julie—but only Lydia Jensen's ("the Old Mother's") is dwelt upon because of her unusual *joie de vivre.* Rather the books set out to show ways in which love can be destroyed. Paulina is ridiculed like all of Hamsun's spinsters. In Marna and Mrs. Hagen natural passion has been perverted by literature; in Lovise Magrete, by social ambition; in Ragna and Cornelia, by religion; in Ane Maria, by her husband's neglect. Similar variations can be found generally in Hamsun's work, and all of them would be described by the author as "unnatural." A special case—and one inspired by Hamsun's personal crisis—is August's old man's love, which is very different from that of the Old Mother, in that August has nothing to offer beyond words. Still, since love means possession, he suffers the pangs of jealousy no less than other people and tries to make up for his physical shortcomings by showering his beloved with gifts, like literature's old men since the beginning of time (and like the troll in Fröding's poem, who ends up eating his beautiful princess, since he does not know what else to do with her).[38] The moment Cornelia is dead, August's jealousy is gone and with it his passion.

August's sterile love, paralleling the unnatural ideas he tries to foist upon an unwilling community, symbolizes the central themes of the book, industry and emigration. Hamsun wrote to Marie of *August:* "It is all an attack upon industry. Now, that's all right, but whether I have managed it from a literary point of view is another matter."[39] He probably has not: the coming and going of industry has become a natural feature of contemporary life, and few readers will heed the author's warning. August in 1930 was a man of the future; in 1980, despite the recent "green waves" (and subsequent attempts to make Hamsun a modern ecologist), August is still not a man of the past. People in north Norway, like twentieth-century people generally, cannot live without industry of some sort, and even if August's herring-meal factory did not succeed, many others have. Much more convincingly argued is the book's major theme of emigration, new in Hamsun's work, but old in Scandinavian literature: even Snorri Sturluson (1179–1241) wrote of two Norwegian kings, Øystein and Sigurd, who discussed the merits of either staying home and building up one's country or gaining glory and renown by foreign travel and warfare.[40] Hamsun's trilogy appeared at a time when Norwegian emigration to America had recently received its finest treatment in the work of O. E. Rølvaag.[41] Hamsun may not have had Rølvaag's knowledge of nineteenth-century Norwegian homesteaders in the Midwest, but he knew the problems of emigration only too well from home. His uncle Hans had emigrated to north Norway and was followed later by the whole Hamsun family. The usual contrast of settler versus vagabond was further represented in his uncles, Hans and Ole, as well as in his brothers Ole, who stayed at home all his life, and Peter, who lost himself in America.[42] Most restless of them all was Knut Hamsun himself, who—if one counts north and south Norway as different provinces—emigrated no less than six times. He could well tell his brother Ole: "You are the only one who has lived quietly in our childhood home, and I have been the worst to roam around."[43]

In Rølvaag's trilogy about Per Hansa and his son, Peter Victorious, the author spoke eloquently about the settlers' gradual loss of national background. However, where it is a question of permanent settlement—be it in tenth-century Iceland or nineteenth-century America—new traditions take the place of old, and later generations do not experience the rootlessness of the first. Hamsun in his trilogy is less concerned with settlers (like Ezra) and more with those thousands of people, like his own brother Peter, who became permanently uprooted and whose tragic fates have often been minimized in contemporary literature—including the fate of Eleseus in Hamsun's own *Growth of the Soil.* More importantly, Hamsun wished to transcend the scope of conventional emigration novels by giving his readers not only the special truth about the rootlessness of many nineteenth-century Norwegian immigrants in the American Midwest, but the much more general truth about a sense of displacement that characterizes life in the twentieth century. This is why Lovise Magrete's case, unlike Barbro's, is irremediable and tragic, why the August trilogy—much more than *Growth of the Soil*—expresses our present reality, and why August, despite the danger he is said to represent, is closer to us than Ezra.

In the trilogy the underlying tragic theme of displacement has been glossed over by Hamsun's humorous characters, humorous incidents, and humorous language—which is often lost in translation. It is said of Edevart and August: "They went on talking things over in their curious Nordland dialect. It has many peculiar words, unexpected words, and was a masterpiece of absurdity, but it expressed their meaning."[44] Thus Paulina is well characterized by her favorite expression of wonder "jeg kan ikke nedlegge det" ("I can't put it down," meaning "I can't stop thinking about it"), and August similarly by his repeated "Now, that is quite another difference" (for "quite a different matter"). That this humorous, essentially antipoetic low style does not preclude poetry is shown time and again throughout a thousand pages, as in the description of Edevart's first two meetings with Lovise Magrete, probably the most naturally poetic in all of Hamsun's work. In the course of time some readers have expressed their enthusiasm over these pages differently: "The one part which rises above the drab," is the opinion of an American reviewer in 1930 who doubted "whether a worse novel than this [*Wayfarers*] could have been written by an American novelist of distinction."[45] But generally the American reception of the August trilogy was good. One critic noted the irony of the fact that "this great exponent of youth is producing his most vigorous work at a time of life which must once have appealed to him only as the 'doddering age,' "[46] and O. E. Rølvaag himself ventured the guess that *Wayfarers* and *August* would outlive *Growth of the Soil.*[47]

The Ring Is Closed

Like Ibsen's last play, *When We Dead Awaken,* Hamsun's last novel, *Ringen sluttet* (*The Ring is Closed,* 1936), sums up its author's life and work while at the same time showing interesting new directions. As in the case of Ibsen, there is also no real falling off in creative powers; Hamsun's own statement, "the best I have ever written,"[48] may be an exaggeration, but he had certainly written many books of less significance.

The setting is much the same as in *The Women At the Pump:* a coastal town in south Norway with its usual range of Hamsun citizens, from rich businessmen and their spoiled daughters to poor factory workers with promiscuous wives. The main character is lazy and optimistic like Oliver but otherwise the very opposite of the eunuch from *The Women At the Pump.* The son of an alcoholic woman and her much older and miserly husband, Abel Brodersen's character is shaped early in childhood: he knows he is totally without a future, yet he is dogged and learns to clench his teeth and rough it. Like Oliver he goes to sea as a young boy, and like Oliver he returns as an entirely changed person, not that his manliness is diminished—quite the contrary—but his motivation for getting on in life is gone for all time. We hear of his life in America, of his good friend Lawrence, and of his beautiful wife, Angèle, with whom he apparently lived very happily in—what many decades later would be termed—a hippie community at Green Ridge, Kentucky, until she died in an accident. During his first visit home, after four years at sea, his mother had died. During his second stay abroad his old father had remarried and then died; the bride (and subsequent widow) was Abel's old acquaintance Lola, who had moved in with the wealthy sea captain because she needed money to save her own family. Lola not only shared her deceased husband's savings with Abel, but in the years to come tried to be a mother to this stepson, who did not want to spend his money wisely but rather wished to go downhill at his own rate. Strangely, Abel, who had never had much luck with the girls in his teens, suddenly appeared to have more sex appeal than he could handle. His stepmother, Lola, lusted for him in vain; even the hopeless love of his childhood, Olga—a woman belonging to the upper class—seemed interested in him, and Lili, married to a working man, Alex, became a frequent companion.

In the remaining four fifths of the novel Olga and Lili exploit Abel's generosity to the point where Captain Brodersen's rich son has spent his father's fortune and lives in a shack in hunger. But this is exactly the old Kentucky style that appeals to Abel, much to the despair of Lola, who knows he could do well in society if he wanted to. In fact, on one occasion he had proved to be the only person in town with sufficient intelligence and courage to save Alex when he was in mortal danger at the sawmill. To help Abel Lola finally buys up the shares in a small coastal steamer, the *Sparrow,* and makes Abel its captain, while she herself signs on as head waitress. For a while Abel seems to like his new position, but people who know his generosity keep asking for free rides—a situation that Lola tries hard to prevent. However, the regularity and predictability of navigating in the calm coastal waters soon reduces the excitement of the job, and after only one year of service Abel suddenly disappears, to return twelve months later—from Kentucky. The *Sparrow* in the meantime has been under the command of its three-member crew until, during a fight over who should wear the captain's cap, Alex and his two companions manage to run the ship aground.

Lola is happily married to Olga's first husband, Mr. Clemens, but Olga herself has less luck in her new marriage to a wealthy businessman. During this time more details of Abel's life in America start to come out. He had shot his wife in a fit of jealousy, and the third party in the imagined love triangle was his own best friend Lawrence, who has since died in prison, where he was serving a sentence for murder. Olga visits Abel in his shack, and when they have made love, she confesses that she had wanted to sleep with a murderer. When Abel sees her again, she at first pretends not to know him, later, when he dresses up like a gentleman, she is less distant, but still not approachable. Even Lola, after she has had a child, loses all interest in Abel. In the end there is still Lili, who loves him as in the past but also, as in the past, wants something in return—this time a bicycle for two of her children (those sired by Abel). At this point the police begin to inquire into Abel's affairs in America and he leaves once more for Kentucky, where he intends to explain the whole case. Tore Hamsun tells us that his father planned to let Abel serve his prison sentence in America and then return home for good. Hamsun was not, however, able to complete a second volume and referred to the novel as a torso.[49]

Among the innovations in *The Ring Is Closed* are its characters. Captain Brodersen—Hamsun's last fictional portrait of old age (except for his portrayals in *On Overgrown Paths*) is entirely unlike the unappetizing Fredrik Mensa *(Rosa)* or the fatuous Old Gihle *(In the Grip of Life)*. The captain is more realistic than either and, for a senior citizen in Hamsun, really quite human—he is almost akin to Alexander Kielland's Skipper Worse, whose erotic escapades at an advanced age also proved to be his undoing. A similarly new creation is the young lawyer Clemens, correct in all his ways, of good family background, though lacking in enterprise and sexual appeal. He is attracted to Lola's voluptuous body and to her motherly instincts. Brighter than Ihlen *(Editor Lynge)* and less naive than Parelius *(Rosa)*, Clemens is the only person in the novel who appreciates the value and uniqueness of its hero Abel Brodersen. Lola mothers Abel, while Lili—like a number of Hamsun's women from Kamma *(Mysteries)* to Ragna *(Wayfarers)*—loves him and exploits him, as does Olga, though she uses a bit more finesse. Although Olga is related to Edvarda *(Pan)* and Fia Johnsen *(The Women At the Pump)*, she is presented this time in the unisex style of the 1920s, a style that Hamsun kept criticizing in his own daughter Ellinor. Like Ingeborg Torsen *(Look Back On Happiness)*, vacillating between an effeminate actor and the brutal male chauvinist Solheim, Olga after her divorce from mild-mannered Clemens marries the businesslike Gulliksen and, when her new husband's indifference finally prompts her to accept Abel's love, her greatest satisfaction is having slept twice with a murderer. "Nothing but sensationalism" is a phrase used of Ingeborg Torsen, but it applies even more to Olga. She is the last of Hamsun's "princesses"—all of whom are concerned with social status—the first being Laura Walsøe, who gave up Knut Pedersen, a poor poet, for the higher status offered by a telegraph operator at Kabelvåg (cf. *Mysteries*, pp. 40–41). Olga will not accept the idea of being inferior to Lola, who has finally experienced happiness as a wife and mother. When Abel sees Olga eight months after their brief love affair, she carries his child, but she ignores its father completely: "All in order, Abel's name expunged."[50]

Abel is different from any other Hamsun character, though he continues a line from Nagel to the more recent Edevart of *Wayfarers*. As in the case of Edevart, the most radical change in Abel seems to occur during a stay abroad. It was indicated, however, that Edevart's resentment might ultimately stem from certain difficulties in his childhood, a theme that has been more fully developed in the case of Abel. For the latter there were no problems at school—since Abel is not only more intelligent than Edevart, but remarkably intellectual for an ordinary sailor—but rather a general sense of being somehow hopelessly disadvantaged, despite a reasonably good social and economic background. Like Johannes in *Victoria,* Abel is both an only child and one isolated from other children, but since his parents are utterly selfish, his childhood is much more pathetic than Johannes's. Furthermore, Abel does not seem, like Johannes, to enjoy the comfort of a creative imagination, even if his small hands ("nimble as a thief's") indicate "artistic" gifts, as well as an aristocratic temperament. Like only very few of Hamsun's protagonists—such as Lieutenant Holmsen in *Children of the Age*—Abel has taught himself extraordinary self-control: when he is shot by Alex, he finishes tying his shoe laces before taking care of his wound. On the other hand, when he has been named after Abel—rather than after his aggressive and artistic brother Cain—this seems to underline the fact that, except for those special occasions when he robs the church, saves Alex, and kills Angèle, Abel has succeeded in taming his will to the point of passivity, and because he is able to intellectualize his passivity, he is much more of a Hamlet figure than any other Hamsun character, including Edevart.[51] In opposition to his socially respected father, but still with some of his father's stubbornness, Abel has made his goal that of becoming nothing whatsoever in life, a goal that the author worked into a whole philosophic system, quite different from anything he had lately professed, though it pointed back to the cultural pessimism of Hamsun's early novels and helped explain the title *The Ring Is Closed.*

Geissler in *Growth of the Soil* presented Isak Sellanraa's stable universe as an ideal for others, since he knew that rootlessness and resentment had ruined his own career. Edevart of *Wayfarers,* though less reflective than Geissler, felt the same loss of direction as he listened to Joakim's theories on the meaning of roots. Abel is similarly touched by the story of a cow that was hauled by ship to the nearest town, where she broke loose and found her way home. In his comments on the story, Clemens—and he speaks here with Hamsun's voice—tries to teach Abel something about the importance of roots, a lesson that is not lost on him. Abel is above all a person of extraordinary loyalty—to the memory of Kentucky, of Angèle, of Lawrence, and, in the end, to the memory of his childhood town. On being asked by Lola why he is back after only one year abroad, he gives as his reason the story of the cow. Even so, Abel has succeeded not only in transcending the early loss of ties to home but in attaining some sort of sovereignty. He is not a tippler like Geissler, nor one of the living dead like Edevart, neither is he a potential suicide like Hamsun's early misfits. He tells Olga, "Then I became rootless in a foreign land, and that continued the process of development. Then I married Angèle and with her, thank God, my independence became complete. I am content with my lot."[52] The reason for this new freedom is that Abel, unlike other Hamsun protagonists, has stripped himself completely of social ambition, a sentiment often symbolized by dress—Knut Sonnenfield's cap (*The Enigmatic Man,* 1877), Nagel's yellow suit, Glahn's uniform, Lieutenant Holmsen's military cape, Geissler's lacquered boots, Edevart's gold rings, etc. Olga judges Abel by his dress, and Lola keeps buying him new clothes in order that he can be judged according to his true worth. Abel, however, is a master at messing up his clothing (a special gift inherited even by his illegitimate offspring) and speaks with nostalgia of his simple outfit in Kentucky: "All we ever wore where I come from was shirt and pants and a revolver. Lola, you can't imagine how much more natural that is than to wear a whole lot of clothes."[53]

Thinking perhaps of Hamsun's personal pedantry in all matters of form, including clothing, some critics have taken Abel's plight to mean that the gradually more misanthropic novelist was at the end of his tether, with a hero who was nothing but an animal.[54] However, no one who reads *The Ring Is Closed* can miss a note of admiration in the author's description of Abel:

> In the depths of his obscurity he was not lacking in character. This was something. He possessed a sublime indifference toward all conditions he encountered. And this was something. He could endure, he could do without. He did not cling to any living person for protection, for he was broadminded and uncritical and did not feel that he himself had anything that needed to be shielded. His weak ambition and mediocre intelligence, these had been his sole equipment to start with, but together they had come later on to be a very bulwark of defence which, because it was both enduring and complete, rendered him independent—a sovereign in his own way.[55]

Hamsun was never lavish with his praise, and only one of his protagonists—Lieutenant Holmsen—received as high a recommendation.

Optimism and restless activity are qualities Hamsun had earlier associated with the West—August's temperament was typically American—while a Stoic's ability to suffer and yet retain his peace of mind is mostly found in Hamsun's descriptions of the East: "The Turk has time to celebrate Friday according to old customs. And he has time for several hours of devotion each day. And in the evening he sits outside his little home until late at night, giving himself up to pleasant rest and dreams."[56] In his last novel, however, Hamsun had the East meet the West in Green Ridge, Kentucky. Nagel's romantic cabin in the woods, where he would live with his silver-haired Martha had been replaced by a shack, and Hamsun in 1936—possibly recalling his own life in a shed in Oslo's Møller Street fifty years earlier—showed an appreciation of the American hippie of the 1960s which is still (1984) beyond most members of Norway's prosperous society: "He had cut to the bone his standard of living and had become to a degree original; he did not think it so awful to chill his hide a little or to go for a day on an empty stomach."[57]

Living in luxury at Nørholm and seeing finally all his social dreams fulfilled, Hamsun may have realized that he had bartered away the inspiration that filled him when he slept in a hovel and lived the life of *Hunger*. Perhaps that was another reason for his title *The Ring Is Closed* and for his statement that he would gladly give up Nørholm with its magnificent 400 acres for the ability to write again.[58] Like few people in world literature, Hamsun was granted that wish in his ninetieth year, when he wrote the story of a man's trial and final return home, not as part 2 of *The Ring Is Closed,* but in the form of his own moving autobiography.

On Overgrown Paths

Hamsun's final work is not his only attempt at autobiographical writing, nor is it conventional autobiography. On the one hand, there were his travel accounts from the years 1903–5, where personalities and events were similarly authentic; on the other hand, there is in most parts of *På gjengrodde stier* (*On Overgrown Paths,* 1949) an admixture of what could well be fiction, which calls to mind

Hamsun's earlier first-person novels, such as *The Wanderer* and, particularly, *Hunger.* It is really not until *On Overgrown Paths* that "the ring is closed": Andreas Tangen's trials and tribulations in Kristiania come back here as the rough treatment of the old Hamsun at the hands of Norwegian lawyers and psychiatrists. A 175-page chronicle of contemporary events and impressions without chapter divisions, *On Overgrown Paths* lacks the intensity and artistic form of the earlier work. However, *Hunger*'s chief compositional device—the protagonist's gradual displacement, from the pleasures of the Palace Gardens to the slums behind the East Station—is also felt in the changing places and fortunes of the old author Knut Hamsun as he is being moved around as a political prisoner. In this sense the book is a documentary novel—like those many gripping accounts of imprisonment and deportation that appeared in the wake of World War II.

The reader is told that, in May 1945, Hamsun was driven from Nørholm to Grimstad Hospital, where he suffered the indignity (which he gradually enjoyed) of having to walk around in a pair of worn-out shoes, but where he also experienced certain pleasures, such as a gift of Javanese cigars sent him from a secret admirer. From the Grimstad Hospital he was taken to the Landvik Old Age Home, where he tried with poor results to show off his old-fashioned charm and gracious demeanor: he was denied access to the library, even though he had most likely written some of the books there. In October 1945 there followed his long and painful railroad journey to the Oslo Psychiatric Clinic, where he was subjected to seemingly senseless examinations by medical specialists and where—as in the prison scene of *Hunger*—his physical and mental resistance was temporarily broken down. The stay at the clinic later inspired him to write an indignant letter to the attorney general (a letter with overtones of Tangen's attack upon God in *Hunger*). From the Oslo Psychiatric Clinic Hamsun was taken back to the Landvik Old Age Home in February 1946 and at the end of that year was permitted to spend Christmas with friends and relatives in Oslo. That vacation turned out to be both bracing and exciting, even if the ostensible purpose of the trip—to get new spectacles—confirmed his old impression of medical doctors as incompetent and unfriendly people. The following year, 1947, turned out to be better. He seemed to have recovered his balance of mind after the months in the Psychiatric Clinic and enjoyed meeting a Hamarøy compatriot visiting in south Norway, he tried his hand at writing—poetry, drama, prose—and saw his dream of appearing in court come true when he was finally summoned to the Grimstad Municipal Court, where he presented his own case, freely confessing his old admiration of the Germans and pleading ignorance of their war crimes. After the sentence on 23 December Hamsun was moved back to Nørholm, where during the following year—the last recorded in the book—he continued taking his daily walks and reporting his experiences and reflections with the detachment and disarming irony of a true philosopher. The story ends abruptly with the news that Norway's supreme court, on 23 June 1948, had confirmed the Grimstad sentence.

What seems at first nothing but a day by day account of trivial events suddenly reveals the art of a great novelist, his sense of scene and dialogue, of humor and pathos, and beneath it all the insidious *j'accuse*. The old Hamsun must have been about as proud and obstinate as the hero of *Hunger*. But though to most people he seemed not to regret what he had done, his memoir shows time and again that he was upset by the animosity of *young* people; to them he had become a bugaboo, so that they turned away in dismay whenever he asked them for assistance. However, that unfriendly attitude changed soon after the war, and the remarkably therapeutic effect of Hamsun's stay in Oslo during the Christmas vacation of 1946 may well have had to do with the fact that many people had recognized him on the streets and treated him in a kindly manner: "I was neither hated nor despised by people. And that is good." But he added characteristically, "if it had been otherwise, I should not have cared. I am so old."[59]

In a play about the old Hamsun, *Ice Age* (1974),[60] Germany's Tankred Dorst emphasizes above all the author's intense stubbornness; indeed, his deafness is symbolic: he does not *want* to hear. Also telling are scenes showing Hamsun's pedantic preoccupation with meaningless detail—not being able to read the fine inscription on a table knife infuriates him—[61] but Hamsun's renaissance mind was not as perverted as Dorst makes it in *Ice Age. On Overgrown Paths* shows Hamsun inspecting new and old buildings, criticizing people's carpentry as well as their vocabulary, and deploring modern spelling or the lack of old-fashioned respect in modern forms of greeting. There are also cases of actual involvement, as when he takes great trouble to guard a *young* pine tree against an *old* poplar, and there are scenes showing some of Hamsun's former ecstasy over the mysteries of nature, as when he watches the mating sparrows in spring or the first open water on the Nørholm inlet or the moon "climbing up from the sea like a jellyfish dripping with gold."[62] Actually, his gratitude for the favor of receiving life at all had not diminished since *The Wanderer.* He could no longer enjoy the splendor of the soughing of the forest, but "there was a friendly breeze blowing all about me even though I was deaf and could no longer hear it."[63] Not being able to read was worse, but he was thankful for being able to use his eyes at all and ended his book with touchingly humorous reflections on the blessings of what in Nordland was called "walking sight"—sight enough to walk by.

As the title *Ice Age* indicates, Tankred Dorst in his book presents Hamsun as a person almost totally without human contact. Dorst makes only two exceptions, when he brings in an old friend from Hamsun's vagabond days and a young man and former admirer who symbolizes Hamsun's need for contact with the new generation (the latter person—Oswald—is not in Hamsun's memoir, but the vagabond is based on an acquaintance, Martin Enevoldsen). *On Overgrown Paths,* however, does not leave the reader with a picture of Hamsun as a misanthrope; instead, as the author rejoices in Nature's wonders, he recalls old friendships, and he establishes new throughout the book. Martin Enevoldsen—an actual lay preacher who later reported his meeting with the novelist in the press[64]—becomes Hamsun's Prince Myshkin, his only picture of a modern saint. Martin's story of unselfish and unrequited love is told by Hamsun in a spirit of conciliation and humor which permeates also the other semifictional accounts in the memoir—the amusing scene with Ol' Hansa who wanted to be a teacher but could not spell, or the sentimental tale of homesickness among Russians and Americans in Helsinki, or the rivalries of Pat and Knut over Bridget from Elroy, Wisconsin. The locus of these delightful tales—narrated with the art of Hamsun's best short stories—is that of the overgrown paths of the book's title, an indication that the author had aimed at some special kind of documentary, in which daily events are finally viewed as memories of things past.

Superficially, *On Overgrown Paths* may remind the reader of *John Gabriel Borkman*—Ibsen's play about old age and loneliness, which the painter Munch referred to as "the mightiest winter landscape in Scandinavian literature." Hamsun's rambling account lacks Ibsen's conscious composition and poetry, but it has both the special appeal of authenticity and a roguishness not found in Ibsen's work. "You are right, deceiving one another, that's friendship," John Gabriel tells his long-time companion Vilhelm Foldal. Typically, Hamsun presents his case more good-humoredly: "What did I need a cane for? It was merely a kind of affectation, like setting my hat on my head a little rakishly and so on. Was the cane any support to me? No, we had become companions, but nothing more. When we fell, we always lay far apart from one another in the snow. As might be expected of companions."[65] And, again typically, he blames no one—neither people nor institutions nor social conditions—loneliness is a part of old age, which is also, as Hamsun at last seems to agree, a part of life. *On Overgrown Paths,* though it deals with a very old man in icy isolation, thus exudes a warmth that served to remind Norwegian readers of what they owed this once so beloved writer and to make them ask whether the old sinner could not have been treated in the more gentlemanly style he used toward his own heroes. The question may not have interested Hamsun, though no doubt he would have liked to have lived to see his prophecies confirmed: *On Overgrown Paths* soon led not only to a renewed interest in his other writings, but to new collected editions and translations of his work, as well as to critical and biographical writings, films, compositions, paintings, and a Hamsun Society.[66] In a moving speech on 16 December 1947 Knut Hamsun told members of the Grimstad Court, "[My speech] has not been meant as any defense; I have therefore not hinted anything of my evidence, to which I might well have turned. Nor have I mentioned all the rest of the material which I might also have made use of. Let it be. It can wait until another time, perhaps until better times and for another court than this. Another day dawns tomorrow, and I can wait. I have time on my side."[67]

Chapter Six
Conclusion

"I can wait. I have time on my side," were Knut Hamsun's last words to the members of the Grimstad Municipal Court which, in 1947, sentenced him for his sympathies with Nazi Germany. Two years earlier he had been declared a person with "permanently impaired mental faculties"; now he was made to pay fines amounting to $80,000—virtually all he owned. No Norwegian writer had ever suffered a similar ignominy. In 1950, at the news that the Gyldendal Publishing House would begin printing his books again, the ninety-year-old novelist broke down and cried with emotion: his worst torture had been the total neglect shown him by readers and scholars in the immediate postwar years.

After all, Hamsun had had a name and lost it. His novels had been discovered by the Germans in the 1890s, and from Germany their fame spread to the Mediterranean countries and the Middle and Far East. After receiving the Nobel Prize in 1920 he won a name for himself also in the English-speaking world. By 1939 his works had appeared in more than thirty languages. Of Scandinavian writers who won the Nobel Prize, some are already forgotten. Hamsun, on the other hand, seems to have profited from the enforced neglect after World War II: since his death in 1952 an increasing number of books and articles on his life and works has appeared every year. He is today the only Norwegian writer besides Ibsen and Undset who belongs to world literature. He is also the best known Scandinavian novelist, with an international reputation surpassed only by such towering names as Hans Christian Andersen, Henrik Ibsen, and August Strindberg. Time has indeed been on Hamsun's side.

Hamsun's new position receives its strength from two sources. One is his place in the development of literary modernism. His manic-depressive heroes, his elitism, his emphasis on the unconscious life of the mind, his stream of consciousness techniques—

make him at the same time a disciple of Dostoevski and Nietzsche, and a precursor of Kafka and Joyce.

Very different is his popular appeal, resulting from the melodrama of his love stories and above all, and particularly for Norwegians, from the central place of Nature in all his work. To average Norwegians it is not only Hamsun's "I belong to the woods" that speaks to their hearts, but his idealization of a simple life-style, his emphasis on *trivsel*—a Scandinavian term denoting well-being and peace of mind—and his insistence that, in the the last resort, industry and materialism do not hold a promise for the future.

In this study I have attempted to present Hamsun as an aesthete, a stylist, a writer as much concerned with his medium as with his message. I have emphasized the importance of Hamsun's American stay for the development of his style, with its strong reliance on rhythm and repetition, and I have tried to show how Hamsun mastered this essential element of his art till the end of his days, even if his lyricism gradually gave way to a more epic manner of presentation. Finally, I hope I have been able to point out the message of joy that, strangely, accompanies Hamsun's lifelong theme of alienation. Henry Miller wrote, "It was from your Knut Hamsun that I derived much of my love of life, love of nature, love of men. All I have done, or hope I have, in relating the distressing story of my life, is to increase that love of life, nature and all of God's creatures in those who read me."[1]

Notes and References

Preface

1. Thomas Mann, *Gesammelte Werke,* vol. 10 (Berlin: Fischer, 1960), p. 620.

2. In *Illustreret biografisk leksikon,* ed. Nanna With (Oslo: With, 1920).

3. Johan Langaard and Reidar Revold, *Edvard Munch: Fra år til år* (Oslo: Aschehoug, 1961), p. 83.

4. Hamsun, "Fra det ubevidste Sjæleliv" (From the unconscious life of the mind), *Samtiden* (Bergen) 1 (1890):325–34; translated by Marie Skramstad De Forest.

5. Isaac Bashevis Singer, "Knut Hamsun: Artist of Skepticism," in *Hunger,* by Knut Hamsun, trans. Robert Bly (New York, 1967), p. ix.

Chapter One

1. A number of biographies of Knut Hamsun have appeared, from Carl Morburger's (1910) to Tore Hamsun's (1959). Einar Skavlan's (1929) is a classic, Tore Hamsun's the richest in details from Hamsun's early life.

2. Hamsun not a genuine *nordlending:* see Paul Knaplund, "Knut Hamsun: Triumph and Tragedy," *Modern Age* (Chicago) 9 (1965):165–74.

3. Of Hamsun's very sparse childhood memories, some are contained in the short story "Blandt dyr" (Among animals) from the collection *Stridende liv* (Struggling life) (1905), in *Samlede verker,* 15 vols. (Oslo, 1954–56), 4:209–13; hereafter this work cited as *SV.*

4. The short story "Et spøkelse" ("An Apparition") from the collection *Kratskog* (Brushwood, 1903), *SV,* 4:46–50), has been analyzed by Eduard Hitschmann in *Imago* (Vienna) 12 (1924):336–60.

5. In Sten Sparre Nilson, *En ørn i uvær* (Oslo, 1960).

6. *SV,* 4:51

7. *Den Gaadefulde* (The enigmatic man), reprinted in *Det første jeg fikk trykt,* ed. Eli Krog (Oslo, 1950), pp. 100–21.

8. From a letter to Bolette C. Pavels Larsen, 10 October 1890; in Olaf Øyslebø, *Hamsun gjennom stilen* (Oslo, 1964), p. 122.

9. *Bjørger* (Bodø: Albert F. Knudsen, 1878). Knudsen also printed "Et Gjensyn" (A reunion) as a broadsheet.

10. "I Nød" (In distress) by Knut Pedersen, in *Norsk Familje-Blad* (Oslo), 6 December 1879, p. 155; reprinted in Skavlan, pp. 77–78.

11. On Bjørnson in the Midwest, see Eva and Einar Haugen, *Land of the Free* (Northfield: Norwegian-American Historical Association, 1978).

12. On Knut Hamsun in America, see my *Knut Hamsun og Amerika* (Oslo, 1969).

13. Letter to Ernst Sengebusch, 8 April 1882; ibid., p. 26.

14. Harry Hart in *La Crosse Tribune and Leader Press,* 2 March 1924; John Hart in *Elroy Leader Tribune,* 21 February 1924.

15. Formerly in the possession of Grace Schultz Hart, Reedsburg, Wisconsin.

16. Letter of 21 April 1883, describing lecture in Stoughton: Wisconsin State Historical Society.

17. *Skandinaven* (Chicago), 8 May 1883.

18. See Georg Brandes, introduction to *Main Currents in Nineteenth Century Literature* (London: Heinemann, 1901).

19. W. T. Ager, "Incidents in the Early Life of Knut Hamsun," *Kvartalskrift* (Eau Claire) 12 (January 1916):2–7; reprinted in Næss (1969), pp. 248–49.

20. "Rædsel" ("Fear") from *Kratskog* (Brushwood, 1903); in *SV,* 4:36–39.

21. I have stated in my book on Hamsun in America that he stayed with the Jansons for about a year. From a collection of letters recently discovered in Elroy by Lawrence Berge, it appears that Hamsun began working with Janson in March or April 1884. By 23 September he was back in Norway.

22. *Life Story of Rasmus B. Anderson* (Madison, Wisc., 1915), p. 308. The Hamsun chapters were originally printed in the Grand Forks periodical *Eidsvold* for 1909.

23. Ibid., pp. 309–10.

24. Hamsun originally refuted Anderson's account in *Dagbladet* (Oslo), 11 August 1909, and again in an interesting letter now in the Martin B. Ruud Papers, University of Minnesota Library.

25. On Hamsun's relationship to Erik Frydenlund, see my "Knut Hamsuns brevveksling med Postmester Erik Frydenlund," *Edda* (Oslo) 59 (1959):225–68.

26. *Dagbladet* (Oslo), 12 December 1884.

27. *Aftenposten* (Oslo), 21 January, 12, 14 February 1885.

28. *Ny Illustreret Tidende* (Oslo) 12 (1885):91–94, 102–3, 107–8, 110.

29. *Dagbladet* (Oslo), 4–5 July 1886 ("On a Lecturing Tour"); 24 August ("Sin").

30. From *Kratskog* (Brushwood, 1903), in *SV,* 4:104–22.

31. *Edda* 59 (1959):230–32.

32. Cecil Krøger (Krøger Johansen), "Knut Hamsun. Hans Læreaar," *Dagbladet* (Oslo), 18 January 1903.
33. *America* (Chicago), 20 December 1888.
34. *Life Story of Rasmus B. Anderson,* p. 315.
35. Letter of 13 January 1889, in Oslo University Library.
36. *Verdens Gang* (Oslo), 25 August 1881.
37. Bergen University Library MS 943 fol; published by Johannes Dale in *Bergens Tidende,* 29 January 1953, p. 5.
38. Letter to Mrs. Alette Gross, Hamburg, 23 November 1914, in Oslo University Library.
39. See Arild Hamsun, ed., *Om Knut Hamsun og Nørholm* (Oslo, 1961).
40. Nothing reveals Hamsun's personal charm better than his letters to his lifelong friend Erik Frydenlund. See *Edda* 59 (1959):225–68.
41. Tore Hamsun, ed., *Knut Hamsun som han var* (Oslo, 1956), p. 110.
42. Ibid., pp. 159–60.
43. Sigrid Stray, *Min klient Knut Hamsun* (Oslo, 1979).
44. In Knut Hamsun, *Artikler* (Oslo, 1939), pp. 148–57.
45. In *Morgenbladet* (Oslo) 15 January 1915.
46. In *Knut Hamsun: Festskrift* (Oslo, 1929), p. 133.
47. On America, including American literature: "Festina Lente," in *Artikler,* pp. 217–29.
48. Leo Lowenthal's important article was originally published in *Zeitschrift für Sozialforschung* (Frankfurt am Main) 6 (1937):295–345, and later included in Lowenthal, *Literature and the Image of Man* (Boston, 1957). Lowenthal's study has inspired a recent Danish publication *Det reaktionære oprør* (Copenhagen, 1975) by Morten Giersing, John Thobo-Carlsen, and Mikael Westergaard Nielsen. In Norway Arild Haaland has written several studies, including "Nazisme, litteratur og Knut Hamsun," in *Nazismen og norsk litteratur* ed. Bjarte Birkeland and Stein Ugelvik Larsen (Oslo, 1975), pp. 57–69.
49. Most of Hamsun's wartime articles have been printed in Nilson, *En ørn i uvær.* A German translation is entitled *Knut Hamsun und die Politik* (Villingen, 1964); page numbers in parenthesis are to the German edition.
50. Article on Ossietzky in *Aftenposten* and *Tidens Tegn,* 22 November 1935, has been reprinted in *En ørn i uvær,* pp. 134–35 (154–55).
51. Nilson, *En ørn i uvær,* pp. 198–200 (204–6).
52. Ibid., p. 200 (207).
53. Ibid., pp. 200–201 (208).
54. Ibid., pp. 201–5 (209–14).
55. Ibid., pp. 205–6 (216–17).
56. Ibid., p. 207 (218).

57. The following account relies largely on Thorkild Hansen's detailed treatment in *Prosessen mot Hamsun* (Oslo, 1978). On Fangen and Hamsun, see Hansen, pp. 89–94.

58. Nilson, *En ørn i uvær,* pp. 213–14 (225–26).

59. Hansen, *Prosessen mot Hamsun,* pp. 124–26.

60. Nilson, *En ørn i uvær,* p. 215 (228–30).

61. Hansen, *Prosessen mot Hamsun,* p. 153–56.

62. Nilson, *En ørn i uvær,* p. 217 (231–32).

63. Ibid., p. 218 (234)

64. *Arbeiderbladet* (Oslo), 18 October 1945.

65. Hansen, *Prosessen mot Hamsun,* pp. 319–37. The complete text of the psychiatric examination is now available in Gabriel Langfeldt and Ørnulv Ødegård, *Den rettspsykiatriske erklæring om Knut Hamsun* (Oslo, 1978).

66. Hansen, *Prosessen mot Hamsun,* p. 731.

67. Ibid., p. 732.

68. Ibid., p. 741.

Chapter Two

1. In Hamsun's article about Mark Twain, *Ny Illustreret Tidende* (Oslo) 12 (1885):108; reprinted in the Minneapolis paper *Budstikken,* 27 April, 4 May 1887.

2. Hamsun in a letter to the *Overland Monthly* (San Francisco) 87 (April 1929):108.

3. For examples, see my *Knut Hamsun og Amerika,* pp. 224–25.

4. Cf. Georg Brandes in his review of *The Cultural Life* (in *Verdens Gang* (Oslo), 9 May 1889): "the form of the book—despite the author's continuous attack on all that is American—because of his unconscious and nervous impressionability, has become really American—incoherent, cutting, humorous in its exaggerations, hunting for effect and normally finding it" (my translation).

5. See Harald Beyer, *Nietzsche og Norden* (Universitetet i Bergen: Årbok 1958), p. 68f.

6. Hamsun, *The Cultural Life of Modern America,* trans. Barbara Gordon Morgridge (Cambridge, Mass., 1969), pp. 33–34.

7. Ibid., p. 82.

8. Harald S. Næss, "The Three Hamsuns," *Scandinavian Studies* 32 (1960):139; original text in Hamsun, *Knut Hamsun,* pp. 281–82.

9. Translated by Marie Skramstad De Forest.

10. Arne Garborg, "Svært til Kar" (Braggadocio), *Dagbladet* (Oslo), 2 April 1893; quoted from Johannes Dale, *Garborg-studiar* (Oslo, 1969), p. 20.

11. *Budstikken* (Minneapolis), 17 July 1889 (my translation).

12. Hamsun, *The Cultural Life of America,* pp. 69–70.

13. On the use of repetition as a lyric device in Hamsun's prose, see Olaf Øyslebø in *Edda* (Oslo) 65 (1965):1–25.

14. Hamsun, *Pan,* trans. J. W. McFarlane (London: 1955), p. 147.

15. Hamsun, *On Overgrown Paths,* trans. Carl L. Anderson (New York, 1967), p. 91.

16. For a careful textual analysis, see Rolf Nyboe Nettum, *Konflikt og visjon* (Oslo, 1970), pp. 59–104. Very important for a modern understanding of Hamsun's works from the 1890s is J. W. McFarlane's "The Whisper of the Blood," *PMLA* 71 (1956):563–94.

17. *Edda* (Oslo) 59 (1959):232.

18. Ibid., p. 233.

19. On Hamsun and Edvard Brandes: *Svenska Dagbladet* (Stockholm), 10 December 1920; reprinted in Axel Lundegård, *Sett och känt* (Stockholm, 1925), pp. 100–106.

20. In his December 1888 article about Strindberg in *America* (Chicago), Hamsun quotes from *Jäsningstiden* (*Fermentation Time,* which is the title of vol. 2 of *Son of a Servant*).

21. "The future literature will be *journalism;* only the exact report in journalism is true, and a step toward this true report is, of late, the increasing number of biography—and memorandum—literature all over the world" (*America* [Chicago], 20 December 1888, p. 30.)

22. Hamsun, ed., *Knut Hamsun som han var,* p. 75.

23. Hamsun, *Hunger,* trans. Robert Bly (New York, 1967), p. 132.

24. Ibid., p. 15.

25. Martin Nag has shown (convincingly, I think) how the heroine's peculiar name is a variation of the word y-Jalali (from Akhlakyjalali) which appears in Hamsun's *The Cultural Life of Modern America* (on page 97 of the 1889 edition). Hamsun here is quoting from Emerson's *Representative Men* (chapter on Plato).

26. Hamsun, ed., *Knut Hamsun som han var,* p. 75.

27. Martin Nag in *Verdens Gang* (Oslo), 8 September 1966, p. 11.

28. Nettum, *Konflikt og visjon,* p. 83f.

29. Hamsun, *Hunger,* pp. 217–18.

30. In addition to Nettum's and McFarlane's treatment of the novel (see note 16), there is Gregory Nybo's interesting *Knut Hamsuns Mysterier* (Oslo, 1969).

31. Gabriel Scott, "Mens Hamsun skrev Pan: En erindring," in *Knut Hamsun: Festskrift* (Oslo, 1929), pp. 151–62.

32. Names like Stenersen, Grøgaard. The parsonage is Vestre Moland.

33. See my "A strange meeting and Hamsun's Mysterier," *Scandinavian Studies* 36 (1964):48–58.

34. Ibid.

35. Now available in *Paa Turné,* ed. Tore Hamsun (Oslo, 1960); it is also in a German translation, *Psychologie und Dichtung* (Stuttgart: Kohlhammer, 1964).

36. Short story "Over Havet" (Across the ocean), *Dagbladet* (Oslo), 14, 21 November 1886.

37. See Olaf Øyslebø, *Hamsun gjennom stilen* (Oslo, 1964), p. 122.

38. T. de Vere White, ed., *A Leaf from the Yellow Book* (London: Richard Press, 1958), p. 18.

39. *Ny Jord* (Copenhagen) 2 (1888):384 (my translation).

40. *Paa Turné,* ed. Hamsun, p. 35.

41. Hamsun, *Mysteries,* trans. Gerry Bothmer (New York, 1971), p. 74.

42. Ola Hansson, *Friedrich Nietzsche: Hans Personlighed og hans System* (Oslo:Cammermeyer, 1890).

43. *Paa Turné,* ed. Hamsun, pp. 56–64.

44. Interview with *Evening Post* (New York), reprinted in *Verdens Gang* (Oslo), 20 October 1918, p. 14.

45. See J. E. Cirlot, *A Dictionary of Symbols* (New York: Philosophical Library, 1962), p. 52.

46. Henry Miller in *Dagens Nyheter* (Stockholm), 3 August 1959, p. 3.

47. Henry Miller, *Plexus* (New York: Grove Press, 1965), pp. 318–19.

48. See, for example, Knut Faldbakken in *Dagbladet* (Oslo), 17 May 1974, p. 2.

49. Hamsun, *Mysteries,* p. 6.

50. Letter to Bolette C. Pavels Larsen; quoted in Johannes Dale, *Garborg-studiar* (Oslo, 1969), p. 23.

51. *Verdens Gang* (Oslo), 22 April 1893, p. 1; reprinted in Arne Garborg, *Tankar og utsyn,* vol. 2 (Oslo: Aschehoug, 1950), pp. 128–31.

52. *Dagbladet* (Oslo), 2 April 1893, p. 1.

53. *Samtiden* (Bergen) 3 (1893):177–91.

54. The resemblance between "Glahn's Death" and Dostoevski's nouvella *Krotkaja* has been pointed out by Rolf Vige in his study *Knut Hamsuns Pan* (Oslo, 1963), p. 74. Alfred Turco proposes that "Glahn's Death" is written by no other person than Glahn himself: *Scandinavica* 19 (1980):13–29.

55. *Knut Hamsun som han var,* ed. Hamsun, p. 103.

56. Bernhard Herre died, like Glahn, after a shooting accident. See Leiv Amundsen in *Norsk biografisk leksikon,* vol. 4 (Oslo: Aschehoug, 1934), p. 41. Herre's *En Jægers Erindringer (A Hunter's Memoirs)* appeared posthumously in 1849.

57. Boganis's first collection of *Jagtbreve* had been very favorably reviewed by Georg Brandes. Dinesen's other writings include an article (*Tilskueren* [Copenhagen, 1887], pp. 778–936) about his stay in America ("Fra et Ophold i de Forenede Stater), which begins, "It was during the late summer of 1872 that I traveled to America. I was sick at heart. . . ." See Richard B. Vowles, "Boganis, Father of Osceola; or Wilhelm Dinesen in America 1872–1874." *Scandinavian Studies* 48 (1976):369–83.

58. *Blomstermålningar och djurstycken: Samlade skrifter,* vol. 22 (Stockholm, 1914), p. 234. Hamsun wrote to Victor Nilsson, "His very latest book, *Flower Paintings,* I have still not read, but Brandes admired it, he said. . . ." (*Knut Hamsun som han var,* p. 58).

59. Letter to Erik Skram, 28 July 1890, in *Knut Hamsun som han var,* ed. Hamsun, p. 101.

60. Johannes V. Jensen, *Den ny Verden* (Copenhagen, 1907), pp. 175–86.

61. Hamsun, *Pan,* pp. 34–35.

62. The significance of the name Iselin is often brought up and never solved. The name is one of many examples of Hamsun's concept of euphony, as Ylajali ("a name with a smooth nervous sound") is probably from Emerson's *Representative Men* (see note 25), so Iselin could be from a New York city directory! To a Norwegian the name could contain the elements "ice" and "mild" ("is" and "linn"), but above all it is reminiscent of certain medieval folk ballads about princesses and rejected suitors, with names like Iselilja, Sylvelin, etc. In a ballad-inspired poem, the Danish novelist J. P. Jacobsen introduces the name Irmelin. It should not be overlooked that words ending in *-lin* are favorite Norwegian cow names, indicating Iselin's connection with the Norwegian wood nymph *(hulder)* and with wild nature in general. Iselin returns—as a real person—in the play *Friar Vendt* (see page 75); there she is surrounded by other characters of her Nordland myth, including Dundas (the same name as that of the father of the poet Petter Dass, 1647–1707?).

63. Hamsun, *Pan,* pp. 148–49.

64. Ibid., pp. 90–91.

65. Ibid., p. 124.

66. For a full discussion of the Pan symbolism, see Henning K. Sehmsdorf, "Knut Hamsun's Pan: Myth and Symbol," *Edda* (Oslo) 74 (1974):345–93.

67. Hamsun, *Pan,* p. 125.

68. Ibid., p. 122.

69. Ibid., p. 127.

70. Ibid., p. 123.

71. Letter to Georg Brandes, Christmas Eve 1898, in *Knut Hamsun som han var,* ed. Hamsun, p. 105.

72. Hamsun, *The Cultural Life of Modern America,* preface.

73. Examples of "surreal" characters in Hamsun's own works are, for example, Thy in *The Game of Life* and Åse in *The Road Leads On.*

74. "Kjærlighetens slaver," *Kratskog* (Brushwood, 1903), in *SV,* 4:9.

75. Hamsun, *Victoria,* trans. Oliver Stallybrass (New York, 1969), p. 167.

76. *The Oxford Ibsen,* ed. J. W. McFarlane, vol. 8 (London: Oxford University Press, 1977), p. 259.

77. Hamsun, *Victoria,* pp. 65–66.

78. See Beverley D. Eddy, "Hamsun's *Victoria* and Munch's *Livsfrisen:* Variations On a Theme," *Scandinavian Studies* 48 (1976):156–68.

79. Letter to Gerda Welhaven, 23 August 1898, in *Knut Hamsun som han var,* ed. Hamsun, p. 87.

80. Hamsun, *Victoria,* p. 37.

81. *Redaktør Lynge,* in *SV,* 2:60–61.

82. 22 April 1893; text available in Arne Garborg, *Tankar og utsyn,* vol. 2 (Oslo: Aschehoug, 1950), pp. 128–31.

83. Hamsun, *Shallow Soil,* trans. Carl Christian Hyllested (London: Duckworth, 1914), p. ix.

84. Ibid.

85. This situation reflects the Copenhagen discussion of Nietzsche between Georg Brandes and Professor Harald Høffding. See Beyer, *Nietzsche og Norden,* 1:68–92.

86. *Livets spill* (The game of life), in *SV,* 14:88, 96, 116.

87. Letter dated 8 June 1896, in *Knut Hamsun som han var,* ed. Hamsun, p. 133.

88. *New York Times,* 9 December 1927, p. 28.

Chapter Three

1. "Aandens Afblomstringstider," *Ateneum* (Helsingfors) 3 (1900):24–34.

2. *I æventyrland* (*In a Wondrous Land;* unpublished translation by Kenneth Hoem); *Dronning Tamara* (Queen Tamara); *Kratskog* (Brushwood).

3. "Ærer de Unge," reviewed in *Aftenposten* (Oslo) 28 April 1907, and widely discussed in Norwegian and Danish papers.

4. Knut Hamsun's letter to the German translator Heinrich Goebel, used as preface to the German edition of *Det vilde Kor: Das Sausen des Waldes* (Leipzig: Xenien-Verlag, 1909), pp. 1–4; reprinted in Hamsun, *Knut Hamsun,* pp. 167–68 (my translation).

5. Herman Wildenvey, who struck a new note in Norwegian poetry with his collection *Nyinger* (Bonfires, 1907), was much indebted to Hamsun. His greeting on Hamsun's seventieth birthday, "Hamsuns bøker" (Hamsun's books) from 1929, shows the influence of Hamsun's poem to

Bjørnson on his seventieth birthday, 1902. Poetry by Hamsun has been set to music by more than twenty composers. See Arvid Østby, *Knut Hamsun: En bibliografi* (Oslo, 1972), pp. 274–76.

6. Hamsun, "Skjærgårdsø," trans. Martin S. Allwood, in *Twentieth Century Scandinavian Poetry* (Marston Hill, Mullsjö, Sweden, 1950), pp. 119–20.

7. Hamsun, *Knut Hamsun,* p. 163 (my translation).

8. Trygve Braatøy, *Livets cirkel* (1929; reprint ed., Oslo, 1954), pp. 42–47.

9. *New York Times,* 9 December 1923, sec. 9, p. 1. A translation by Graham and Tristan Rawson was published as *In the Grip of Life* (London, 1924).

10. Hamsun, *On Overgrown Paths,* trans. Carl L. Anderson (New York, 1967), pp. 157–74.

11. Hamsun, "Teologen i Æventyrland" (The theologian in a fairytale land), *Artikler* (Oslo, 1939), pp. 148–57.

12. Hamsun, *Brev til Marie* (Oslo, 1970), p. 125: "Say—I'm changing a few things in the proof that you read, actually changing quite a lot, and then I'm continuing the whole book so that it gets big."

Chapter Four

1. In Minneapolis Hamsun lectured on Strindberg on 29 January 1888, and in December of the same year he published in the Chicago journal *America* the first article in English on the Swedish dramatist. The most complete discussion of Hamsun and Rousseau can be found in Dolores J. Buttry, "Knut Hamsun: A Scandinavian Rousseau," (Ph.D. diss., University of Chicago, 1978).

2. Hamsun, *Mysteries,* pp. 65, 49.

3. Hamsun, *Artikler,* p. 207.

4. *Knut Hamsun som han var,* ed. Hamsun, p. 201.

5. Hamsun, *Artikler,* pp. 110–37.

6. Jensen, "Bondekulturen," in *Den ny Verden,* pp. 158–218.

7. "Var byen iblandt på din motstanders side med hujen og hvin / stod landet desmere på din" (*SV,* 15:225).

8. Hamsun, *Growth of the Soil,* trans. W. W. Worster (New York, 1972), p. 428.

9. Ibid., p. 348.

10. Jean Jacques Rousseau, *Émile,* trans. Barbara Foxley (London: Dent, 1911), p. 26.

11. Hamsun, *Children of the Age,* trans. J. S. Scott (New York, 1924), p. 82.

12. Matthew Arnold, *Culture and Anarchy* (Cambridge: Cambridge University Press, 1950), p. 84.

13. In *Men livet lever* (*The Road Leads On,* 1933) (*SV,* 12:8) we get to know that Willatz Holmsen had to sell out and that Mariane, after many disappointments, finally got herself a job as a housekeeper in Tromsø!

14. Hamsun, *Segelfoss Town,* trans. J. S. Scott (New York, 1925), p. 14.

15. Ibid., pp. 167–68.

16. Ibid., p. 328.

17. See J. W. McFarlane, *Ibsen and the Temper of Norwegian Literature* (London: Oxford University Press, 1960), p. 155.

18. See Brian Downs, *Modern Norwegian Literature 1860–1918* (Cambridge: Cambridge University Press, 1966), p. 187.

19. H. G. Wells, *The Salvaging of Civilization* (London: Cassell, 1921), p. 124.

20. Hamsun, *Growth of the Soil,* p. 435.

21. Ibid., p. 429.

22. Ibid., p. 428.

23. Knut Hamsun, "Barnet" (The child), *Morgenbladet* (Oslo), 16 January 1915. The provocative article led to a prolonged discussion in a number of Norwegian papers.

24. See Allen Simpson, "Hamsun and Camus: Consciousness in Markens Grøde and The Myth of Sisyphus," *Scandinavian Studies* 48 (1976):272–83.

25. Hamsun, *Growth of the Soil,* p. 428.

26. Ibid., pp. 178–79.

27. Ibid., pp. 95–96.

28. O. E. Rølvaag, *Giants in the Earth* (New York: Harper, 1927); the original Norwegian version is *I de dage* (Oslo, 1924–25); Halldór K. Laxness, *Independent People* trans. J. A. Thompson (New York: Knopf, 1946); original Icelandic version, *Sjálfstætt fólk* (Reykjavik, 1934–35.)

29. Wells, *The Salvaging of Civilization,* p. 124.

30. See G. M. Gathorne-Hardy, *Bodø-saken* (Oslo: Dybwad, 1926).

31. Hamsun reads "Terje Vigen": told by Johan Filseth in "Fra Knut Hamsuns ungdom," *Aftenposten* (Oslo), 2 May 1916, p. 16.

32. Hamsun, *The Women at the Pump,* trans. Oliver and Gunnvor Stallybrass (New York, 1978), p. 252.

33. "Small-Town Life" (Småbyliv) is the title of one of Hamsun's early short stories (1890, reprinted in *Kratskog, SV,* 4:96–109). It has several features in common with *Mysteries* and, particularly, with *The Women at the Pump.*

34. Hamsun, *The Women at the Pump,* p. 351.

35. Ibid., p. 383.

36. Ibid., p. 7.

37. Ibid., pp. 380–81.

38. Hamsun, *Chapter the Last,* trans. Arthur G. Chater (New York, 1929), p. 285.

39. Ibid., pp. 281–82.

40. Rousseau, *Émile,* p. 320.

Chapter Five

1. Embodied in the character Odin of the six-volume *The People of Juvik* (1918–23).

2. An expression first used of Danish conditions by novelist Jacob Paludan.

3. Nordahl Grieg published a perceptive essay about Hamsun as artist and political journalist in his periodical *Veien frem* (Oslo, 1936); Sigurd Hoel wrote extensively about Hamsun between 1920 and 1959; he edited the Hamsun festschrift in 1929, to which he also contributed an article on Hamsun and America.

4. *Fritt folk* (Oslo), 17 October 1936; reprinted in Nilson, *En ørn i uvær,* p. 195.

5. *Aftenposten* (Oslo), 12 December 1928, p. 1 (same day in the *St. Louis Post Dispatch*); reprinted in Hamsun, *Artikler,* p. 226.

6. See *Knut Hamsun som han var,* ed. Hamsun, pp. 126–29.

7. The psychoanalyst was Johannes Irgens Strømme. Hamsun reports his progress in letters to his wife. See *Brev til Marie* (Oslo, 1970), pp. 203–27.

8. Ibid., p. 223.

9. Ibid., p. 214–15.

10. Ibid., p. 225.

11. Øystein Rottem, *Knut Hamsuns Landstrykere* (Oslo, 1978), p. 15.

12. The chronology is based upon certain events described in the text, such as the first transatlantic cable (1866) and the transition from dollar *(daler)* to *kroner* (1877) in Norway.

13. Hamsun, *Wayfarers,* trans. J. W. McFarlane (New York, 1980), p. 239.

14. Hamsun, *Brev til Marie,* pp. 223–24.

15. Hamsun, *Pan,* p. 144.

16. Hamsun, *The Road Leads On,* trans. Eugene Gay-Tifft (New York, 1934), p. 463.

17. Hamsun, *Wayfarers,* pp. 412–13. This special form—name + adverbial phrase + colon + quote (August, startled by his tone: "H'm?")—found sporadically in Hamsun's other novels, is used extensively in the August trilogy, particularly in the middle volume, *August.*

18. Hamsun, *The Road Leads On,* p. 33. The sentence in brackets has been left out by the translator.

19. Nordahl Grieg in *Veien frem* (Oslo) 1, no. 7 (1936):28–32.

20. Critics like Lowenthal in *Literature and the Image of Man.*

21. Hamsun to Professor Langfeldt; see Hamsun, *Knut Hamsun,* p. 281.

22. See Allen Simpson, *Edda* (Oslo) 77 (1977):273–93.

23. Hamsun, *August,* trans. Eugene Gay-Tifft (New York, 1931), p. 327.

24. Ibid., p. 434.

25. Hamsun, *The Road Leads On,* p. 229.

26. Hamsun, *August,* pp. 320–21.

27. Hamsun, *Wayfarers,* p. 91.

28. Hamsun, *The Wanderer,* trans. Oliver and Gunnvor Stallybrass (New York, 1975), p. 273.

29. Dolores Buttry gave a paper, "The Passive Personality: Hamsun's Hamlets," at the annual meeting of the Society for the Advancement of Scandinavian Study, 1979.

30. One such sailor was Pider Ro, whose stories were first published in 1905 by Gabriel Scott (under the pseudonym of Finn Fogg).

31. Hamsun, *August,* p. 421.

32. "I traveled once with a ship's officer who had a little bottle of snow-white pills. There was quicksilver in them, and he used them on his wife when he was home, he said. But he didn't dare leave them at home. Oh, no! For then his wife could run around all she wanted while he was away, just using these pills. He showed me the bottle. It said *Secale cornutum* on the label. I've always remembered that" (*Wayfarers,* p. 420). Secale cornutum is the fungus Ergot, used in obstetrics as well as for the production of LSD.

33. Hamsun, *The Road Leads On,* p. 465.

34. Ibid., p. 126.

35. Hamsun, *August,* p. 433.

36. Hamsun, *The Road Leads On,* p. 193.

37. Hamsun, *Wayfarers,* p. 339.

38. Gustaf Fröding, "Ett gammalt bergtroll" ("An Old Mountain Troll" 1896).

39. Hamsun, *Brev til Marie,* p. 237.

40. *Heimskringla* (*History of the Sons of Magnus,* chapter 21). See Marlene Ciklamini, *Snorri Sturluson* (Boston: Twayne Publishers, 1978), p. 155.

41. The Norwegian original of *Giants in the Earth* (1927) appeared in two sections in 1924 and 1925.

42. See my *Knut Hamsun og Amerika,* pp. 26–29.

43. Hamsun, *Knut Hamsun,* p. 265.
44. Hamsun, *Wayfarers,* p. 110.
45. *Nation* 131 (1930):528.
46. *Springfield Republican,* 24 June 1934, p. 7e.
47. *New York Herald-Tribune Books,* 25 October 1931, p. 5.
48. Gyldendal's Christmas Catalog *(Julekatalog)* (1936), p. 11.
49. Hamsun, *Knut Hamsun,* p. 262.
50. Hamsun, *The Ring Is Closed,* trans. Eugene Gay-Tifft (New York, 1937), p. 318.
51. See note 29 above.
52. Hamsun, *The Ring Is Closed,* p. 281.
53. Ibid., p. 55.
54. In his 1937 review of the novel (reprinted in *I kunstens tjeneste* [Oslo, 1964]) the Norwegian poet and anthroposophist Alf Larsen admires the artist and criticizes what he considers to be Hamsun's nihilism. A similar line of thought can be found in Aasmund Brynildsen's four important essays on Hamsun in *Svermeren og hans demon* (Oslo, 1973).
55. Hamsun, *The Ring Is Closed,* pp. 229–30.
56. In "Under Halvmånen" (Under the half moon) from the collection *Stridende liv* (1905), in *SV,* 4:272.
57. Hamsun, *The Ring Is Closed,* p. 298.
58. Hansen, *Prosessen mot Hamsun,* p. 268.
59. Hamsun, *On Overgrown Paths,* p. 76.
60. Dorst's play *Ice Age* (*Eiszeit*—which has also been filmed) is based upon *On Overgrown Paths* as well as on other writings by and about Hamsun. Dorst's portrait—inspired by the line "You must be young. When you are young you are a different person" (Suhrkamp edition, no. 610, pp. 36, 70)—is effective, but does not portray the Hamsun readers meet in *On Overgrown Paths.*
61. Dorst has this and other details from Hamsun, *Knut Hamsun,* pp. 256–58, where Tore Hamsun tells of his father's anger and irritability during a stay abroad in 1931.
62. Hamsun, *On Overgrown Paths,* p. 175.
63. Ibid., p. 10.
64. Jørgen Grave described his meeting with Hamsun in *Vestmar* (Kragerø, 28 April 1947). The article was reprinted in two Oslo newspapers.
65. Hamsun, *On Overgrown Paths,* p. 175.
66. A listing of all material by and on Knut Hamsun can be found in Østby's comprehensive Hamsun bibliography *(Knut Hamsun: En bibliografi),* A Hamsun Society (Hamsun-Gesellschaft) has existed in Mölln in Lauenburg, West Germany, since 1955. Its periodical, *Die Waldhütte* (edited by Hilde Fürstenberg), contains mostly reprints of older articles.
67. Hamsun, *On Overgrown Paths,* pp. 146–47.

Chapter Six

1. Thomas H. Moore, ed., *Henry Miller on Writing* (New York: New Directions, 1964), p. 209.

Selected Bibliography

PRIMARY SOURCES

1. In Norwegian

Samlede verker. Femte utgave. 15 vols. Oslo: Gyldendal, 1954–56. Contains the following works: (1) *Sult* (1890); *Mysterier,* (1892); (2) *Redaktør Lynge* (1893); *Ny jord* (1893); *Pan* (1894); (3) *Siesta* (1897); *Victoria,* (1898); *I æventyrland,* (1903); (4) *Kratskog* (1903); *Sværmere* (1904); *Stridende liv* (1905); *Under høststjernen* (1906); (5) *Benoni* (1908); *Rosa* (1908); *En vandrer spiller med sordin* (1909); (6) *Børn av tiden* (1913); *Segelfoss by* (1915); (7) *Den siste glæde* (1912); *Markens grøde* (1917); (8) *Konerne ved vandposten* (1920); (9) *Siste kapitel* (1923); (10) *Landstrykere* (1927); (11) *August* (1930); (12) *Men livet lever* (1933); (13) *Ringen sluttet* (1936); (14) *Ved rikets port* (1895); *Livets spill* (1898); *Aftenrøde* (1898); *Munken Vendt* (1902); (15) *Dronning Tamara* (1903); *Livet ivold* (1910); *Det vilde kor* (1904); *På gjengrodde stier* (1949).

Den Gaadefulde: En Kjærlighedshistorie fra Nordland. Af Kn. Pedersen. Tromsø: M. Urdal, 1877. Reprinted in *Det første jeg fikk trykt,* edited by Eli Krog. Oslo: Aschehoug, 1950.

Bjørger. Fortælling af Knud Pedersen Hamsund. Bodø: Printed privately, 1878. Reprint. Brooklyn, N.Y.: Knudsen Printing, 1925.

Fra det moderne Amerikas Aandsliv. Copenhagen: Philipsen, 1889. Reprint. Oslo: Gyldendal, 1962.

Lars Oftedal. Udkast. Bergen: Mons Litlere, 1889.

Artikler. Oslo: Gyldendal, 1939. Fifteen articles, 1889–1928.

Paa Turné. Tre foredrag om litteratur. Oslo: Gyldendal, 1960. Three lectures, 1891.

Brev til Marie. Oslo: Aschehoug, 1970. Letters, 1908–38.

Knut Hamsun som han var. Edited by Tore Hamsun. Oslo: Gyldendal, 1956. Letters, 1879–1949. German edition: *Briefe.* Munich: Langen-Müller, 1957.

2. Translations

a. Novels

August (*August,* 1930). Translated by Eugene Gay-Tifft. New York: Coward McCann, 1931.

Benoni (*Benoni,* 1908). Translated by Arthur G. Chater. New York: Knopf, 1925.

Chapter the Last (*Siste kapitel,* 1923). Translated by Arthur G. Chater. New York: Knopf, 1929.

Children of the Age (*Børn av tiden,* 1913). Translated by J. S. Scott. New York: Knopf, 1924.

Dreamers (*Sværmere,* 1904). Translated by W. W. Worster. New York: Knopf, 1921. Same translation with title *Mothwise* published in London: Gyldendal, 1922.

Growth of the Soil (*Markens grøde,* 1917). Translated by W. W. Worster. New York: Knopf, 1920.

Hunger (*Sult,* 1890). Translated by Robert Bly. New York: Farrar, Straus & Giroux, 1967. Earlier translation by George Egerton (Mary Chavelita Dunne), 1899.

Look Back on Happiness (*Den siste glæde,* 1912). Translated by Paula Wiking. New York: Coward McCann, 1940.

Mothwise. See *Dreamers.*

Mysteries (*Mysterier,* 1892). Translated by Gerry Bothmer. New York: Farrar, Straus & Giroux, 1971. Earlier translation by Arthur G. Chater, 1927.

Pan (*Pan,* 1894). Translated by J. W. McFarlane. London: Artemis Press, 1955; New York: Farrar, Straus & Giroux, 1956. Earlier translation by W. W. Worster, 1920.

The Ring Is Closed (*Ringen sluttet,* 1936). Translated by Eugene Gay-Tifft. New York: Coward McCann, 1937.

The Road Leads On (*Men livet lever,* 1933). Translated by Eugene Gay-Tifft. New York: Coward McCann, 1934.

Rosa (*Rosa,* 1908). Translated by Arthur G. Chater. New York: Knopf, 1925.

Segelfoss Town (*Segelfoss by,* 1915). Translated by J. S. Scott. New York: Knopf, 1925.

Shallow Soil (*Ny jord,* 1893). Translated by Carl Christian Hyllested. New York: Scribner, 1914.

Vagabonds. See *Wayfarers.*

Victoria (*Victoria,* 1898). Translated by Oliver Stallybrass. New York: Farrar, Straus & Giroux, 1969. Earlier translation by Arthur G. Chater, 1923.

Wayfarers (*Landstrykere,* 1927). Translated by J. W. McFarlane. New York: Farrar, Straus & Giroux, 1980. Earlier translated as *Vagabonds* by Eugene Gay-Tifft, 1930.

The Women at the Pump (*Konerne ved vandposten,* 1920). Translated by Oliver and Gunnvor Stallybrass. New York: Farrar, Straus & Giroux, 1978. Earlier translation by Arthur G. Chater, 1928.

b. Plays

In the Grip of Life (*Livet ivold,* 1910). Translated by Graham and Tristan Rawson. New York: Knopf, 1924.

c. Short Stories

"An Apparition" ("Et spøkelse," *Kratskog,* 1903). Translated by Agnes Emilie Petersen. In *International Short Stories,* edited by Virginia W. F. Church. Dallas, 1934, pp. 43–51.

"Call of Life" ("Livets røst," *Kratskog,* 1903). In *Told in Norway,* edited by Hanna Astrup Larsen. New York: American-Scandinavian Foundation, 1927, pp. 125–32. Also in *Great Stories by Nobel Prize Winners,* edited by Leo Hamalian and E. L. Volpe. New York: Noonday, 1960.

"Fear" ("Rædsel," *Kratskog,* 1903). Translated by Sverre Arestad. In *Norwegian-American Studies* (Northfield, Minnesota) 24 (1970):166–70.

"Feminine Victory" ("Kvindeseir," *Stridende liv,* 1905). Translated by Sverre Arestad. In *Norwegian-American Studies* (Northfield, Minnesota) 24 (1970):158–66.

"Just an Ordinary Fly of Average Size" ("En ganske almindelig flue av middels størrelse," *Siesta,* 1897). In *An Anthology of Scandinavian Literature,* edited by Hallberg Hallmundsson. New York: Collier, 1965, pp. 144–48.

"On the Island" ("På Blåmandsø," *Stridende liv,* 1905). Translated by W. W. Worster. *Dial* (New York) 75 (1923):209–24.

"On a Lecturing Tour" ("På turné," *Kratskog,* 1903). In *Tales from Far and Near,* edited by Ernest Rhys and Catharine A. Dawson. New York: D. Appleton, 1930, pp. 187–209.

"On the Prairie" ("På prærien," *Kratskog,* 1903). Translated by Sverre Arestad. In *Norwegian-American Studies* (Northfield, Minnesota) 24 (1970):171–79. Another translation in *Living Age* (Boston) 310 (1921):549.

"The Ring" ("Ringen," *Siesta,* 1897). In *Told in Norway,* edited by Hanna Astrup Larsen. New York: American-Scandinavian Foundation, 1927, pp. 133–34.

"Slaves of Love" ("Kjærlighetens slaver," *Kratskog,* 1903). Translated by J. W. McFarlane. In *Slaves of Love and Other Norwegian Short Stories,* edited by J. W. McFarlane. Oxford: Oxford University Press, 1982, pp. 30–36.

"Zachæus" ("Sachæus," *Kratskog,* 1903). Translated by Sverre Arestad. In *Norwegian-American Studies* (Northfield, Minnesota) 24 (1970): 180–92.

d. Essays

"August Strindberg." *America* (Chicago), 20 December 1888, pp. 29–31.

The Cultural Life of Modern America (*Fra det moderne Amerikas Aandsliv,* 1889). Translated by Barbara Gordon Morgridge. Cambridge: Harvard University Press, 1969.

"Festina Lente." *St. Louis Post Dispatch,* 12 December 1928.

SECONDARY SOURCES

Numbers in parentheses refer to items in the list of secondary sources below. Secondary literature in English is indicated by an asterisk.

Bibliography. An indispensable tool for the Hamsun scholar is Østby's retrospective bibliography (95), a 300-page listing of Hamsun editions, translations, letters, and scholarly books and articles published in the West before 1970. Of current bibliographies, Jorstad's (58) in *NLÅ* (annually since 1966) is the most complete. Surveys of Hamsun scholarship have been given by Beyer, Popperwell, and Stenström. Beyer's (8) is short and systematic; Popperwell's (100*) is particularly good on the period before 1920; Stenström's (114) gives the fullest description of each title.

Editions. There is no scholarly edition of Hamsun's works. The fifth and later editions of his *Samlede verker* (Collected Works) do not contain his first two published "novels" nor his book on America; neither do they contain his essays, lectures, and letters from various periods. Some of this material, which has been published separately, is included in the list of primary sources. Additional letters from Hamsun can be found in articles by Engen (29), Gierløff (35), Grieg (41), Knutsen (64), Langfeldt (68), Næss (86), Stray (117), and Svarstad (119).

Biography. While there is no scholarly biography of Knut Hamsun, several surveys of his "life and works" have appeared since Carl Morburger's pioneering study (1910). Noteworthy among these is Berendsohn's (5) for its valuable documentation, Landquist's (66) for its analysis of Hamsun's hero, and Skavlan's (112) for its lucid and unsentimental style. Hamsun's older son, Tore, has given what is still the most complete account of the author's life (49). Of special periods in Hamsun's life, the America years have been treated by Andersen (1*), Flanagan (31*), Hildeman (32), Hoel (54), and Næss (85); his year in Finland by Dale (24). Knut Hamsun as a husband, father, and friend from 1908 to 1952 is described in books by his wife, Marie (47–48), his sons, Arild (46) and Tore (50), and by his publisher, Harald Grieg (40). Hamsun's life during and after World War II is the subject of books by Gierløff (35), Langfeldt (68), and Stray (117), but first and foremost of a massive, well-written, and controversial study by the Danish writer Thorkild Hansen (51). A selection of the many polemical articles following the publication of Hansen's work in Denmark, Norway, and Sweden can be found in a book edited by Skjønsberg (113).

Criticism. Textual analyses of psycho-stylistic features in Hamsun's prose can be found in studies by Johnsen (57) and, particularly, by Øyslebø, whose well-documented major work on Hamsun (97) contains a wealth of philological information. More eclectic in their approach are three American studies, by Wiehr (128*, the earliest and most substantial), Gustafson (43*), and Larsen (70*). Larsen's book pays special attention to Hamsun's women. The fullest discussion of Hamsun's women, however, can be found in van Marken's dissertation (77).

A thematic approach is characteristic of studies by Lange (67), Bolckmanns (13, "The Individual and Society"), and Marstrander (78, "The Lonely Man"). Marstrander's work has been an important inspiration for Rolf Nettum, whose book (90) contains the most detailed psychological analysis to date of Hamsun's early work. Psychological in a more general sense are studies by Johannes V. Jensen (56) and Storstein (115–16), while in a German article, Hitschmann (53) provides a psychoanalytic treatment of the author's personality, as does the Norwegian Braatøy in his impressive study from 1929 (16). Tiemroth in a more recent work (122) continues Marstrander's and Nettum's existentialist line with the aid of phenomenology and Jungian psychology.

An investigation, like Haaland's (44), of the degree of social contact between Hamsun's characters is part of a larger discussion of the social structure of his universe—as in the pioneering works of Christensen (21) and Lowenthal (73*)—and this again has led to studies of his ideology, a subject that has dominated Hamsun scholarship for some time. An antidemocratic streak in Hamsun's work has been noted by critics in Russia (Plekhanov, 99), Germany (Mendelssohn, 79), Denmark (Giersing, 36; Kierkegaard, 60), and Norway (Nordahl Grieg, 42; Eystein Eggen, 28).

Hamsun's nihilism has been the subject of several sensitive articles by Brynildsen (18), whereas the possible anti-Semitism in his work has been discussed in an article by Simpson (110*). The best treatment of Hamsun's political involvement is Sten Sparre Nilson's book (91).

Of special periods in Hamsun's writing career, Friese has treated his relationship to the Jugendstil (34), while McFarlane in a seminal article (74*) has treated his major works from the 1890's which are also the subject of an anthology by Rottem (106). Hamsun's relationship to other writers and artists is the subject of a series of studies, such as Hamsun and Ibsen by Popperwell (104*), H. and Nietzsche by Harald Beyer (10), H. and Garborg by Dale (23), H. and Rousseau by Buttry (19*) and Kejzlar (59), H. and Johannes V. Jensen by Andersen (2), H. and Kafka by Friedrich (32), H. and Pasternak by Barksdale and Popp (4*), H. and Henry Miller by Bolckmanns (11), H. and Martin A. Hansen by Ingwersen (55*), and H. and Camus by Simpson (109*). Hamsun's place in the world of letters has been treated in a number of articles—his position in postwar Norway by Beyer (6) and Stuberg (118), in Germany by Carlsson (20) and Friese (23), in Russia by Nag (89), and in America by Næss (84*).

Hamsun's poetry has been discussed in articles by Kommandantvold (65) and Noreng (92); his short stories are treated by Kierkegaard (60, "The Queen of Sheba") and Kittang (62, "Call of Life"). Hamsun's plays are the subject of a chapter in Fechter's book about European drama (30) and of several articles by Waal (126–27*). Braatøy (16) has analyzed *Queen Tamara;* and Tiemroth (122), *Friar Vendt;* Popperwell (103*) has treated Hamsun's last play, and Grabowski (38*)—in a great number of articles—has discussed the second part of the Kareno trilogy.

Of Hamsun's novels, *Hunger* has been treated in studies by Breiteig (17), Einar Eggen (27), Mishler (81*) and Musarra Schrøder (82*). *Mysteries* is the subject of dissertations by Nybo (94)—who treats the novel as a detective story—and Faith Ingwersen (55*)—who compares it to Martin A. Hansen's *Løgneren.* Beyer (9) writes about the relationship between Nagel and the Midget; Thiess (121), about the Werther motif in the novel; Borgen (15) discusses the character Nagel. Other articles include titles by Magris (76), Næss (87*), and Popperwell (102*). *Pan* is the subject of a small book by Vige (125) and a long article by Sehmsdorf (108*), who treats the novel's mythological allusions. Linneberg (72) uses the novel for a study of Hamsun's fascism. *Victoria* is the subject of an interesting article by Kittang (61). The social structure of society in *Benoni* and *Rosa* is the subject of an article by Gimnes (37) and a book by Knutsen (63). *The Wanderer* has been treated by Norseng (93*), partly in response to a review by John Updike (124*). Granaas (39) has written about *Children of the Age;* Unruh (123*), about *Segelfoss Town,* and Popperwell (101*) about *Growth of the Soil,* which is also used by Rumbke (107) to illustrate "regressive social criticism." The August novels have been treated in studies by Bolckmanns (14) and Andersen-Næss (3), as well as in two books, one of which (Rottem, 105) is concerned with ideology, while the other (Simpson, 111*) discusses point of view technique and disagrees with critics who make the author responsible for opinions expressed in the text. Hamsun's last novel, *The Ring Is Closed,* is the subject of an article by Alf Larsen (69), and *On Overgrown Paths* of articles by Thiess (120) and Bolckmanns (12), as well as of a play by Tankred Dorst (25), which has been analyzed in a perceptive article by Magris (75).

1. **Andersen, Arlow W.** "Knut Hamsun's America." *Norwegian-American Studies* 23 (1967):175–203.
2. **Andersen, Harry.** "Knut Hamsun og Johannes V. Jensen." *Nordisk tidskrift* 40 (1964):485–516.
3. **Andersen-Næss, Reidar.** "Landstryker-motivet i Hamsuns diktning." *Nordisk tidskrift* 37 (1961):444–56.
4. **Barksdale, E. C.,** and **Popp, Daniel.** "Hamsun and Pasternak: The Development of Dionysian Tragedy." *Edda,* 1976, pp. 129–38.
5. **Berendsohn, Walter A.** *Knut Hamsun. Das unbändige Ich und die menschliche Gemeinschaft.* Munich: Albert Langen, 1929.
6. **Beyer, Edvard.** *Hamsun og vi.* Oslo: Aschehoug, 1959.
7. ———. "Hamsun und das Hamsun-Problem." *Nordeuropa* 11 (1978):49–65.
8. ———. "Knut Hamsun." In *Norsk litteraturhistorie,* by Harald and Edvard Beyer. Oslo: Aschehoug, 1972, pp. 441–44. Bibliography.
9. ———. "Knut Hamsuns Mysterier." In *Profiler og problemer.* Oslo: Aschehoug, 1966, pp. 38–58.
10. **Beyer, Harald.** "Knut Hamsun." In *Nietzsche og Norden.* Vol. 2. Bergen: Universitetet i Bergen, Årbok, 1959, pp. 94–106.
11. **Bolckmans, Alex.** "Henry Miller's *Tropic of Cancer* and Knut Hamsun's *Sult.*" *Scandinavica* 14 (1975):115–26.
12. ———. "Het laatste boek van Knut Hamsun: *Paa gjengrodde Stier.*" *Studia Germanica Gandensia* 6 (1964):273–80.

13. ———. *Individu en maatschappij in het werk van Knut Hamsun.* Antwerp: Standard wetenschappelijke uitgewerij, 1967.
14. ———. "Knut Hamsuns August-trilogie." In *Studies in Skandinavistiek.*Groningen: Brouwer International Publishing, 1977, pp. 103–19. Festschrift for Amy van Marken.
15. **Borgen, Johan.** "Nagel." *Vinduet* 13 (1959):119–28.
16. **Braatøy, Trygve.** *Livets cirkel.* 1929. Reprint. Oslo: Cappelen, 1954.
17. **Breiteig, Byrge.** "Det erotiske i *Sult.*" *Edda,* 1972, pp. 329–35.
18. **Brynildsen, Aasmund.** *Svermeren og hans demon.* Oslo: Dreyer, 1973.
19. **Buttry, Dolores.** "Knut Hamsun: A Scandinavian Rousseau." Ph.D. dissertation. University of Illinois at Urbana-Champaign, 1978. See also *Scandinavica* 19 (1980):121–50.
20. **Carlsson, Anni.** *Ibsen, Strindberg, Hamsun.* Kronberg: Athenäum, 1978.
21. **Christensen, Alf.** *Litteratur og klasse.* Oslo: Fram, 1935.
22. **Dahl, Willy.** "Knut Hamsun og datteren på Sirilund." In *Perspektiver: Essays om norske klassikere.* Bergen: Eide, 1968, pp. 56–81.
23. **Dale, Johannes A.** "Garborg og Hamsun." In *Garborg-studiar.* Oslo: Samlaget, 1969, pp. 9–25.
24. ———. "Knut Hamsun i Finland." In *Menn i motstraum.* Oslo: Noregs boklag, 1973, pp. 80–96.
25. **Dorst, Tankred.** *Eiszeit.* Frankfurt: Suhrkamp, 1973.
26. **Eddy, Beverly D.** "Hamsun's *Victoria* and Munch's *Livsfrisen:* Variations on a Theme." *Scandinavian Studies* 48 (1976):156–68.
27. **Eggen, Einar.** "Mennesket og tingene. Hamsuns *Sult* og den nye roman." *Norsk litterær årbok,* 1965, pp. 82–106.
28. **Eggen, Eystein.** "Knut Hamsuns vei til fascismen." *Edda,* 1969, pp. 341–44.
29. **Engen, Arnfinn.** "Knut Hamsun og Zahl på Kjerringøy." *Edda,* 1977, pp. 255–62.
30. **Fechter, Paul.** "Die erste existentielle Wendung Knut Hamsun." In *Das europäische Drama.* Vol. 2. Mannheim: Bibliografisches Institut, 1956, pp. 162–68, 191.
31. **Flanagen, John T.** "Knut Hamsun's Early Years in the Northwest." *Minnesota History* 20 (1939):397–412.
32. **Friederich, Reinhard H.** "Kafka and Hamsun's *Mysteries.*" *Comparative Literature* 28 (1976):34–50.
33. **Friese, Wilhelm.** "Das deutsche Hamsun-Bild." *Edda,* 1965, pp. 257–76. Anni Carlsson's reply in *Edda,* 1966, pp. 278–88.

34. ———. "Hamsun und der Jugendstil." *Edda,* 1967, pp. 427–49.
35. **Gierløff, Christian.** *Knut Hamsuns egen røst.* Oslo: Gyldendal, 1961.
36. **Giersing, Morten, Carlsen, John Thobo,** and **Westergaard-Nielsen, Michael.** *Det reaktionære oprør: Om fascismen i Knut Hamsuns forfatterskab.* Copenhagen: GMT, 1975.
37. **Gimnes, Steinar.** "Knut Hamsuns *Benoni* og *Rosa.*"*Edda,* 1976, pp. 139–47.
38. **Grabowski, Simon.** "Kareno in Nordland: A Study of *Livets Spil.*" *Edda,* 1969, pp. 297–321; 1972, pp. 337–59.
39. **Granaas, Rakel Kristina.** "Ironi og ideologi: Ein analyse av Knut Hamsuns *Børn av tiden.*" *Norsk litterær årbok,* 1979, pp. 56–76.
40. **Grieg, Harald.** *Hamsun: Et kapitel av En forleggers erindringer.* Oslo: Privately published, 1954. Reprinted in *En forleggers erindringer* (Oslo: Gyldendal, 1958), 2:461–543.
41. ———. "Knut Hamsun: Brev fra Hamarøy til Christian König." *Vinduet* 13 (1959):64–75.
42. **Grieg, Nordahl.** "Knut Hamsun." *Veien frem* (Oslo) 1, no. 7 (1936):28–32. Reprinted in *Vinduet* 13 (1959):137–40.
43. **Gustafson, Alrik.** "Man and the Soil." In *Six Scandinavian Novelists.* New York: American-Scandinavian Foundation, 1940, pp. 226–85.
44. **Haaland, Arild.** *Hamsun og Hoel: To studier i kontakt.* Bergen: John Grieg, 1957.
45. ———. "Nazisme, litteratur og Knut Hamsun." In *Nazismen og norsk litteratur,* edited by Bjarte Birkeland and Stein Ugelvik Larsen. Oslo: Universitetsforlaget, 1975, pp. 57–69.
46. **Hamsun, Arild.** *Om Knut Hamsun og Nørholm.* Oslo: Aschehoug, 1953.
47. **Hamsun, Marie.** *Regnbuen.* Oslo: Aschehoug, 1953. German edition, 1954.
48. ———. *Under gullregnen.* Oslo: Aschehoug, 1959.
49. **Hamsun, Tore.** *Knut Hamsun.* Oslo: Gyldendal, 1959.
50. ———. *Mein Vater.* Leipzig: Paul List, 1940.
51. **Hansen, Thorkild.** *Prosessen mot Hamsun.* Oslo: Gyldendal, 1978.
52. **Hildeman, Per-Axel.** "Knut Hamsun och Amerika under 1880-talet." Ph.D. dissertation, Stockholm University, 1955.
53. **Hitschmann, Eduard.** "Ein Gespenst aus der Kindheit Knut Hamsuns." *Imago* (Vienna) 12 (1924):336–60.
54. **Hoel, Sigurd.** "Knut Hamsun og Amerika." In *Knut Hamsun. Festskrift.* Oslo: Gyldendal, 1929, pp. 84–97.

55. **Ingwersen, Faith.** "The Truthful Liars: A Comparative Analysis of Knut Hamsun's *Mysterier* and Martin A. Hansen's *Løgneren*." Ph.D. dissertation, University of Chicago, 1974.
56. **Jensen, Johannes V.** "Bondekultur." In *Den ny Verden*. Copenhagen: Gyldendal, 1907, pp. 175–86.
57. **Johnson, Egil Eiken.** *Stilpsykiske studier i 1890–årenes norske litteratur*. Oslo: Gyldendal, 1949.
58. **Jorstad, Anne Lise.** "Bibliografi over norsk litteraturforskning." *Norsk litterær årbok*. Oslo: Samlaget, 1966–. Published annually.
59. **Kejzlar, Radko.** "Les conceptions du monde ideal chez J. J. Rousseau et chez Knut Hamsun." *Recontres et courants littéraires franco-scandinave*. Paris: Lettres modernes, 1972, pp. 225–34.
60. **Kierkegaard, Peter.** *Knut Hamsun som modernist*. Copenhagen: Medusa, 1976.
61. **Kittang, Atle.** "Kjærleik, dikting og sosial røyndom: Knut Hamsuns *Victoria*." In *Litteraturhistoriske problem*. Oslo: Universitetsforlaget, 1975, pp. 203–33.
62. ———. "Problemstilling og metode i den strukturelle litteraturanalysen." In *Strukturalisme og semiologi*, edited by Kjell S. Johannesen and Arild Utaker. Grenaa: GMT, 1973.
63. **Knutsen, Nils M.** *Makt-avmakt: En studie av Hamsuns Benoni og Rosa*. Oslo: Aschehoug, 1975. Short German version in *Skandinavistik* 5 (1974):25–36.
64. ———. "Tre ukjente Hamsun-brev fra 1880." *Edda*, 1972, pp. 321–27.
65. **Kommandantvold, Kristian Magnus.** "Lyrikaren Knut Hamsun i *Det vilde Kor*." *Norsk litterær årbok*, 1972, pp. 10–25.
66. **Landquist, John.** *Knut Hamsun: Sein Leben und sein Werk*. 1917. Reprint. Tübingen: Fischer, 1927. Swedish edition, 1929.
67. **Lange, Wolfgang.** "Hamsuns Elementargeister." *Euphorion* 50 (1956):328–40.
68. **Langfeldt, Gabriel, and Ødegård, Ørnulv.** *Den rettspsykiatriske erklæring om Knut Hamsun*. Oslo: Gyldendal, 1978.
69. **Larsen, Alf.** "Hamsuns ånd." In *I kunstens tjeneste*. Oslo: Dreyer, 1964, pp. 113–23.
70. **Larsen, Hanna Astrup.** *Knut Hamsun*. New York: Knopf, 1922.
71. **Lavrin, Janko.** "The Return of Pan." In *Aspects of Modernism*. London: S. Nott, 1935.
72. **Linneberg, Arild.** "Hamsuns *Pan* og fascismen." *Ventil* 4 no. 1 (1976):14–27.

73. **Lowenthal, Leo.** "Knut Hamsun." In *Literature and the Image of Man.* Boston: Beacon Press, 1957, pp. 190–220.
74. **McFarlane, James W.** "The Whisper of the Blood: A Study of Knut Hamsun's Early Novels." *PMLA* 71 (1956):563–94.
75. **Magris, Claudio.** "Gefangener der Vitalität." In *Werkbuch über Tankred Dorst,* edited by Horst Laube. Frankfurt: Suhrkamp, 1974, pp. 181–205.
76. ———. "Zwischen den Spalten des Ich. Hamsuns *Mysterien.*" *Edda,* 1978, 345–54.
77. **Marken, Amy Van.** "Knut Hamsun en de vrouwenfiguren in zijn werk." Ph.D. dissertation, Ghent State University, Groningen, 1970.
78. **Marstrander, Jan.** *Det ensomme menneske i Knut Hamsuns diktning: Betraktninger omkring Mysterier og et motiv.* Oslo: Det Norske Studentersamfunds kulturutvalg, 1959.
79. **Mendelssohn, Peter De.** "Erleuchtung und Verblendung des Zerrissenen." In *Der Geist in der Despotie.* Berlin: F. A. Herbig, 1953.
80. **Miller, Henry.** "Hamsun—min förebild." *Dagens Nyheter* (Stockholm), 3 August 1959, p. 3.
81. **Mishler, William.** "Ignorance, Knowledge and Resistance to Knowledge in Hamsun's *Sult.*" *Edda,* 1974, pp. 161–77.
82. **Musarra-Schrøder, Ulla.** "Monologisk og dialogisk fremstilling i *Sult.*" In *Studies in Skandinavistiek.* Groningen: Brouwer International Publishing, 1977, pp. 137–50. Festschrift for Amy van Marken.
83. ———. "Tankegengivelsen i *Sult,* et bidrag til jeg-fortællingens teori." *Edda,* 1974, pp. 145–59.
84. **Næss, Harald.** "American Attitudes to Knut Hamsun." *Americana-Norvegica* 3 (1971):338–60.
85. ———. *Knut Hamsun og Amerika.* Oslo: Gyldendal, 1969.
86. ———. "Knut Hamsuns brevveksling med Postmester Erik Frydenlund." *Edda,* 1959, pp. 225–68.
87. ———. "A Strange Meeting and Knut Hamsun's *Mysteries.*" *Scandinavian Studies* 36 (1965):48–58.
88. ———. "Who Was Hamsun's Hero?" In *The Hero in Scandinavian Literature,* edited by John M. Weinstock and Robert T. Rovinsky. Austin: University of Texas Press, 1975, pp. 63–86.
89. **Nag, Martin.** *Hamsun i Russisk åndsliv.* Oslo: Gyldendal, 1969.
90. **Nettum, Rolf Nyboe.** *Konflikt og visjon: Hovedtemaer i Knut Hamsuns forfatterskap 1890–1912.* Oslo: Gyldendal, 1970.

91. **Nilson, Sten Sparre.** *En ørn i uvær.* Oslo: Gyldendal, 1960. German translation: *Knut Hamsun und die Politik* (Villingen: Ring-Verlag, 1964).

92. **Noreng, Harald.** "Knut Hamsuns hylningsdikt til Bjørnstjerne Bjørnson i 1902." In *Studies in Skandinavistiek.* Groningen: Brouwer International Publishing, 1977, pp. 121–35. Festschrift for Amy van Marken.

93. **Norseng, Mary Kay.** "The Startling Vagueness of Knut Pedersen (From an American Point of View)." *Edda,* 1979, pp. 157–73.

94. **Nybø, Gregory.** *Knut Hamsuns Mysterier.* Oslo: Gyldendal, 1969.

95. **Østby, Arvid.** *Knut Hamsun. En bibliografi.* Oslo: Gyldendal, 1972.

96. **Øyslebø, Olaf.** "Gjentakelse som lyrisk middel hos Hamsun." *Edda,* 1965, pp. 1–26.

97. ———. *Hamsun gjennom stilen.* Oslo: Gyldendal, 1964.

98. ———. "Hamsuns merkverdige at-setninger." *Maal og minne,* 1964, pp. 64–87.

99. **Plekhanov, Georgy.** "Doktor Stockmanns Geisteskind." In *Kunst und Literatur.* Berlin: Dietz, 1955.

100. **Popperwell, Ronald.** "Critical Attitudes to Knut Hamsun, 1890–1969." *Scandinavica* 9 (1970):1–23.

101. ———. "Growth Contra Independence: A Study of Knut Hamsun's *Markens Grøde* and Halldór Kiljan Laxness' *Sjálfstætt Fólk.*" In *Studia Centenalia.* Reykjavik: 1961, pp. 134–44. Festschrift for Benedikt S. Þórarinsson.

102. ———. "Interrelatedness in Hamsun's *Mysterier.*" *Scandinavian Studies* 38 (1966):295–301.

103. ———. "Knut Hamsun's *Livet ivold.*" In *Twentieth Century Drama in Scandinavia: Proceedings of the Twelfth Study Conference of the International Association for Scandinavian Studies.* Helsinki, 1979, pp. 211–18.

104. ———. "The Problem of Influence: A Specific Case." In *Proceedings of the Fifth International Study Conference on Scandinavian Literature.* London: 1964, pp. 1–22.

105. **Rottem, Øystein.** *Knut Hamsuns Landstrykere: En ideologikritisk analyse.* Oslo: Gyldendal, 1978.

106. ———, ed. *Søkelys på Knut Hamsuns 90-årsdiktning.* Oslo: Universitetsforlaget, 1979.

107. **Rumbke, Eberhard.** " 'Træskeens tidsalder': Regressive Gesellschaftskritik in Knut Hamsuns Roman *Markens grøde.*" *Skandinavistik* 3 (1973):39–59.

108. **Sehmsdorf, Henning.** "Knut Hamsun's *Pan:* Myth and Symbol." *Edda,* 1974, pp. 345–93.
109. **Simpson, Allen.** "Hamsun and Camus: Consciousness in *Markens grøde* and 'The Myth of Sisyphus.' " *Scandinavian Studies* 48 (1976):272–83.
110. ———. "Knut Hamsun's Anti-Semitism." *Edda,* 1977, pp. 273–93.
111. ———. *Knut Hamsuns Landstrykere.* Oslo: Gyldendal, 1973.
112. **Skavlan, Einar.** *Knut Hamsun.* Oslo: Gyldendal, 1929.
113. **Skjønsberg, Simen,** ed. *Det uskyldige geni?* Oslo: Gyldendal, 1979.
114. **Stenström, Thure.** "Gammal och ny Hamsun-forskning." *Samlaren* 94 (1973):41–69.
115. **Storstein, Olav.** "Knut Hamsun og patriarkatet." In *Fra Jæger til Falk.* Oslo: Tiden, 1950, pp. 111–17.
116. ———. "Litt om Hamsun og 'skuespilleriet.' " *Vinduet* 13 (1959):153–60.
117. **Stray, Sigrid.** *Min klient Knut Hamsun.* Oslo: Aschehoug, 1979.
118. **Stuberg, Tore.** "Fra landssviker til dikterkonge: Knut Hamsun i norsk offentlighet 1945–55." *Norsk litterær årbok,* 1978, pp. 144–62.
119. **Svarstad, Christianne Undset.** "Noen brev fra Knut Hamsun til hans ungdomsvenninne Caroline Neeraas." *Ord och Bild* 63 (1954):25–32.
120. **Thiess, Frank.** "Hamsuns *Auf überwachsenen Pfaden.*" *Die Waldhütte* (Mölln in Lauenburg), no. 17 (1968), pp. 2–14.
121. ———. *Das Werther-Thema in Hamsuns Mysterien.* Mainz: Akademie der Wissenschaften und der Literatur, 1957.
122. **Tiemroth, Jørgen E.** *Illusionens vej: Om Knut Hamsuns forfatterskab.* Copenhagen: Gyldendal, 1974.
123. **Unruh, Kathryn I.** "The long dark summer in *Segelfoss Town.*" *Edda,* 1977, pp. 263–72.
124. **Updike, John.** "A Primal Modern." *New Yorker,* 31 May 1976, pp. 116–18. On *The Wanderer.* For reviews of *Hunger* and *On Overgrown Paths,* see *New Yorker,* December, 1967.
125. **Vige, Rolf.** *Knut Hamsuns Pan.* Oslo: Universitetsforlaget, 1963.
126. **Waal, Carla.** "Hamsun's *Ved Rigets Port* on the Norwegian Stage." *Scandinavian Studies* 41 (1969):138–49.
127. ———. "The Plays of Knut Hamsun." *Quarterly Journal of Speech* 57 (1971):75–82.
128. **Wiehr, Joseph.** "Knut Hamsun: His Personality and his Outlook upon Life." *Smith College Studies in Modern Languages* 3 (1921–22):1–129.

Index